The
Law-Gospel
Debate

Gerhard O. Forde

The Law-Gospel Debate

An Interpretation of Its
Historical Development

FORTRESS PRESS
Minneapolis, Minnesota

THE LAW-GOSPEL DEBATE
An Interpretation of Its Historical Development

Fortress Press ex libris publication 2007

Cover design: JoAnn L. Ohma

ISBN: 978-0-8006-6230-1
The Library of Congress Catalog Card Number: 68-25804

The paper used in this publication meets the minimum requirements of American National Standard for Information Sciences—Permanence of Paper for Printed Library Materials, ANSIZ329.48-1984.

Manufactured in the U.S.A.

TO MY FATHER

Preface

The problem of law and gospel has been one focus of contemporary discussions of theology and ethics. Karl Barth's essay of 1935 on gospel and law [1] called for a wholesale re-evaluation of traditional Protestant thinking; more recently, "contextual" ethicists have seriously questioned whether law can be relied upon as a guide for proper Christian action under the gospel. The prophets of the "new morality" likewise advise casting off traditional standards of morality in favor of a more "honest" approach to ethical decisions. We hear many voices advising us to consider anew the old questions relating to the law and the gospel.

No doubt this is all to the good. Unfortunately, however, the discussions for the most part have been rather confusing, and the arguments have seemed to generate more heat than light. It is not my intention here to add yet another voice to this confusion; instead, the study which follows is an attempt to clarify the discussion by investigating its historical background. I am convinced that at least some of the confusion today is the result of an insufficient understanding of the historical roots of the contemporary debate. The purpose of the study, therefore, is to probe into this historical background in the hope that doing so will shed light on

---

[1] Karl Barth, "Gospel and Law," *Community, State and Church* ("Anchor Books"). Garden City: Doubleday and Company, Inc., 1960.

the contemporary problems and contribute to more fruitful discussion.

This study, of course, cannot pretend to be exhaustive. That would be far too ambitious an undertaking. Rather, what I have attempted is an interpretation of the development of the problem of law and gospel through concentrating on the decisive moments which have helped to shape the modern debate. Many theologians other than those treated could have been included. In general, I have limited myself to those who have significantly advanced the argument and/or who have attempted to draw conclusions for systematic theology from their understanding of the relationship between law and gospel.

The concern of the study is primarily theological. That is, it is concerned primarily with the understanding of the relationship between law and gospel in the theological system; only secondarily does it deal with the related problems of ethics. The justification for such an approach, if indeed one is needed, is my conviction that the contemporary discussion suffers from a lack of theological clarification. Much is said today, for instance, about the law and its relevance or irrelevance, but seldom does anyone take the trouble to investigate what was traditionally meant by law in the theological system or to see the kinds of transformation the understanding of law has undergone in recent years.

It is the contention of this study that a major source of the difficulty in understanding the historical background is to be traced to that point where Protestant theology rejected the non-historical supernaturalism of the older Orthodoxy and turned to a strictly conceived *Heilsgeschichte* approach. This shift brought about a crisis, especially in the conception of law and gospel, the dimensions of which have not yet been fully realized. The change necessitated a reformulation of the relationship between law and gospel which had both positive and negative results. On the positive side it brought about a justifiable rejection of the strict legalism of the orthodox position; on the negative side, though, it left Protestantism ill-prepared to cope with the neo-Kantian liberalism and the historicism of the late 19th and early 20th centuries. In attempting to find its way out of these difficulties, contemporary theology has not paid enough attention to the kind of willy-nilly development the understanding of law and gospel has undergone in the process.

In looking for what could be called a decisive starting point for the modern debate, one is soon led to the famous Erlangen theologian, J. C. K. von Hofmann (1810-1877), often called the father of modern *Heilsgeschichte*. By attempting a thoroughgoing reconstruction of Lutheran theology in terms of salvation history, Hofmann provoked a controversy centering around the doctrine of the atonement which became the genesis of several lines of theological development. This study is an attempt to follow the lines of development which followed Hofmann's work, to interpret them, and to conclude by making some constructive suggestions which may lead to a better understanding of the law and gospel today.

I am indebted especially to Professors Richard R. Niebuhr and Herbert Richardson, both of Harvard Divinity School, for their help in the writing of this book. All translations from the Latin and German are my own with the exception of those from the writings of Karl Barth.

G.O.F.

Introduction

Do not be misled by the modesty of this book's title. Professor Forde has disguised his achievement in the conventional robes of *another* historical study of *another* doctrine. Several such studies on greater or lesser doctrinal issues appear each year: studies on Christology, church and sacraments, eschatology, the Holy Spirit, Scripture and revelation, and so forth. To the extent that his book focuses on doctrinal questions, it too belongs in this genre. And by his sorting out, pointing out, and working out the questions and consequences involved in 150 years of debate on the law-gospel problem, Professor Forde has provided us with a definite and decisive work.

However, it would be unfortunate if the reader's delight in the author's advertised purposes were to distract his attention from other, less obvious, achievements of this work. For like the good cook who is also a good woman, Professor Forde's volume possesses certain unobtrusive virtues that may not appear at once, but will only be savored in the course of a long acquaintance. The more I have dipped into this book, the more I have meditated upon these unobtrusive, even hidden, strengths, the more I have come to regard it as a unique and towering achievement—not just *another* historical study of *another* doctrine, but as THE BOOK that best demonstrates how a progressive deepening of Christian understanding does take place when serious theologians, in thoughtful (even technical) conversation with one another over many generations, seek to conform themselves to the truth of God's Word.

I ask you, reader, to give me testimony from your own experience. Haven't you read histories of this or that aspect of Christian theology that seemed to be no more than a *seriatim* listing of individual opinions, a listing that seemed to hint the motive behind all theology to be the passion of individual theologians for novelty and conflict rather than any serious love for the truth of God's Word? Or haven't you read histories which suggest that the breakthrough to Christian understanding comes when *one great man* finally overthrows a defective tradition perpetrated by theological parrots who sought thereby to justify the pretensions of papal power and protect their own preferred positions? But where have you found a historical study like the one you now hold in your own hand, a study showing that true Christian theology is neither the once-and-for-all achievement of a *great man* nor a parade of vain novelties, but the achievement of many dedicated and competent thinkers who gradually discover the mind of Christ even as they listen to and criticize one another?

I do not—God forbid!—suggest that the achievement of the theologians Professor Forde analyzes is the consequence of their religious piety. All the vanity and foolishness of the world is their portion, too. But I do sense that the intrinsic logic developed in the course of their ongoing discussion, a logic that grows out of their seriously sustaining themselves and their reflection in relation to one another, seems to suggest that *one single mind* is thinking out certain problems through their thinking. I myself am inclined to such a mystical metaphor. But for those who demur at this expression, let me express the matter otherwise: what Professor Forde has shown is that the theological discussion of the law-gospel question over the past 150 years has an organic, corporate character (so that the gains of one generation provide the assumptions of the next); and the theological discussion attains this organic, corporate character because the many thinkers involved did not separate themselves from one another (each trying to develop his own "private theology"), but maintained themselves in Christian community by working critically over against one another.

Briefly, then, what is the deepened understanding towards which the 150 years of theological debate gradually moved? What is finally at the heart of the law-gospel question? It is in his patient, expansive, and brilliantly illuminating analysis of this point that Professor Forde makes his decisive contribution. He shows that the law-gospel question is, finally, *the question* about the meaning of theology (on the one hand) and faith (on the other). Theologians, preachers, and language-using creatures endure the constant occupational hazard of supposing that true religion finally is a matter of right understanding, that the meaning of the cross is finally a matter of *the meaning* of the cross rather than *the cross itself.* The temptations to make man's salvation upon some gnosis are ever-present and very subtle. This is something Professor Forde has really taught me.

Now the law-gospel question is the question how rational beings can escape this constant occupational hazard. How can we escape confusing our understandings of Jesus Christ, his cross and resurrection, with Jesus Christ crucified and raised from the dead? It sounds so simple, almost as if it were no problem at all. And, in fact, I confess that only this book has made me see its weightiness and unavoidable character. Only this book has made clear to me the extent to which theologians and preachers and hearers of the Word tend to confuse their understandings of redemption with redemption itself—thereby separating themselves from the power of the gospel and the life of faith. It is against this confusion, against this tendency of men to alienate themselves from the possibility of faith that every preacher must struggle. And he must struggle against this tendency at the heart of his own preaching, in the very acts of thinking out and saying aloud the things he is calling men to affirm. For only thereby will his preaching lead men to the cross rather than away from it.

Since every theology, by its very rational character, can become a surreptitious gnosis—an unobtrusive but constricting kind of "law" —the law-gospel question must be faced by every theologian in relation to all his understanding over and over again. In a sense, then, there is no such thing as a "doctrine" about the right relationship between the law and the gospel (as there might be said to be a doctrine about Jesus Christ). Rather, the law-gospel question concerns the basic relationship between doctrine itself and the fact of being redeemed, i.e., between all human understanding and faith in God. It is a mistake—Professor Forde has shown me—to think that a right understanding of the law-gospel question requires first a definition of the law and then, in relation to this, a proper understanding of the gospel, after which we move on to other topics. *Rather, the theologian discovers what the law is for him, in his situation, precisely as he discovers the alienating tendencies within his own theology,* as he discovers the extent to which he makes faith impossible by his own theologizing about it. To have shown clearly the existence of this tendency in many theologies and to have shown the Christian theological community struggling against it in order to gain, ever and again, a firm grip on *the fact of redemption in Jesus Christ* is the momentous teaching of Professor Forde's book.

You hold it now in your hand. May you find as much wisdom in it as I both have and shall.

HERBERT W. RICHARDSON
St. Michael's College
Toronto, Canada

Contents

Part One

ORTHODOXY
VERSUS
HEILSGESCHICHTE:

*The Genesis
of the
Law-Gospel
Debate*

CHAPTER I

THE POSITION OF ORTHODOXY[1]

The beginning of the modern debate about law and gospel took the form of a controversy over the doctrine of the atonement. The controversy erupted when J. C. K. von Hofmann attacked the orthodox doctrine of vicarious satisfaction in the name of a *heilsgeschichtliche* theology. Although the law-gospel issue is seldom mentioned as such, when we look back on the controversy from our present vantage point it is apparent that this was really the central issue. In this more or less forgotten chapter of 19th century theology *Heilsgeschichte* confronts Orthodoxy, and this confrontation begins a crisis of major proportions—so much so that it is still a key to understanding many later developments, most especially the debate over law and gospel.

Before turning to the controversy over the atonement precipitated by Hofmann, it will be necessary briefly to outline the orthodox position against which he directed his attack. This will lead us into the orthodox conception of the relationship between law and gospel.

The key to the traditional orthodox position is the understanding of the place of the law in the theological system. Protestant orthodoxy

---

[1] We shall use the term "Orthodoxy" in this study primarily with reference to the orthodox doctrine of law and gospel. Even though many of the theologians we refer to could not be classified as "orthodox" in the 17th century sense, nevertheless they were orthodox in their view of law, gospel, and atonement, and it is to this complex of ideas that I refer.

operated with what we shall refer to in this study as a static-ontological concept of divine law. This idea of law provides the basic structure for the whole orthodox system and so determines the understanding of all other related doctrines—the nature of the gospel, revelation, and of course, the doctrine of the atonement.

The orthodox understanding of law stemmed, no doubt, from its theology of justification. Orthodoxy made the doctrine of justification of central importance; this led quite naturally to a system based on divine law and justice,[2] for the theology of justification by faith posits a God who alone justifies and decides man's fate. In his absolute freedom (*agens liberrimum*), God acts according to his own good pleasure;[3] to the orthodox this freedom could make him seem almost arbitrary in his motives and actions. There was, consequently, a pronounced attempt in Lutheran dogmatics, to avoid assigning God this whimsical freedom. God, they said, acts freely indeed, but only in accordance with the inner law of his own essence.[4]

If in his essence God is righteous and acts only according to the law of his own being, then this must also be true in God's relationship with man. God's righteousness, God's claim upon man, expresses itself in the form of law, and justification must take place in accordance with this law. Law is, therefore, an eternal, objective order, a *lex aeterna* which sets forth the ideal to which human life must attain in order to find favor with God.[5] In the law man encounters the personal will of God, so that relationship to this will becomes the decisive problem of his existence. Only a righteousness which is *absoluta conformitas* with the divine law can count in justification. Here the basic structure of the orthodox system is already given; the entire orthodox theology of sin and grace is formulated against this background.[6]

---

[2] Hans Emil Weber, *Reformation, Orthodoxie und Rationalismus* (3 vols.; Gütersloh; C. Bertelsmann Verlag, 1937-51). II, 1-11. Cited hereafter as *Reformation*.

[3] *Ibid.*, p. 3.

[4] *Ibid.*, p. 3.

[5] Lauri Haikola, *Studien zu Luther und zum Luthertum*, Uppsala Universitets Aarsskrift, 1958, No. 2; (Uppsala: Lundequistika Bokhandeln, 1958), p. 9. Cited hereafter as *Studien*.

[6] Weber, *Reformation*, pp. 5-7.

Furthermore, this divine law finds its "echo" in the "natural law," the law which speaks in the conscience of man. The righteousness of God makes its claim upon man, demanding absolute conformity, threatening the conscience. The remnant of the divine law in the conscience of man, the natural law which has persisted even after the fall, provides the point of contact. This basic understanding of the law enabled the orthodox to build a rationally coherent system.[7]

The law provided, therefore, the structure which governed the understanding of other doctrines. This is most apparent in the doctrine of the atonement. The law is, in effect, the "way" of salvation, but because of his sin man cannot traverse this "way." Since he cannot meet God's demands, he is guilty and subject to just punishment under the law. Atonement takes place only when another as man's "substitute" bears the punishment and succeeds in going the "way" instead of man. Since the law was understood as an objective scheme of demands and prohibitions, as a legal order which must be fulfilled, it was quite easy to conceive of a substitutionary fulfillment by Christ.[8]

Vicarious satisfaction of the demands of the divine law is therefore the heart of the orthodox doctrine of the atonement.[9] Here orthodoxy follows mainly in the tradition of Anselm, although with some alterations.[10] Their main point is Anselmian: that Christ made the satisfaction which was necessary to allow God to meet man in mercy.

The alterations come in two places. First, the Anselmian alternative, either punishment or satisfaction *(poena aut satisfactio)*, was rejected. The law demands punishment for sin, so that satisfaction can be made only if the necessary punishment has been suffered. For orthodoxy the punishment *is* the satisfaction. Second, orthodoxy differs from Anselm in its emphasis upon active obedience in the fulfillment of the law as well as passive obedience. If man cannot fulfill the law, Christ must do it actively as man's substitute; the

---

[7] See Ernst Troeltsch, *Vernunft und Offenbarung bei Johann Gerhard und Melanchthon* (Göttingen: Vandenhöck & Ruprecht, 1891), pp. 135-140.

[8] Haikola, *Studien*, pp. 10-11.

[9] Gustav Aulen, *Das Christliche Gottesbild* (Gütersloh: C. Bertelsmann Verlag, 1930), p. 256.

[10] *Ibid.*, p. 257.

demands of the law must be fulfilled under all circumstances. It is important to note here that both alterations serve the same end: they strengthen and magnify the place of law in the system.[11]

Thus the elevation and insistence upon the law as *lex aeterna* were the distinctive features of the orthodox system. The demand for satisfaction was even more insistent than it was in Anselm; the Anselmian view is magnified and made more legalistic. This is shown by the position of some of the orthodox teachers on the necessity of the atonement. Quenstedt, for instance, rejected the "scholastic" idea that God could forgive by virtue of his absolute power without satisfaction[12]; because his essence is righteousness God can do nothing other than be wrathful against sin until satisfaction has been made. Others, like Hollaz, admitted that God could, as absolute Lord, forgive without satisfaction, but they went on to say that in justification God acts not as absolute but as a righteous judge *(iudex iustissimus)* who has the law in himself and whose righteousness is part of his nature. For Hollaz, then, the absolute power to forgive without satisfaction is only an abstract possibility which can have no actuality. The idea that God's righteousness necessarily demands satisfaction is still basic.[13]

I shall refer to this orthodox doctrine of the atonement as a speculative construction based on the static-ontological concept of divine law. I do this because, in contrast with the more historically orientated view of Hofmann, orthodoxy understood the atonement against the background of a concept of the law which is rooted in the divine being as an eternal and unchangeable standard. The law provides the rational framework for understanding what takes place in the atonement. This can be called a speculative construction because it seeks to posit what is necessary "from God's point of view" before atonement can take place. By using this framework orthodoxy is forced to think in terms of a rational equivalence between the punishment inflicted on Christ, the divine-human substitute, and the demands of the divine righteousness.

This orthodox doctrine of law has several consequences for the rest of the theological system. These consequences are evident in the

---

[11] *Ibid.*, p. 257.
[12] *Ibid.*, p. 258.
[13] *Ibid.*, p. 258.

orthodox conception of the relationship between the law and the gospel, for Orthodoxy was driven to make what can be called an abstract and material distinction between the law and the gospel. Law was distinguished from gospel in the same way that one group of propositions is distinguished from another according to the given content or matter of each proposition. Those propositions which contain the *demands* of the divine righteousness are law whether they be "natural" or "revealed." On the other hand, those propositions which contain the divine promises and gifts are "gospel," and come, of course, only through "revelation." This distinction can be called abstract and material because, as we shall see later, it is to be contrasted with a more concrete and formal type of distinction which emerges from the modern debate.

The fact that law and gospel were understood as composed of propositions had the further consequence that revelation itself was understood quite strictly in a propositional sense. Orthodoxy said that revelation is the impartation of divine truth in the form of propositions which "must be believed" if one is to "be saved." Faith, therefore, is understood as an act of cognition—the acceptance of the propositions of revelation—and one is led quite necessarily into the knowledge, assent, trust *(notitia, assensus, fiducia)* scheme characteristic of the orthodox system.

Since revelation is propositional, the law-gospel distinction as such has little or nothing to do with the problem of how revelation is to be received and validated; as a result the distinction never affected the dogmatic prolegomena of orthodoxy and was relegated to the practical sections having to do with the preaching of the word.

This meant that orthodox theology had to depend upon some other means for validating the propositions of revelation. Here it was the doctrine of scriptural infallibility which filled the breach. Since revelation was propositional truth, the orthodox theologians had to establish first the reliability of the propositions before they could go on to other matters. They were virtually driven therefore to a doctrine of verbal infallibility. Starting from assumptions about the eternal standard of the law, the system produced a chain of consequences which are difficult, if not impossible, to avoid—up to and including a view of scripture which could hardly survive the crisis presented by the development of the historical-critical method.

In addition to these more or less formal consequences of the orthodox conception of law and gospel, there are consequences more intrinsic to the system itself which became the object of considerable attention in the controversy over the atonement. Because the law was seen as a static, eternal order, orthodoxy committed itself to a system which became extremely difficult to operate.

This difficulty is evident in the orthodox doctrine of justification itself. In order to guarantee a justification *sola gratia,* faith had to be described as the appropriation of the entirely "objective" work of Christ. Justification had to be purely "forensic." One therefore became entangled in the difficult question of "objective" versus "subjective." Justification is supposed to be entirely the work of God, something "outside of" man and therefore entirely "objective." But this makes it seem as though man subjectively has nothing whatever to say about it and that God's justifying action is entirely arbitrary. On the other hand, if one reacts to this by asserting the place of man's subjectivity, seeking a place for man's "decision" or "response," and making justification somehow dependent on such subjective response, one is hard pressed to avoid the charge of synergism. Thus traditional piety was torn between the poles of orthodoxist "objectivism" and pietistic "subjectivism."

The nature of the ethical life is also obscured by the orthodox view of law. Works must be excluded from justification; consequently, careful distinctions must be made between justification and sanctification, even if they tend artificially to fragment the Christian life.

Starting from certain assumptions about the law, then, the orthodox system spun a web from which it was difficult to escape. When the law is thought of as a static-ontological scheme, atonement must be understood as an "entirely objective" act, a satisfaction of the demands of the law. The gospel then becomes a proposition to the effect that the demands of the law have been met, that a "once-for-all" act has occurred within an eternally fixed scheme. God's action in Christ then loses any dimension of present actuality; one is confronted instead with a doctrine about a past event which "must be believed." In order that the doctrine possess credibility the reliability of the historical sources must be assured; thus the doctrine of scriptural infallibility must be added. All this follows quite naturally and inevitably from the original starting point. The orthodox system was a system wedded to a particular conception of law; this meant that the entire edifice was permeated by a stringent legalism which it could not avoid.

Admittedly, this sketch of the orthodox system is exceedingly brief; as is the case with most brief sketches it runs the risk of caricature. There are no doubt many devices and dictinctions which the orthodox theologian could and did use to ameliorate the difficulties of the system, but those are not our concern here. What I have sought to do is simply to expose the main structural components which bear upon the problem of law and gospel and which lead into a controversy about the atonement. It is necessary to do this in order to understand that when the battle was joined over the doctrine of the atonement it was really the fundamental structure of orthodoxy that was being attacked, and that that structure is based upon a particular conception of law and gospel.

Of course, the orthodoxy of the early 19th century was not exactly that of the 17th century. The orthodoxy of the early 19th century, variously called Biblicism, Supernaturalism, or Repristination Theology, arose out of the religious awakenings of the time and was a reaction to the erosion of the traditional theology by the Enlightenment. It was inspired by different conditions and used a somewhat different methodology, but the end result was in most cases the same as the orthodoxy of the 17th century. This is especially true in the areas of our concern here, the doctrine of law and gospel and the doctrine of the atonement.

A good example of 19th century orthodox theology can be seen in the work of E. W. Hengstenberg (Professor in Berlin, 1828-69), a theologian whom Hofmann attacks in much of his early work. In opposition to the Enlightenment and the encroachment of historical criticism, Hengstenberg sought to base his theology entirely and objectively on the Bible. From the religious awakening he drew the belief that rebirth is necessary for true theological work and that obedience to the word of scripture is the only possible

procedure.[14] In opposition to the rationalists he held that there
was no philosophical road to the knowledge of God. Revelation, in
his view, was contrary to human reason and so could not be but-
tressed by appeal to universal truths.[15] Unlike the orthodox of the
17th century, he made no attempt at a synthesis of natural and
revealed truth.

To avoid the charge that he based his theology purely on subjective experience, Hengstenberg appealed to the Bible as the sole
objective basis for faith. His aim, which involved excluding all
subjectivity and human reason, was to listen simply and completely to the words of the Bible as the objectively given source of
revelation. His only goal was to learn to think and to teach bibli-
cally.

Hengstenberg made a kind of substitution of biblical objectivity
for rational objectivity. Rationalism sought its "scientific" objectivity in the universally valid truths of reason. Hengstenberg's
repristination theology sought its objectivity solely in its object,
the Bible. This kind of Biblicism, Hengstenberg thought, could be
the only real defense against historical criticism. Historical criticism, he felt, was contaminated by alien subjective concerns stemming from human reason. Like other Biblicists, he carried on a kind
of negative apologetic in that he sought to defend the authenticity
of scripture by demonstrating that the arguments of the critics were
not necessarily conclusive.

The complete subjection of man's mind to the objective authority of scripture brought with it for Hengstenberg a return to orthodoxy in doctrine. The Bible became the sourcebook for church doctrine. In Hengstenberg's view, the doctrine of the Bible and that
of the Church Confessions (The Augsburg Confession) were
one.[16] The Bible was treated, even more than in orthodoxy, as a
compendium of doctrines.

As a theologian and as an influential church politician, Heng-

---

[14] Werner Elert, *Der Kampf um das Christentum* (München: C. H. Beck,
1921), p. 87.

[15] Emanuel Hirsch, *Geschichte der neueren Evangelischen Theologie* (Gütersloh: C. Bertelsmann Verlag, 1954). V. 119-123. (Cited hereafter as *Geschichte.*)

[16] *Ibid.*, p. 122.

stenberg worked unceasingly for the renewal of orthodoxy. It is significant that he devoted a good share of his theological energy to a renewal of the orthodox doctrine of vicarious satisfaction.[17] The net result of Hengstenberg's work was simply a restoration of orthodoxy under the aegis of Biblicism. This meant, of course, the reinstatement of the orthodox position on law and gospel.

Through men like Hengstenberg, orthodoxy was revitalized and offered to the "awakened Christian" of the 19th century as an alternative to the rationalism of the Enlightenment and as a defense against historical criticism. But for those who really took historical criticism seriously and who could not simply dismiss the developing historical world view as something antithetical to Christianity, Hengstenberg's Biblicism could hardly be a viable alternative.

To attack this Biblicism, though, meant to attack the entire system of which it was a part. The man who saw this most clearly was J. C. K. von Hofmann. His attempt to reconstruct the entire system on the basis of a *heilsgeschichtliche* scheme was an attack on the basic presuppositions of the orthodox-biblicistic system.

---

[17]*Ibid.*, p. 127.

CHAPTER II

HOFMANN'S
HEILSGESCHICHTLICHE SCHEME

The piety of J. C. K. von Hofmann, like that of Hengstenberg, was shaped by the religious awakenings of the early 19th century. Yet, unlike Hengstenberg, Hofmann was much more decisively influenced by the developing historical world view and by the emerging science of historical criticism. After a period of initial studies at Erlangen, Hofmann went to Berlin, where he studied under the "giants" of the day: Hegel, Schleiermacher, and Ranke. It is significant that of these three Ranke seems to have attracted him the most.

The crisis of historical criticism was dramatically punctuated for him by the appearance in 1835 of D. F. Strauss's *Leben Jesu.* As a serious student of history Hofmann apparently felt that it was impossible for the Christian simply to turn his back on the new science and take refuge in the doctrine of scriptural infallibility as Hengstenberg and the Biblicists had done. Yet the problem for Hofmann was how to assure oneself of the basic facts of the historical revelation—how to understand revelation as history—without succumbing either to the unhistorical legalism of scriptural infallibility or to the skepticism of radical historical criticism. A statement made early in his career reveals the essential motive behind Hofmann's theology:

> When the facts to which theology owes its existence are lost, then theology loses its justification and its source of nourishment. It becomes nothing more than the shadow of a vanished body.

Whatever crumbs it may pick up from the tables of the worldly sciences can indeed give it the appearance of life, but it is really a shame when it must say to itself, "I don't want to be buried, so I am not ashamed to beg." But how shall theology, in a time in which it has been declared to have lost its rights to its entire possession, assure itself once again of its content, a content which is not doctrinal opinion, but history? [18]

Theology for Hofmann has to do with historical facts, not (as for Hengstenberg) with doctrines. Yet because of radical historical criticism the facts themselves are in danger of being lost. This was Hofmann's dilemma. How was it to be met? The only way, he felt, was to develop a new and independent theological method which would establish both a new relationship to the facts of revelation and a new approach to scripture. For him this meant an approach dependent on neither the doctrine of biblical infallibility nor the results of historical criticism.[19] But how was such an independent method to proceed? Hofmann saw only "two ways," one which begins from the experience of salvation and works out the implications of that experience, and another which he called "the historical," which works with the interpretation of scripture.

I see only two ways worthy of an independent method. The first and most immediate way starts from the most general form of the personal experience of salvation, that which makes a Christian to be a Christian, and leads from the immediately certain fact which forms its content to the presuppositions for that fact, which also must themselves be facts. Just as the historian knows essentially from a given situation in time what must have happened to bring it about, just as the natural scientist knows from the result the series of natural transformations which caused it, so also the theologian finds the essential events of the entire Holy History comprehended in the fact of rebirth and he can reproduce the beginning and process from that antici-

---

[18] Johannes Haussleiter (ed.), *Grundlinien der Theologie J. v. Hofmanns in seiner eigenen Darstellung* (Leipzig: A. Deichert, 1910), pp. 1-2.

[19] In seeking an independent method Hofmann earned for himself a place which has not been sufficiently recognized. See Martin Schellbach, *Theologie und Philosophie bei v. Hofmann* (Gütersloh: C. Bertelsmann, 1935), p. 23; also Martin Kähler, *Geschichte der Protestantischen Dogmatik im 19. Jahrhundert,* edited by Ernst Kähler (Theologische Bücherei; München: Chr. Kaiser Verlag, 1962), p. 212.

patory end of the history (i.e., the rebirth). Or does the relationship of God in Christ to us, of which we are certain by personal experience, not have as its presupposition, and is it not the result of, all that which constitutes the essential content of the history of salvation?

The second way is the historical, in which one puts together the whole of the Holy History as it is transmitted in scripture in the sense of scripture itself, i.e., from the vantage point of what scripture itself declares to be the mid-point of that history. The unity and completeness of this history will provide a guarantee of its truth which will have validity and power for everyone who through the personal experience of salvation is in a position to understand it. For where this is missing, there there is no theological calling.[20]

We must look at these "two ways" more carefully to discover how they work and how they are related.

It is evident from all of Hofmann's work that it is really the first way, the way of experience, that he took as basic; this was the point from which everything began. Through Christ, he maintained, the Christian is aware of being brought into an absolutely new and personal relationship with God.[21] Christianity is not, as Hengstenberg's restored orthodoxy implied, a matter of subscribing to doctrines, but rather an experience. As Hofmann put it it is an "actual situation" [22] mediated by Christ through the church as a historical community. The Biblicistic position, Hofmann said, should be rejected because it is

> . . . not a personal relationship to and attitude towards God, such as the Christian is conscious of, but a legalistic relationship to a thing. For whether it be that which is given or the giving of it, it is always a mere something that is believed. Christianity ends up in this legalistic poverty by way of Supernaturalism, because that makes out of Christianity a historical revela-

---

[20] Johannes Haussleiter (ed.), *Grundlinien der Theologie J. v. Hofmanns in seiner eigenen Darstellung* (Leipzig: A. Deichert, 1910), pp. 2-3.

[21] J. C. K. von Hofmann, *Encyclopädie der Theologie*, ed. H. J. Bestmann (Nördlingen: C. H. Beck, 1897), p. 5. Cited hereafter as *Encyclopädie*.)

[22] The word which Hofmann used is *Tatbestand*. It implied for him a situation which is the result of a historical act, a *Tat*. Thus I have chosen to translate it as "actual situation."

tion the content of which must be believed simply because it is divinely revealed.[23]

Thus at the outset Hofmann voiced his opposition to the legalism inherent in the orthodox structure, an opposition which he carried through consistently to an attack on the doctrine of vicarious satisfaction.

By making personal experience basic, Hofmann showed his debt both to the pietism in which he was raised and to Schleiermacher. As a consequence it has been his fate, and the fate of the Erlangen school which he was instrumental in founding, constantly to be accused of extreme subjectivism in theology. Perhaps he cannot be completely exonerated from this charge, but there are several things which must be said in his defense—things which also help to clarify the nature of the relationship between experience and history.

First, for Hofmann the experience is never self-generated; the Christian experience is mediated by the church. It is an experience *into which* one is incorporated when one becomes a Christian.[24]

Second, one must note carefully the manner in which Hofmann proceeded on the basis of this experience. It was his conviction that theology will be truly independent only when it starts from the newness and uniqueness of the Christian experience and occupies itself with expounding that experience. This is the significance of Hofmann's oft-quoted but little-understood statement about the nature of theology:

> Theology is a truly free science, free in God, only when precisely that which makes a Christian to be a Christian, his own independent relationship to God, makes the theologian to be a theologian through disciplined self-knowledge and self-expression; when I the Christian am for me the theologian the essential material of my science.[25]

For Hofmann, then, the experience is never merely a subjective or individual experience but *the Christian experience*. It is not merely

---

[23] Hofmann, *Encyclopädie*, p. 6.
[24] *Ibid.*, pp. 8-9.
[25] J. C. K. von Hofmann, *Der Schriftbeweis* (2 vols.; 2nd ed. rev.; Nördlingen: C. H. Beck, 1857-1860), I, 10.

the faith of the individual that comes to expression, but *the* Christian faith.

> For it is Christianity *(das Christentum)* that is to be expressed,
> not faith that expresses itself. The self-expression of faith would,
> to be sure, be only a subjective confession, as is falsely charged
> of my system, and not a science of Christendom.[26]

It is therefore a *communal* experience. Faith is, of course, the theologian's own experience, but he has the experience only to the degree to which he personally is incorporated into the church.

> Not *a* Christianity, *his* Christianity, is to set itself forth; which,
> however, to the degree that he personally is adapted to the
> community of God through Christ, will be *the* Christian experience.[27]

Finally, since the Christian experience is mediated by the church and is a communal experience into which one is incorporated, one must also understand its *historical* nature. The experience is a historical *fact* and must be understood as such. It carries within itself its own internal guarantee[28]; it is, as one would say today, "self-authenticating." That means for Hofmann that the history carries its own guarantee of truth with it because it is not merely a past history, a "once upon a time it happened," but rather a "present" which happens again. The history of which one speaks reaches into the present to create the experience anew. The historical revelation is therefore related to faith not merely as a set of teachings to a knower, but as a history which has a "present" in the experience of the believer. It "authenticates itself," proves itself, by happening once again in the present to the believer. The object of faith, therefore, Hofmann insisted, is not a record about a past event, not a doctrine, but the present mode of divine activity in history, which in the case of the Christian must be not merely the Christ of past history but the present Christ, the resurrected and living Christ.[29]

---

[26] J. C. K. von Hofmann, *Schutzschriften für eine neue Weise, alte Wahrheit zu Lehren* (4 parts; Nördlingen: C. H. Beck, 1856-1859), IV, 31. (Underlining mine.) (Cited hereafter as *Schutzschriften.*)

[27] Hofmann, *Der Schriftbeweis* (2nd ed.), I, 8.

[28] Hofmann, *Encyclopädie*, p. 7.

[29] Paul Wapler, *Johannes v. Hofmann* (Leipzig: A. Deichertsche Verlagsbuchhandlung Werner Scholl, 1914), p. 69.

For Hofmann, then, the history to which the believer is related always has a present dimension. This present dimension is assured by the fact that it is the church which mediates the experience to the believer in the present. God's action in history continues in the present through the church. When faith is created, this means that God's historical activity has reached its appointed *telos* in the believer.

> To this communion of God and man pertains, because it is mediated not objectively but personally, not through something but through Christ, the most perfect simplicity. It is the resolution and decision towards which everything that has happened between man and God is straining, the simple issue *(einfache Ergebnis)* in which all history finds its end *(Abschluss)*.[30]

It was this understanding of the relationship between history and faith that gave Hofmann his unique stance and furnished him with the vantage point from which he could view the history of salvation. Since the history which has produced the Christian experience carries its own internal guarantee, and since this history has reached its *telos* in the experience of the individual, this means that the individual is free from any sort of legalistic relationship to the past, in either scripture or tradition. Furthermore, since in this experience the history has reached its simple issue or goal, all the essential moments of that history must be, for him, contained within the experience itself. The content of the history of salvation, therefore, is to be developed by a careful examination of the Christian experience itself. This, for Hofmann, was the basic task of systematic theology—to analyze the nature and content of the Christian experience.[31] Theology is born out of the Christian's own desire to understand and give expression to that which makes him to be a Christian. The Christian experience is a *historical fact* which must have as its presupposition previous *historical facts* which account for its existence.

Thus, as Hofmann said, his "first way" starts from

---

[30] Hofmann, *Der Schriftbeweis* (2nd ed.), I, 12.
[31] *Ibid.*, p. 10.

> . . . the personal experience of salvation, that which makes a
> Christian to be a Christian, and leads from the immediately cer-
> tain fact which forms its content to the presuppositions for this
> fact, which also must themselves be facts.[32]

The most important point is that for Hofmann a proper consideration of the Christian experience leads to *Heilsgeschichte*—a
process of historical cause and effect which itself makes up the content of the Christian experience. Understanding the Christian experience in terms of a *heilsgeschichtliche* process quite independently from scripture, tradition, or the results of historical criticism
is the "first way" to insure a free and independent theology, a
theology free from all types of legalism.

But how is this "first way" related to the "second way"—the way
of historical exegesis? It was Hofmann's conviction that this question too could be answered only by the analysis of the nature of
Christian experience. That is to say, it is only through a proper
understanding of the Christian experience that one could establish
a correct relationship to exegesis. Since the Christian experience is
self-authenticating and carries within itself its own content, one
cannot approach scripture with a view to culling out authoritative
doctrines which "are to be believed." Nor can it be the case that
the teachings of scripture are to be imposed by virtue of a doctrine
of infallibility. Exegesis cannot be allowed to tyrannize experience
in a legalistic fashion. Nevertheless, since the experience is communal, and scripture belongs to the community, there is a necessary
relationship to scripture. Hofmann formulated this relationship by
saying that the communal nature of the experience dictates that the
understanding of this experience be *compared with,* and if necessary
corrected by the understanding of the experience as it is found in
scripture.[33] Even though the development of the content of experience is an independent task, nevertheless it must be recognized
that one can make mistakes; this method, then, must be open to
comparison with other expressions of the nature of the experience.

The point is that the Christian experience *by its very nature*
leads one to the "second way," the way of historical exegesis—to a

---

[32] Haussleiter, *Grundlinien*, p. 2.
[33] Hofmann, *Encyclopädie*, pp. 26-27.

comparison of one's own experience with the experience of the community which procedes and conditions it. This was also one of the main points of Hofmann's defense against the charge of subjectivism:

> Systematic theology has its justification by virtue of the fact that Christianity is a personal matter. But it is at the same time a community matter and therefore it must be augmented by historical investigation. If not, Christianity moves from being a personal matter to being a subjective matter.[34]

So the "first way" leads necessarily to the "second way"; understanding the experience leads to historical exegesis. Such exegesis, for Hofmann, consists in the fact that

> . . . one puts together the whole of holy history as it is transmitted in scripture in the sense of scripture itself, i.e., from the point of view of what scripture itself declares to be the midpoint of that history.[35]

In other words, one must exegete scripture as a unified whole, as a *heilsgeschichtliche* continuum. When this is done, Hofmann felt that scripture will ratify experience just as experience ratifies the content of scripture. As he put it in his statement about the "second way":

> The unity and completeness of this history will provide a guarantee of its truth which will have validity and power for everyone who through the personal experience of salvation is in a position to understand it.[36]

Hofmann followed this dual method in his major work, *Der Schriftbeweis*. First, in a brief *Lehrganze*, Hofmann develops the content of the Christian experience. Then follows, in the main part of the work, the scriptural "proof," the demonstration that the experience agrees with scripture.

Hofmann also recognized the tradition of the church, which might be called a "third way"; the communal nature of the experi-

---

[34] *Ibid.*, pp. 32-33.
[35] Haussleiter, *Grundlinien*, p. 3.
[36] *Ibid.*

ence also dictates that one take the history of the church into account. Since he was primarily a biblical exegete, however, Hofmann never really undertook a "proof" from the tradition even though he recognized its place. Thus, for Hofmann, and for the Erlangen School following him, systematics (unfolding the content of experience), scriptural exegesis, and church history were the three pillars of theological science. In these three operations theology has both a threefold possibility for discovering the truth and at the same time a threefold possibility for falling into error. But in this life, theology can attain to no closer approximation to the truth than these three disciplines afford:

> Between the threefold possibility of knowing the truth and also succumbing to error, theological science remains in the balance until by the hand of the Lord who leads his church and also her theology she will reach that goal towards which she strives, the unity of faith and the knowledge of the Son of God.[37]

It is from this point of view that Hofmann undertook his reinterpretation of basic Christian doctrines and launched his attack on the Orthodox-Biblicist system. It was his conviction that the Christian experience is the experience of being incorporated into an absolutely new reality, one so new, in fact, that it demands a new systematic method, a new understanding of the nature of the history of salvation and, consequently, a reinterpretation of such basic doctrines as the atonement. In what follows I shall try to demonstrate how at every point Hofmann built up his case against the orthodox system and how this culminated in his attack on the doctrine of vicarious satisfaction.

Theological Method. To begin with, Hofmann insisted that the Christian experience makes a unique method necessary. The peculiar nature of the experience, its absolute newness, requires a particular kind of thinking. It is not that one thinks *about* the experience so as to produce *Lehrmeinungen* (doctrinal opinions), but rather that one must *think in* the actual situation of being a Christian.

---

[37] Hofmann, *Encyclopädie*, p. 27.

But now in order to allow the thus explicated fact of Christianity to attain to the exposition of its manifold content, a *thinking in* the situation is required. No concepts which, as always, spring up outside of Christianity may be allowed to have determinative influence in the self-unfolding. If one allows this [thinking in the situation] freely to happen, one will nowhere end up with isolated concepts which calculating reason must then first bring into relationship with one another. It is an actual relationship that is our concern, *in which,* not about which we think.[38]

For Hofmann this was a very important point because, as we shall see, his constant complaint about the orthodox doctrine of the atonement is that it is the result of a type of thinking inappropriate to the Christian experience.

But what does such thinking in the situation of being a Christian involve? Hofmann says that it involves an *unfolding* of the content of the experience. The systematic method to be used is that of evolution—allowing the content of the experience to unfold or evolve out of itself.[39] How is this to be done? First of all, one must remember that it is *the Christian experience* which is to be unfolded. Second, since this experience is communal and at the same time the completely simple result of God's dealing with mankind in history, it must be possible, Hofmann felt, to express this experience in a general or universal statement which would be acknowledged by all Christians.[40] The first task of thinking in the Christian experience, then, is to arrive at the most simple and universal expression of that experience. Having done this, one can proceed to unfold its content.

But what is this simple and universal statement of the Christian experience? It involves several factors.[41] First, one is aware as a Christian that he stands in a personal relationship to God. Second, he is aware that this relationship is mediated by Jesus Christ and that without this mediation it would not have come about. Third, he is aware that this relationship is one which has brought peace

---

[38] Hofmann, *Der Schriftbeweis* (2nd ed.), I, 12-13 (Italicizing mine.)
[39] Hofmann, *Encyclopädie*, p. 48.
[40] *Ibid.*, p. 49.
[41] *Ibid.*, pp. 50-51.

to his conscience so that he aspires to nothing other than the full realization of the relationship. It is therefore a relationship of love (Liebesgemeinschaft). Fourth, in this relationship of love he is a participant in a visible community whose basis is the relationship of God to Christ. Putting all this together, Hofmann arrived at the statement which perfectly comprehends the nature of the Christian experience:

> In bringing Christianity to its most simple expression, we arrive . . . at the result that it is the living personal communion between God and sinful mankind mediated, indeed, mediated in the present, in Christ Jesus.[42]

The statement is repeated in even more brief form in Der Schriftbeweis: "The personal communion of God and mankind mediated in Jesus Christ."[43]

It is from this statement that the content of the experience is to be unfolded. What does this mean? Since this experience is the result of a mediation in history, a historical fact, one must ask what must necessarily be presupposed for this experience to be what it is. One must ask what God must have done in history in order to make the Christian experience possible. By developing the presuppositions necessary for the experience one unfolds the content of the experience itself.[44]

---

[42] Hofmann, Encyclopädie, p. 51.

[43] Hofmann, Der Schriftbeweis (2nd ed.), I, 12.

[44] One is reminded here of Schleiermacher, who develops his systematic out of propositions presupposed by and contained in the antithesis of sin and grace. Hofmann undoubtedly is indebted to Schleiermacher at this point. He felt, however, that by taking as his starting point the most general statement of the Christian experience and then unfolding the content of this statement, he had escaped the "subjectivism" of Schleiermacher. "The unfolding of the content of this proposition is something other than Schleiermacher's description of pious self-consciousness, i.e., it is not the Sosein of the Christian that comes to expression, but always the actual situation which exists objectively but has realized itself in me." (Encyclopädie, p. 51.) (Italicizing mine.) Paul Wapler, Hofmann's biographer, makes the same point: "For him, therefore, the material of dogmatics is not as for Schleiermacher the condition of pious feelings, . . . but the historical objectivity of the living reality created through Christ, which allows it to be deduced by each individual because of rebirth as a system of heilsgeschichtliche development (Johannes von Hofmann, p. 93). For Hofmann unfolding the content of the experience leads to Heilsgeschichte.

There are basically three kinds of such presuppositions in Hofmann's system.[45] First, since it is a relationship *to* God that is mediated, there are some *eternal* presuppositions, that is, presuppositions having to do with how God must have disposed himself *eternally* in order to enter into a relationship with historical man. Second, since it is a relationship *established through history,* there must be some *historical* presuppositions, that is, presuppositions about man's history with God, a history of salvation. Finally, since the historical experience is *not yet perfected,* it must be presupposed that it will be perfected in the *future.* Hence on the basis of experience, one is led to hold a future hope.

For Hofmann, then, the unfolding of the content of the Christian experience leads to a *heilsgeschichtliche* system built up out of eternal presuppositions, historical presuppositions, and future hope. The Christian experience is thus the experience of historical life-forces *(Lebensmächte)* in which God himself is active; it is participation in a historical-suprahistorical continuum of life *(Lebenszusammenhang).*[46]

From this it can be seen that Hofmann developed a systematic method quite opposed to that of an orthodox Biblicist like Hengstenberg. It was a thoroughgoing departure from the orthodox system. It has a different way of validating the facts of Christian experience, it understood the nature and function of theology differently, and it established a different relationship to scripture and the tradition. At every point it tried to avoid any suggestion of a legalistic understanding of faith.

The basic theme: Heilsgeschichte. A second point at which Hofmann's difference from the orthodox system becomes apparent is in the basic theme of his theology, the *heilsgeschichtliche* scheme. The Christian experience must be understood as the result of a chain of historical events issuing from God and culminating in the creation of faith. As we have seen, Hofmann believed that all the essential moments of the *Heilsgeschichte* must be contained in the experience of faith as its presupposition. The content of faith is therefore *Heilsgeschichte;* the *history* is therefore the "doctrine" of

---

[45] Hofmann, *Der Schriftbeweis* (2nd ed.), I, pp. 13-14.
[46] Wapler, *Johannes v. Hofmann,* p. 93.

Christianity. Everything must therefore be understood in a historical sense, as a continuum of historical cause and effect. *Heilsgeschichte* provides the "system" for understanding the "doctrines of
Christianity."

What does this system look like? Consonant with Hofmann's
method of "thinking in" the Christian experience, it consists of the
three types of "presupposition" necessary to understanding that
experience. It begins with the presuppositions which must be made
about God, the eternal presuppositions, then goes on to the historical
presuppositions and ends with those dealing with the future hope.
To get a picture of this system I shall here present a brief résumé
of Hofmann's *Lehrganze* as it appears in *Der Schriftbeweis*.[47]

The system begins with Hofmann's understanding of the Trin-
ity (the eternal presuppositions).[48] Since the relationship established with God through Christ is a personal one, it must be presupposed that God is a self-determining person. Since it is mediated by Christ, one must presuppose that Christ stands in a relationship to God which is itself not in need of mediation, hence a
relationship internal to the divine life itself. Thus one must presuppose the eternal relationship of the Father and the Son. Furthermore, since in Christ the relationship of God and mankind is perfected, it must be the realization of God's eternal attitute *(Verhalten)* towards mankind, so that that which supports the life of
Jesus Christ must also support man's life. This leads to the concept
of Spirit. God as Spirit is the ground of life, the immanent life
force *(inweltlich wirksamen Lebensgrund)*, which must also be internal to the divine life.[49] That which God intends for mankind
must be perfect and eternal in him. The eternal content of God's
will for mankind, therefore, must be perfectly embodied in Jesus
Christ. The eternal object of the divine will is Jesus Christ as true
man. Since this will is realized in history, mankind is the temporal
object of God's will. God's will is that man should be his own in
Jesus Christ.

This leads to the historical presuppositions. From the fact that in

---

[47] pp. 33-57.
[48] *Ibid.*, pp. 35-36.
[49] *Ibid.*, p. 37.

Jesus Christ the will of God for mankind has reached the beginning of its perfection in history, one must presuppose that God has willed a historical process of self-realization *(Selbstvollziehung),* moving from eternal identity to historical differentiation *(Ungleichheit).*[50] Since Christ is the perfection of this process, he must be both its beginning and end. In him, therefore, the world must have been created and in him the world is perfected. Christ is both archetype and *telos* of the world *(Urbildlichen Weltziels).*[51]

This leads to the doctrine of sin, which of course will be of importance for the doctrine of the atonement.[52] Since man is aware that his relationship to God is mediated by Christ, one must presuppose that the original relationship set by creation was broken. This means that man must have allowed himself to be determined in a manner contrary to the original divine will. But where could such determination come from? Certainly not from God, for that would be self-contradictory. Nor could it come from man, for that would mean that man deliberately denied his relationship to God and cut himself off permanently from God. Nor could it come from nature as such, for nature is impersonal and could not affect man in a personal way. Only one alternative is left: It must have come from the realm of spirit.

Hofmann has a rather complicated doctrine of spirit which comes, apparently, from German 'Idealism, especially Schelling.[53] God as Spirit is the immanent life-ground. In the created and natural world this life-force is divided, so to speak, into a plurality of spirits accounting for plurality and variety in the world. These finite spirits (angels) carry out the rule of God in the world and are one with the Divine Spirit insofar as they are dedicated to the goal and completion of the world in man as God's. Man is the apex, the *telos* of creation, and hence the one in whom creation finds its unity and purpose. When the plurality of spirits is directed toward

---

[50] *Ibid.,* p. 37.

[51] *Ibid,.* p. 37.

[52] *Ibid.,* pp. 38-40.

[53] See Schellbach, *Theologie und Philosophie bei v. Hofmann,* p. 104; also Paul Wapler, "Die Theologie Hofmanns in ihrem Verhältnis zu Schellings positiver Philosophie, *Neue Kirchliche Zeitschrift,* 16 (Sept. 1905), pp. 716-718.

this goal, creation is in harmony. When this is not so, creation threatens to collapse into a chaos of competing spirits.[54]

If man has allowed himself to be determined otherwise than was intended by God in the original creation, this must have come about because as part of the created world he is open to activity stemming from among the plurality of spirits. What must have happened was that a revolt in the spirit world came to focus on man to defeat the divine purpose. It must have been directed towards deceiving man about the divine plan, towards making man fail to understand his perfection, his creation in the image of God as the *telos* of the created order. Sin could enter, therefore, only in the form of a *deception* stemming from spirits in revolt against the divine plan. It could come about only through a temptation enticing man to transcend the creaturely limitation placed upon him.[55] Hofmann believes it possible to "unfold" the nature of this temptation even down to the details of the temptation of the first woman by Satan and the subsequent temptation of man by the woman.

Thus we have Hofmann's unfolding of the concept of sin as a presupposition for the present Christian experience. What happened—and this can be taken as his definition of sin—was that because man succumbed to a desire and an activity which went contrary to the divine order, he exchanged, as far as was possible for him, his relationship to God and the world established by creation for one in which he is in personal dependence to the contra-divine spirit, becoming an object of God's wrath instead of his love. Sin has two sides. In the relationship to the world, man has become subject to the spirit which wills its dissolution; this means that he finds himself in a world captive to dissolution (death) rather than one which has its unified *telos* in himself as God's. In relationship to God, man is aware that God excludes him, that he has become a stranger and an enemy. This means that he is aware of sin, guilt, and death.

Since, however, we see from the present experience of Christianity that God has made provision for the ultimate realization of his

---

[54] Hofmann, *Der Schriftbeweis* (2nd ed.), I, pp. 38-39.
[55] *Ibid.*, pp. 39-40.

will, we must presuppose that God must have foreordained the possibility of a fall whose eventuality could not frustrate his will.[56] The fact that this is so, however, must be seen as God's doing, as an act of his grace. It is by no means due to man's inherent goodness. It is only because God is Triune that the possibility of salvation remains open.

From here, Hofmann went on to unfold the historical presuppositions prior to the appearance of Jesus Christ. The Christian is aware that the relationship established in Jesus Christ did not originate in himself. Consequently between the fall and the restoration in Christ an activity of God must have taken place which was actually the self-disclosure and self-realization of the relationship interior to the divine life. The task here, therefore, is to ascertain the steps which were necessary for this to have come about. Since the appearance of Jesus Christ is itself the end *(Abschluss)* of this history, one must presuppose a series of preparatory steps. The history must therefore be a prefiguring of the final end.[57]

With this the basis for the temporal *Heilsgeschichte* is established and Hofmann can "unfold" the content of this history. He proceeded through successive stages—family, the Israelite nation, Christ, and finally the church.[58] The family (Abraham and his descendants) was the original unit which could have provided the arena in which to prefigure the reunion of God and man. We know

---

[56] *Ibid.*, p. 40.

[57] *Ibid.*, pp. 40-41.

[58] *Ibid.*, pp. 40-45. It should be noted at this point that Hofmann does not believe it possible to unfold *all* these historical facts from the Christian experience as such. There are, he maintained, a number of purely historical and sociological facts available to anyone, Christian or not, which cannot be doubted and can be used by the Christian in unfolding the system. Such facts are, for instance, the existence of the Israelite nation with its history and its persistence outside the church since the time of Christ, the fact that Jesus came from this nation, the existence of the church as a purely sociological entity, etc. The point seems to be that for Hofmann these facts as such are not in need of mediation and therefore do not need to be unfolded from the *Christian* experience. This indicates that for Hofmann it is only the *heilsgeschichtliche* aspect of the "history" that needs to be unfolded from the Christian experience, i.e., those facts (fall, incarnation, resurrection, consummation, etc.) which are not evident to everyone and can be subject to scientific doubt. See Hofmann, *Encyclopädie*, pp. 51-52.

from history, however,[59] that Jesus was not only a member of a family but of a nation. This assumes that the family of man must have been separated into a number of nations and that the righteousness of certain individuals was not enough to prepare for Christ. Thus Hofmann introduced the history of the Israelite nation with its institutions (King, Priest, and Prophet) as the prefiguring of the appearance of Christ.

The climax of the scheme was reached, of course, in Jesus Christ. In Jesus Christ the relationship between God and man internal to the divine life is disclosed and realized. The self-determination of Jesus involves the fact that he, as archetypal-world *telos*, entered human nature to be the mediator of the new relationship. Consequently, he must have participated in human nature as it is because of sin, yet without sin himself. Born an Israelite, he was the incarnate Son of God and the counterfigurative end *(gegenbildlicher Abschluss)* of the pre-figurative history *(vorbildlichen Geschichte)*.[60]

Thus a new stage in the *Heilsgeschichte* was reached through Christ. Its purpose was to overcome the contradiction between the divine love-will and the sin which calls forth the divine wrath. In the incarnation God makes himself into the antithesis *(Gegensatz)* of God the loving Father and God the Son subject to the divine wrath.[61] What occurs therefore will have to be that the Son preserves his personal relationship with the Father to the end—in the face of all that results from sin—and in so doing removes the contradiction in his own person. Jesus endured to the end in that he suffered in the most extreme manner the full force of the opposition focused on him because of sin (the activity of the contra-divine forces acting through man). His act was the perseverance in the attitude towards God *(Verhalten gegen Gott)* which made good *(gut macht)* what sin had corrupted *(übel gemacht)*.[62] In this act reconciliation *(Sühnung)* is accomplished *in* mankind *(in der Menschheit)*, and thus in him true righteousness is realized.[63]

---

[59] See preceding note.

[60] Hofmann, *Der Schriftbeweis* (2nd ed.), p. 46.

[61] *Ibid.*, p. 47.

[62] Hofmann, *Encyclopädie*, p. 85.

[63] *Ibid.*, p. 85.

The point of all this, as we shall see more completely in the discussion of the atonement, is that Jesus' life and death must be understood strictly from a *heilsgeschichtliche* point of view. Jesus is the realization of the divine will to love mankind. As the incarnate Son of God, he suffered under the contra-divine forces which sought to frustrate the divine will. These contra-divine forces acted through a mankind which has become enslaved. By persevering in his divine calling and eventually through his resurrection, Jesus Christ established a *new humanity*, a new righteousness in which the eternal will is realized.[64] Jesus' death was a translation into a new kind of human existence in which his nature now becomes the means through which a new and unconditional relationship between God and man can be realized. Hofmann refers to this existence as a transfigured (*verklärten*) existence, the existence of the resurrected Christ.[65]

To be a Christian is to be conscious of one's participation in this new exsitence, to be included in the body of Christ, the church. The final sections of Hofmann's *Lehrganze* deal with the life in this new community, with its past, present, and future.[66] Here he gives attention to life "in the spirit." This is a new kind of existence in which the Spirit of God, the immanent life force, becomes the determining force in man's personal and natural life so that he is freed from captivity to the contra-divine spirits; through the Spirit the unity of creation which was lost in the fall is restored. In the future the Christian looks for the complete perfection of this life and the final defeat of the contra-divine forces.

From this rather brief summary it can be seen that Hofmann unfolded a system quite different from that of orthodoxy. It was the unfolding of a historical continuum on a grand scale, a theology of history, indeed an absolute universal history. Hofmann's system was an attempt to understand all the basic facts of Christianity in terms of the divine love-will realizing itself in spite of all opposition.

Obviously there are many questions which arise at this point—

---

[64] *Ibid.*, p. 86.

[65] *Ibid.*, p. 87.

[66] Hofmann, *Der Schriftbeweis*, pp. 49-57.

questions particularly about theological method. How did Hofmann believe it possible to operate in this manner, and why did he find it necessary? Such questions, however, are beyond the scope of the present study.[67] Suffice it to say that Hofmann felt it necessary to operate in this way in order to establish a truly independent method, one freed from both the legalism of orthodox verbal infallibility and from the skepticism of radical historical criticism. The Christian, who experiences the "new birth," participates in the "new humanity" as a historical reality and must operate independently from all other forms of verification. He must understand his experience only in terms of itself and be true to its content alone. This fact governs all else. One might say that it is an attempt to write a theology strictly from the point of view of the "new humanity" in Christ.

The place of law in Hofmann's system. The point at which Hofmann's disagreement with orthodoxy became most apparent was in his attitude toward the law. As we have seen, law provided for orthodoxy the structure in terms of which God's action in Christ was to be understood. What Hofmann did was to replace law with *Heilsgeschichte.* God's action is to be understood as the realization of the divine will to love, a realization which works itself out in history and can be understood only in terms of a history of salvation. The appearance and activity of Christ can be grasped only when it is understood as the result of a confluence of historical and supra-historical forces.

This means that law is displaced as the structural determinant of the system. In Hofmann's construction, law appears only at that stage in the *Heilsgeschichte* in which Israel existed as a nation. Israel was a prefigure *(Vorbild)* of that which was to come. To serve in this manner, the nation must, Hofmann asserts, have had an origin completely different from other nations; otherwise it

---

[67] For an interesting discussion of these problems with a contemporary colleague see the correspondence between Hofmann and Franz Delitzsch: Franz Delitzsch and Johannes v. Hofmann, *Theologische Briefe* (Leipzig: J. C. Hinrichs, 1891). (Cited hereafter as *Briefe.*) See also E. W. Wendebourg, "Die Heilsgeschichtliche Theologie J. C. K. v. Hofmanns," Dissertation, Göttingen: 1953.

would have brought with it folk-mores contrary to its calling.[68] Thus Israel must have received a self-disclosure from God which would mark it out as God's own people; this would have enabled it to prefigure the final end. Since law gives a nation its distinctive structure and character, Israel must have received a specially revealed law. This meant that for the nation, the attitude demanded of faith necessarily took on a legalistic character.

The point, however, is that the legalistic stance of Israel is purely prefigurative. Since it did not succeed in bringing about the desired goal (the reunion of God and man) it was *superseded*. The next stage in the *Heilsgeschichte* supplanted the legalistic stage and did away with law. Law can be rightly understood, then, only within the *heilsgeschichtliche* scheme. The trouble with Israel, Hofmann felt, was that even though the form of faith consonant with its national life was necessarily a legalistic one, it was tempted to forget the *heilsgeschichtliche* referent, so that its faith tended to become futile.

> The form of the activity of faith therefore is here necessarily a legalistic one. There is thus the possibility that the attitude will allow itself to be determined entirely by the communal order of the people. This would be merely an attitude of legalism, which just as little as lawlessness (*Ungesetzlichkeit*), which the communal order also rejects, is the attitude which God demands. Such legalism gives itself the comfort of salvation in vain, even if it knows the law. For the communal order is only between the times (*ein zwischeneingekommenes moment*) and must be evaluated in relation to the promise contained in the prefigurative realization of salvation and the divine self-witness explicated therein.[69]

Law is peculiar only to Israel's existence as a nation, something which comes "between the times." When this is forgotten and the law has become itself the object of faith, that faith is futile. Law can be understood only in terms of *Heilsgeschichte;* it can never provide the structure for understanding God's action; it cannot be an "eternal standard" for measuring what God must do to save man or what man must do to save himself. When Christ

---

[68] Hofmann, *Encyclopädie*, pp. 77-78.
[69] Hofmann, *Encyclopädie*, p. 81.

comes, the legalistic form of faith is superseded by the "new humanity." Hofmann rejected the old idea of a *lex aeterna;* in its place stands the *heilsgeschichtliche* scheme.

Law is therefore only part of the picture. It belongs only to a particular historical dispensation, given to man in the situation of sin. With this in mind, Hofmann could speak of the giving of the law in connection with the divine wrath: "God's wrath against sin placed Israel under the law of commandments and prohibitions . . . ." [70]

Man's righteousness, consequently, cannot be measured by the degree of his compliance with divine law. Instead, righteousness always consists, for Hofmann, in the penitent acceptance of God's action in history.[71] Man's obligation is to accept whatever form of divine activity is revealed to him at a particular time. The object of faith is always the current mode of the divine activity, that is, faith in the *Heilsgeschichte.* For the Israelite this meant living according to the law in the context of the promise. For the Christian, it means living in the freedom of the "new humanity" given in Christ.

This view of law is amplified in Hofmann's ethics. Theological ethics, he said, is an integral part of systematic theology and not a separate discipline. This is so because like systematics it grows out of the understanding of the "new humanity," not out of the question of "morality"—the question of "the good" in general.[72] The task of ethics, for Hofmann, is to *describe* the reality of the new life and not to *prescribe* what ought to be according to a set of laws. It is natural for the Christian, Hofmann said, simply to allow that life into which he is reborn to be his life; this life should be the expression of the love which he has received. And if it be the case, in particular instances, that demands are made, these must be made in the sense of the apostolic injunction: "Regard yourselves to be dead unto sin, but alive unto God." What is demanded is simply that the Christian remain in that which he has been given

---

[70] Hofmann, *Schutzschriften,* II, p. 95.

[71] Hofmann, "Lutherische Ethik," *Zeitschrift für Protestantismus und Kirche* (N. F. 45, no month given, 1863), pp. 251-256.

[72] *Ibid.,* p. 253.

and allow himself to be determined by that same Spirit who has made him to be what he is.

> Neither a doctrine of duty nor of virtue is *apropos* here. The virtue of the Christian is the new life in which he stands, and his duty is to show himself ever and again as one who stands in such new life. But in the new life itself everything is already included towards which he must evolve.[73]

Just as in systematics one cannot legalistically prescribe what "is to be believed" but rather must unfold the content of the experience, so also in ethics one cannot prescribe duties and virtues; the ethical life must be an unfolding of what the new life really is.

Theological ethics consequently leaves law behind:

> When the science in question here enters the picture—at the point where justifying faith in Jesus and therewith the rebirth is present—every moral condition has been superseded. For justified faith that is already a thing of the past, be it before sin or under sin and law.[74]

Hofmann was not so naive as to believe that the reality of the new life is present in perfect form. What he meant was that the new life is the object of faith and not of sight. It is the *true* life of everyone who is reborn in justifying faith and the sole basis upon which he should act even though it is not *perfectly* present in any Christian.[75] In the new relationship, God's will is so to be realized that it becomes the "internal law" of the Christian. The task of the Christian is simply to maintain himself and to activate himself according to that in which he stands.[76]

> The Spirit of Christ teaches him what he has to do, drives him to do it and enables him to do it. And that which he then does is indubitably right.[77]

Since the starting point for Hofmann's ethic was incorporation into the new humanity, this dictated the structure which he built.

---

[73] *Ibid.*, pp. 253-254.
[74] *Ibid.*, p. 254.
[75] *Ibid.*, p. 256.
[76] J. C. K. v. Hofmann, *Theologische Ethik* (Nördlingen: C. H. Beck, 1878), p. 78.
[77] *Ibid.*, p. 78.

The first consequence is that as a redeemed sinner one is a member of the Christian community, the church. Beyond this follow other given natural relationships such as family, state, and humanity in general. The important fact is that one serves in the wider spheres of family, state, and humanity in general only from the center, from the starting point in the new life. The wider spheres, one might say, are a series of concentric circles extending out from the center in the new life.

In his ethics Hofmann described the disposition or posture (Gesinnung) proper to the Christian in each of the spheres of action. In cases of conflict between spheres the rights and responsibilities of each are to be noted and respected. Were the state, for instance, so to enlarge itself as to threaten either family or church on the one hand, or on the other to attempt forcibly to subject humanity in general to itself in a universal kingdom, it would become despotic and one would be constrained to resist it.[78]

So conceived Christian ethics must by its very nature be social. Because of this there is no need, Hofmann said, to call it specifically a social ethic:

> There is no need to call this a social ethic. It is that which is demanded of ethics—that it should not be merely a personal ethic but a social ethic—completely of itself. The individual does not stand in his individuality over against God, but as an individual who is a man and a Christian, as a member of the church. . . . And as man, he is a member of the humanity which lives in the communal forms of family and state.[79]

This brief sketch is enough to demonstrate that Hofmann's rejection of the traditional orthodox concept of law was complete, and that it was carried through with systematic consistency even in the area of ethics. There is no trace of the traditional idea of the *lex aeterna*, no trace of the traditional scheme of the *usus legis* and no hint of a "third use of the law." Law is displaced entirely by the reality of the new humanity.

The examples I have adduced in theological method, in the basic theme of theology *(Heilsgeschichte)*, and in the view of the law,

---

[78] *Ibid.*, p. 268.
[79] *Ibid.*, p. 23.

demonstrate quite clearly the opposition between orthodoxy and Hofmann's *Heilsgeschichte*. It is not strange, therefore, that if the *heilsgeschichtliche* system were to be consistently worked out, a controversy would ensue, especially over so central a doctrine as the atonement.

Hofmann saw this quite clearly. He saw that if the *heilsgeschichtliche* system were consistently carried through it would have to challenge the idea of an "eternal law" which was basic to the orthodox system; it would provide a different structure for understanding God's action in Christ. He seems deliberately to have provoked a controversy over the doctrine of the atonement. It was at this point that the battle was joined between orthodoxy and *Heilsgeschichte;* this was the beginning of the modern law-gospel debate.

CHAPTER III

HOFMANN ON
THE ATONEMENT

Reconstructing the doctrine of the atonement was the principal doctrinal aim of Hofmann's theology. In one of his letters to Delitzsch he states that the final form of his view of the atonement in *Der Schriftbeweis* was the fruit of 20 years' work, and that he was well aware of the controversy it would arouse.[1] Elsewhere he states that he was convinced that the traditional doctrine ought to be reformulated and that he was determined to work towards that end regardless of the difficulty it would cause.[2] Consequently he did nothing to veil the differences between his view and the tradition, but drew the distinctions sharply at every point.[3] Indeed, he even overstated his case at times to make sure that it would evoke the necessary discussion.[4]

Hofmann expressed the need for revision in 1842, in the first lectures he gave as a 31-year-old docent at Erlangen.[5] The recurring theme of these early lectures is that the traditional doctrine of the atonement does not concern itself with the actual historical forces operative in the life and death of Jesus but rather dissolves

---

[1] Delitzsch and Hofmann, *Briefe,* p. 5.

[2] Letter to Luthardt, quoted in Wapler, *J. v. Hofmann,* pp. 246-247.

[3] See for instance *Der Schriftbeweis* (2nd ed.), II, pp. 333 ff.

[4] Wapler, *J. v. Hofmann,* p. 248.

[5] Paul Wapler, "Die Genesis der Versöhnungslehre J. von Hofmanns," *Neue Kirchliche Zeitschrift,* 25, No. 3 (March, 1914), p. 170. Hofmanns' lectures are partially reproduced as an appendix to this article.

and loses them in logic and abstraction. The reason for this is that the older theology does not start from the historical facts themselves but rather from an extra-biblical conceptual structure; then it forces the facts into this structure. The result is inconsistency, inadequacy, and outright error. One finally ends with a doctrine of satisfaction defined along juridical rather than theological lines, and with a divine righteousness conceived " . . . along human juridical lines as the will of God . . . to give everyone what he deserves." [6] What is needed, Hofmann said, is not merely a few adjustments of the old point of view, but a complete revision in terms of what actually happens in history. [7]

Hofmann believed that the orthodox doctrine of vicarious satisfaction was plagued with the problem of compensatory reckoning, an exact equivalence between what man owed and what Christ must pay. Hofmann rejected all this as unbiblical and logically contradictory. He cited (Rudolph ?) Stier with approval in this connection:

> Stier has very aptly called attention to this error *(Beiträge zur biblischen Theologie)*. He shows how absurd it is to seek to calculate how Christ's merit corresponds to our guilt in order consequently to draw the conclusion that therefore God is gracious to us. For all the while the paramount fact is that God is gracious and therefore has sent Christ. For what after all does "forgiveness" mean? Stier rightly says that if one does not want to exchange empty words for real concepts then "forgiveness" means "not to punish," neither me nor another in place of me. If we had to do here with a balancing of accounts then there would be no forgiveness. Furthermore, if one wanted to force juridical concepts onto theology, then strict justice would demand punishment of the guilty one . . . . Thus that theory of satisfaction as Anselm sets it forth but which the Lutheran dogmaticians first developed fully cannot stand. [8]

Hofmann's objection to the orthodox doctrine of the atonement took the form of a frontal attack on the concept of vicarious satisfaction. Vicarious satisfaction should be rejected, he said, because

---

[6] *Ibid.*, p. 196.

[7] Wapler, *J. v. Hofmann*, p. 248.

[8] Wapler, *Neue Kirchliche Zeitschrift*, 25 (March, 1914), p. 197.

it does not correspond to the view of scripture and because it does not adequately represent what faith affirms. It is impossible, Hofmann insisted, to understand the atonement correctly if one assumes that God's righteousness must first be satisfied before he can be merciful. Atonement must start from the fact of God's originating love.[9] Further, vicarious satisfaction gives a false impression of what happened in the atonement; it introduces the idea of a quantitative reckoning with all its contradictions, and it does not adequately express the true relationship between Christ and mankind. Christ was not "another" alongside of man who then died and suffered "instead of man" what man should have suffered and done, but he was the one "in whom mankind was created and who again enters into mankind" and in whom "mankind finds its second Adam."[10] The importance of this assertion will become more apparent when we see Hofmann's positive reconstruction. The point here is that for Hofmann vicarious satisfaction is quite unable to convey what is really involved in the atonement.

The objections Hofmann made were not new, of course. They trace back at least as far as to the Socinian[11] criticisms uttered when the doctrine was first worked out in Protestant orthodoxy. Unable to arrive at a viable alternative in the face of the Socinian attacks, orthodoxy was driven to an attempt to work out the logic implied in vicarious satisfaction and then to invoke the category of "mystery" when the logic broke down. Hofmann had no patience with this state of affairs.

> The idea that the punishment of our sin is carried out on him instead of on us is a self-made mystery which does not follow from his incarnation. It has its origin in the fact that one constructs his own ideas about how God must have disposed himself to atone for sin instead of learning from holy history how he has in fact atoned for our sin.[12]

What did Hofmann's positive reconstruction of the doctrine of

---

[9] Hofmann, *Schutzschriften*, I, p. 16.

[10] *Ibid.*, pp. 18-19.

[11] An anti-trinitarian movement of Reformation times which rejected the doctrine of vicarious satisfaction.

[12] Hofmann, *Schutzschriften*, II, p. 106.

the atonement look like? He began, as is to be expected, from the experience of the "new humanity" in Christ. Through faith one knows himself to be freed from the dominance of the power of sin. This means that a *new* situation has been brought about, which is in contrast to the old one. What Christ did stands over against what "Adam" did.[13] This basic duality of old and new, Adam and Christ, is the starting point. Thus one is directed immediately to the historical scheme. One must proceed from Adam and the history of his race to Christ and his history. Only by considering the work of Christ in this historical context will one come to a proper appreciation of the nature of the atonement.

Christ's work, then, must be seen in relation to the preceding history of Adam's race. We have already seen the basic outline of this history as it is unfolded in the *Lehrganze;* what remains for us here is a closer examination of Christ's work against this background. It must be remembered at the outset that Christ, for Hofmann, is the eternal Son, the eternal object of the divine love-will in whom man is created and loved. The question which has to be answered here is why his incarnation, death, and resurrection results in atonement.

Hofmann can answer this question only by considering Christ's history. Atonement must be seen in terms of the interplay of actual historical forces.

> In every respect the weight lies upon the concrete historical character of the work of Jesus. It is not, as in the orthodox theory, an objective transaction *(dingliche Leistung),* fulfillment of an abstract demand according to the scheme of forensic justice, but a historically new creation. It does not consist of a string of acts which produce an abstract metaphysical effect, the condition for the gracious attitude of God, but it is a living continuum *(Lebenszusammenhang)* which indeed possesses the highest metaphysical significance but possesses it as eternal religious power, living and immediate, in its concrete historicity. Or dogmatically expressed: Christ's work is not the forensic production of the condition for grace but rather the historical realization of the divine will of grace itself.[14]

[13] Wapler, *Neue Kirchliche Zeitschrift,* 25 (March, 1914), p. 191.
[14] Wapler, *Neue Kirchliche Zeitschrift,* 25 (March, 1914), p. 172.

To understand the atonement in its historical sense one must see it against the background of the entire *Heilsgeschichte*, including the Old Testament history leading up to the event. Here Hofmann finds two categories decisive: the suffering of the righteous and the concept of sacrifice.

The Old Testament shows first of all that under the conditions of mankind after Adam "the righteous one" must suffer the antagonism of the unrighteous.[15] This begins with the slaying of Abel and continues until it reaches its climax in the sufferings of the righteous servant in Isaiah. And in the larger sense, Israel as "the people of God" suffers at the hand of the "unrighteous" nations. This is by no means accidental; in their suffering the righteous are in fact fulfilling the calling which they have from God. From the time of the fall, God began to bear witness to himself through chosen representatives in such a way as to work repentance and faith. This meant that these representatives would have to suffer the antagonism of a mankind enslaved by sin. The suffering of the righteous, then, has two contributing causes: They suffered both because God laid this suffering upon them and because of the opposition of sinful mankind. Their suffering came because of their faithfulness to their calling *(Berufstreue);* in their obedience they stood between God and man in a mediatorial capacity.

The righteous one suffers, in a certain sense, "for the sins of mankind," because he becomes the object of the antagonism of the sinful. He bears the sins of mankind "in his body." In the Old Testament this reaches its climax and fulfillment in the suffering servant, whom Hofmann sees as the fulfillment of the prophetic office and consequently a prophecy (in the sense of *Vorbild*) concerning the sufferings of Christ. The sufferings of the Servant of Yahweh are salutary because they bring about repentance and transformation in those who have caused the suffering. The unrighteous recognize that the servant suffers what they should have suffered. He suffers a fate laid on him by God, to be sure, but one in which he bears the sins of those who attack him. When the

---

[15] Hofmann, *Der Schriftbeweis* (1st ed.), IIa, pp. 115-139.

unrighteous recognize this, the antagonism caused by sin exhausts itself, so that the sufferings of the servant come to have a certain saving efficacy. The servant of Yahweh by being true to his calling brings evil to an end, for he allows it to exhaust itself in his sufferings.[16]

In this interpretation of the sufferings of "the righteous one" it would seem that Hofmann upheld a purely subjective view of the atonement: The sufferings of the servant cause a "change of heart" in the perpetrators of the deed. But the picture is not yet complete. The second category—the concept of sacrifice—must be added to rescue his view from the charge of subjectivity.

The problem of sacrifice was much discussed in Hofmann's time. Two extremes were current.[17] One, represented by Bähr's *Symbolik des Mosaischen Kultus* (1837/39) held a "subjective" point of view. The act of sacrifice symbolically represents the fact that one could not be accepted into God's community without the giving up of human selfhood. The other extreme, represented by Kurtz in *Das Mosaische Opfer* (1842) held that in sacrifice the victim vicariously suffered the punishment due the sinner. The intention of the two views is obvious. One leads to a so-called "subjective" view of the atonement, the other to the orthodox or "objective" doctrine of vicarious satisfaction.

Hofmann did not accept either of these views. He attempted to steer a course which would avoid the necessity for a choice between these undesirable alternatives. This was not an easy task, and it made his concept of sacrifice somewhat difficult to grasp. Sacrifice, as one might suspect for Hofmann, must be seen within its entire historical context and not just as an isolated instance. There seem to be two facets to the act of sacrifice. On the one hand, it is an act of piety on the part of the sinner. God, in the beginning, gave man dominion over creation, and the sinner was to bring the slain animal as an expression of his relationship to God *(Gottesgemeinschaft)*, whether for praise or thanksgiving as in the case of Abel

---

[16] Hofmann, *Der Schriftbeweis* (1st ed.), II a, p. 139.

[17] Paul Bachmann, *J. Chr. K. v. Hofmanns Versöhnungslehre und die über sie geführte Streit* (Gütersloh: C. Bertelsmann, 1910, pp. 14-20.

and Noah, or for petition or on the occasion of some particular sin.[18] On the other hand, sacrifice is an act of God which shows that sin cannot be forgiven merely as a matter of course.

The classification of types of sacrifice and the altered significance of the offering first appears when it becomes the express command of God in the establishment of the holy community through the law.[19] From this point on (a new stage in the *Heilsgeschichte*), all worship of God must be seen within the context of the new relationship established by Moses as God's ordained mediator.

Thus sacrifice must be understood within the context of the covenant. Sacrifice does not *earn* grace—that is already assured by the covenant—but the act of sacrifice, which is an act of piety and worship on man's part, is now taken up within the covenant and made also God's own act through the divinely ordained priest. It is a sign of the fact that sin separates man from God and that this sin cannot simply be overlooked by God. Even though the sacrifice does not "earn" grace, yet it does atone *(sühnen)* the sin counted against the one bringing the offering.

The atonement takes place in the sprinkling of the blood, signifying the release *(Hingabe)* of the life of the animal to God. The blood is sprinkled on the holy place as a covering for sin. Sacrifice, then, is not the execution of divine punishment upon the animal as a substitute, but rather the "covering" of the sinner through a divinely ordained means. Just as God once slew an animal to cover man's nakedness, so now through the priest man's sin is "covered" by God through the act of sacrifice.

Thus a sacrifice is an act which releases man from the consequences of his sin.[20] God through his covenant established a means whereby sin can be covered. In carrying out the act of sacrifice man must give evidence of his piety and obedience so that it can become an experience of reconciliation; through his repentance and faith man participates in the act. An atonement takes place, but not because the animal is punished in man's stead. Rather,

---

[18] Hofmann, *Der Schiftbeweis* (1st ed.), II a, pp. 143-150.

[19] *Ibid.*, pp. 192, 144.

[20] Hofmann, *Der Schriftbeweis* (1st ed.), IIa, pp. 145, 154.

man's act is accepted and taken up into God's act through the covenant.

The important point is, though, that such an action is still only prefigurative. Hofmann said that the sin, which always forms a barrier between God and man, is not removed but only covered. In actuality, sin still remains. Sacrifice does not create a new and permanent situation in which sin is removed, but rather must be repeated again and again while awaiting further divine action. Sacrifice is, like all aspects of the Old Testament history, only *prefigurative;* it does not have the power to remove the situation itself in which sin exists. Nevertheless, sacrifice is an act of God which has "objective" status and is not merely symbolical or "subjective."

To arrive at the complete view of New Testament atonement, the two lines of Old Testament thought—the suffering of "the righteous one" and the act of sacrifice—must be brought together so that each supplies what was missing in the other. What was lacking in the suffering of the righteous one was that it was not a perfect sacrificial act on the part of sinful man; since man is a sinner, such acts always remain incomplete. What was missing in the act of sacrifice was that it was not the vocational suffering of the righteous servant. Neither the suffering of the righteous nor sacrifice alone is able to remove the *situation* in which sin inheres.

It is against this Old Testament background that the work of Christ must be considered and understood. In Christ the movements of sacrifice and suffering are united and fulfilled.[21] As the eternal Son he is "the righteous one" in the absolute sense, a sinless man who took up the calling of the prophet and bore witness to God's will in the world. He suffered the opposition of the forces of unrighteousness; he bore the sin of the world "in his body." He suffered in the most extreme manner *(bis zum Aüssersten)* under the power of evil and sin.[22] By persevering in righteousness he was faithful to his calling to the end, thereby completing and fulfilling the prophetic line of development.

By his acquiescence under antagonism, then, Jesus suffered pas-

---

[21] Hofmann, *Der Schriftbeweis* (1st ed.), IIa, p. 194.

[22] Hofmann, *Encyclopädie*, p. 85.

sively at the hands of men. But it is equally true that Jesus' work was also his own accomplishment; it was a sacrifice. He gave his life freely; no one took it from him against his will. God through Jesus was working out his will so that in Christ's death the prefigurative sacrifice is fulfilled. The fulfillment occurred because in Jesus God's action and man's action converged and met. Evil, working through the hatred and sin of mankind, slew the sinless victim. But at the same time the sinless victim was God's Christ, through whom God met the forces of evil in actual historical combat. The event was no longer just prefigurative; it was an actual meeting of historical life forces—*Lebensmächte*, as Hofmann put it.

In this historical conflict it was God who won the ultimate victory. Christ's resurrection from the dead is the assurance that this is so.[23] Sin and the forces of evil exhausted themselves; they attacked the eternal Son but were defeated. In this total event—cross *and* resurrection—atonement is made. This is so because through his resurrection, Christ has made it possible to be related to God on a new basis. An actual change *in man's situation* has been established in which sin no longer rules.[24] The power of sin and evil has been broken and man stands in a new relationship to God.

As we have seen, this new relationship, this "new humanity," is the key category of Hofmann's entire theology. In the doctrine of the atonement Hofmann has given his explanation of how this new humanity has come about. Atonement is the event in which the transition from the old to the new takes place; it is a transition to a new stage in the history of salvation.

Hofmann, with his penchant for brief dogmatic formulations, was able to sum up his doctrine of the atonement in one sentence which we can paraphrase here: Because man allowed himself to be determined by sin through the working of Satan, he became the object of divine wrath. The triune God, however, was determined that the relationship established at creation between himself and mankind should be brought once again to a full communion of love.

---

[23] Hofmann, *Schutzschriften*, II, p. 91.

[24] *Ibid.*, I, p. 12.

In order to realize this, the triune God projected himself into the most extreme antithesis possible without self-denial, namely that of the Father wrathful toward mankind because of sin and the sinless Son who entered into this mankind. The Son then endured all the consequences of sin even to the extent of the criminal death which met him because of the activity of Satan. Satan did his utmost through sin but could establish nothing but the perseverance of the sinless one. This occurred in order that the relationship of the Father to the Son might once again be a relationship of God to a newly beginning humanity in the Son, a humanity determined no longer by the sin of Adam's race, but by the righteousness of the Son.[25]

The distinctive feature of Hofmann's view as compared with the orthodox view is apparent. First, the action throughout is God's. God is not acted upon so that he can *become* gracious. It is not the case that God's righteousness must be satisfied before he can forgive. Hofmann was concerned to show that his view entailed a new concept of the divine righteousness. It is not, he said, to be understood juridically, but rather as God's steadfastness, his remaining true to his own will.[26] Taking righteousness in this *full* sense, Hofmann maintains, it is impossible to uphold the traditional understanding of satisfaction. To be sure, God's righteousness is fulfilled in the atonement, and it is in one sense satisfied *(eine Genüge ist geschehen der Gerechtigkeit Gottes)*, but it is not fulfilled in a juridical sense.[27] Instead, God's righteousness is "satisfied" in the sense that God remains steadfast in his will, in his decree concerning the blessedness of man. Sin only makes God's original decree of love into a decree of grace, and because it is a decree of grace it is also a decree of enmity towards sin.

If this entirety is God's righteousness, then God's righteousness is not satisfied merely by an act of satisfaction in the death of Christ on the cross, but even more so by what follows, the resurrection.

---

[25] Hofmann, *Schutzschriften*, I, p. 6.

[26] Wapler, *Neue Kirchliche Zeitschrift*, 25 (March, 1914), p. 199.

[27] *Ibid.*, p. 199.

The act of exaltation also belongs to the satisfaction of the divine righteousness.[28] If the term satisfaction is to be used, then it must be used in this sense and not merely in a narrow juridical way. The whole sweep of the *Heilsgeschichte* from beginning to end must be seen as the realization of the divine will of love.

Second, it follows from this that Christ's work should not be seen (as in orthodoxy) in terms of a juridical framework in which he suffers punishment *instead of* man. Christ entered mankind to carry out *his own* calling. His righteousness consisted in being true to his own calling to the end, in his *Berufstreue.* Hofmann rejected the idea that Christ's righteousness could be adequately described by the fact that he fulfilled the law.[29] His righteousness is something more than this because it includes his obedience in self-emptying, in taking the form of a servant and being placed under human ordinances, in suffering, dying, and being raised again. It cannot be said that this entire action of Jesus is the fulfillment of "the law." It is, rather, fulfillment of the divine love-will. Jesus' righteousness must be measured against his higher vocation.[30] The work of Christ, therefore, cannot be understood against a juridical background. The *entire* movement from incarnation through resurrection and the founding of the new humanity must be understood as his "*Beruf*" and thus constitutive of his righteousness.

Jesus' work consisted, then, in his faithfulness to his calling. It is at the same time active and passive. Hofmann rejected the traditional attempt to distinguish between active and passive obedience; Christ's activity is not to be divided and measured according to such an abstract scheme. Jesus did not suffer the punishment due man at all in this sense. The suffering took place *for man's good,* to be sure, but it was Christ's suffering, a suffering laid upon him because of his calling.[31] No juridical transaction took place. It was not, as Hofmann has said, "*an objective transaction, fulfillment of*

---

[28] Wapler, *Neue Kirchliche Zeitschrift,* 25 (March, 1914), p. 199.
[29] Hofmann, *Der Schriftbeweis* (2nd ed.), IIa, p. 123.
[30] *Ibid.,* p. 134.
[31] *Ibid.,* p. 318.

an abstract demand according to the scheme of forensic justice but a historically new creation." [32]

Finally, the relationship of all this to man is different from the orthodox scheme. In Hofmann's system man is not related to God exclusively through a juridical framework—a system which demands satisfaction before he can be freed. Rather, because man has been deceived by Satan and taken captive to hostile forces he suffers under the results of his sin. In this form he experiences the wrath of God—in his enslavement to sin.[33] But now, through the atonement, he has become the object of an activity of the divine will which has as its goal the reparation of the damage done by sin. Christ enters into man's situation, suffers the utmost that the forces of Satan can muster through man's sin, and perseveres, thereby establishing a new humanity which is no longer dominated by sin. In Christ, the conditions under which mankind is related to God are *altered;* a new relationship has been established which does away with the old. In other words, man's relationship to God is not understood in juridical terms—in terms of a legal scheme which regulates his relationship and which, even though satisfied, *is still in effect* as a timeless structure—but rather *an entirely new situation obtains.*[34]

It is apparent from all this that Hofmann attempted to construct a doctrine of the atonement which is more true to the historical picture as he understood it. It is obvious that at every point his attack was directed against the old doctrine of the law and the structure it fostered in the orthodox system. If one were to attempt to classify his view, it would no doubt be closest to what Gustaf Aulén has called the classic or victory motif.[35] Reconciliation occurs when Christ triumphs over the forces of evil and establishes a new and "transfigured" humanity. But is this an adequate doctrine of

---

[32] Above, p. 57.

[33] Hofmann, *Schutzschriften,* III, p. 14.

[34] *Ibid.,* p. 17.

[35] See Gustaf Aulén, *Christus Victor,* tr. A. G. Hebert, New York: The Macmillan Co., 1951.

the atonement? Has Hofmann adequately clarified his view? The representatives of a more orthodox point of view did not fail to take up these questions; in the controversy which followed we have ample opportunity to see the clash between orthodoxy and *Heilsgeschichte.*

CHAPTER IV

THE ATONEMENT
CONTROVERSY

Hofmann's doctrine of the atonement was not accepted by the more conservative and orthodox theologians of his day. To be sure, most of these theologians were no longer orthodox in the old sense, for they realized that the doctrine of scriptural infallibility was no longer viable. Methodologically, at least, they all followed paths influenced by Schleiermacher. But apparently they refused to see any necessary connection between a reconstruction in method and a reconstruction in the doctrine of atonement. For Hofmann this was a glaring inconsistency; a change in method demands whole-sale reformulation of the system. He often expressed dismay over the fact that this was not taken into account in the controversy.

The first reaction to Hofmann's doctrine of the atonement came from F. A. Philippi, a professor at Rostock. He charged Hofmann with a "subjectivistic transposition of the objective biblical and churchly doctrine of atonement and justification," and he called upon Hofmann to use his very apparent gifts to reformulate his views in accordance with the traditional doctrine.[1] The patronizing tone of Philippi's charge evoked a rather acid reply from Hofmann in an article, *"Begründete Abweisung eines nicht begründeten*

---

[1] F. A. Philippi, *Commentar über der Brief Pauli an die Römer* (2nd ed.; Frankfurt: Heyder u. Zimmer, 1856), pp. x-xi.

Vorwurfs,[2] in which he challenged Philippi to substantiate his charge of deviation from the tradition. Hofmann set forth his doctrine in brief form, and discussed point by point the differences between his view and the traditional view.[3] Hofmann did admit that there were differences, but in his defense he made a distinction between the actual faith of the church and the form or theory which expresses that faith. He insisted that he had no intention of altering the basic faith of the church and held that the only question to be decided was whether his formulation conformed better to the actual faith of the church than the traditional one.

In the case of the doctrine of the atonement, Hofmann said, there are two questions to be asked. First, is the event of salvation so presented that it is the presupposition for justification by faith alone? Second, does the form in which it is presented better conform to the righteousness of faith than the previous view? The point, he admitted, at which his view diverged most crucially from the tradition was in the relationship of the work of Christ to the law. He spoke not of the fulfillment of the demands of the law but of Christ's perseverance in his calling, not of a vicarious suffering of punishment but of a suffering under the conditions and results of sin to establish a new humanity through the resurrection.

The traditional view, Hofmann said, actually endangers justification because it inevitably raises the question of the adequacy of Christ's suffering. In attempting to answer this question the traditionalist is forced into a system of compensatory reckoning which must resort to theories about the infinite worth of Christ's suffering. Furthermore, the orthodox position overlooks the fact that man is not only supposed to have *done* something but is also supposed to have *become* something. The juridical framework is inadequate to express this, so that it does not do full justice to the doctrine of justification.

Secondly, Hofmann said, the conceptual framework of the traditional view fails because it actually endangers the idea that the atonement is a work of pure grace. Atonement is the result of a

---

[2] *Zeitschrift für Protestantismus und Kirche* NF 38 (February-March, 1856), pp. 175-182.

[3] The discussion parallels our discussion above, pp. 44ff.

payment, not a free gift. True, the doctrine does not *intend* this, but because of its form this is the way it comes out. The failure lies in the systematic structure.

Furthermore, the idea of vicarious satisfaction gives the impression that payment is made only for the individual *sins* of men and not the *sinfulness* of *mankind*. This is so because it does not indicate how the relationship of mankind to God has actually been *altered* by the work of Christ.

This leads necessarily to the question of the nature of faith. Faith, in the orthodox scheme, is a faith directed towards a past event. But, Hofmann asked, is mere faith in a past event sufficient to enable one to participate in what that event has accomplished? There is no conception of how this faith is mediated and made alive in the present, so that one cannot really experience the reconciliation accomplished in the atonement.

Against the charge of subjectivism, Hofmann hurled back a charge of false objectivism. In the older system, faith becomes merely a passive acceptance of past events. Such a faith will have difficulty maintaining itself against the afflictions of the conscience in the present.[4] The weakness of the traditional formulation is avoided, Hofmann claimed, only when there is a unity between what was accomplished once for all and the benefits of that accomplishment in the present. This unity exists in the present actuality of the new relationship.

Philippi was not satisfied. He answered Hofmann in a pamphlet entitled *Herr D. von Hofmann gegenüber der lutherischen Versöhnungs- und Rechtfertigungslehre*.[5] Persisting in his charge of deviation, Philippi rejected the idea that one can make a distinction between form and content in matters so central as justification and atonement, especially when one has to do with confessional statements. He contended that Luther was the champion of absolute objectivity in the atonement and that the doctrine of justification by faith is dependent entirely upon such objectivity (that is, on vicari-

---

[4] Hofmann, *Zeitschrift für Protestantismus und Kirche* (February-March, 1856), p. 188.

[5] (Frankfurt: Heyder u. Zimmer, 1856), cited hereafter as *Hofmann gegenüber*.

ous satisfaction).[6] The alien righteousness of Christ is imputed to the believer. This, for Philippi, was the heart of the Reformation and that which sets it off from the Roman Catholic *gratia infusa*.[7] He saw in Hofmann's concept of the new humanity a return to the mysticism and subjectivism which the Reformation rejected. Hofmann, Philippi said, overemphasized the *Christ in us* at the expense of the *Christ for us*. Justification as *a forensic act* is displaced by the incorporation into the new humanity.

Philippi went on to defend the orthodox doctrine against what he felt was an unfair interpretation by Hofmann. It is not, he said, a process of abstract reasoning which stands behind the doctrine; rather it evolves from the deepest experience of faith. Where faith experiences the absolute holiness of God it is utterly impossible to grasp the divine love until the "block" which the divine holiness sets up is removed. One experiences the release of the tension between the divine love and holiness only through repentance and faith in the death of the God-man. This *experience,* Philippi said, is the basis for the dogmatic doctrine of the atonement.[8]

Thus Philippi saw the roots of the traditional doctrine in the consciousness of guilt. Only the certainty that another has borne this guilt vicariously can set a man at peace. To be sure, the possibility for atonement is rooted in the divine love (in the principle of divine self-giving), but God cannot give himself in such a way that he compromises his holiness (the principle of divine self-preservation).[9] Hence he cannot give himself to man before his holiness is satisfied. This is not quantitative reckoning but simply the necessity that the full gravity of God's holiness be maintained over against sin. Hofmann simply takes his place in the long line from Socinus to Strauss which objects to the orthodox teaching because it supposedly emphasizes God's righteousness at the expense of his love.[10] Wrath, Philippi maintained, had no reality for Hofmann. It is simply presupposed that the sinner as sinner can

[6] Philippi, *Hofmann gegenüber*, pp. 7-8.

[7] *Ibid.,* p. 28.

[8] *Ibid.,* pp. 32-37.

[9] *Ibid.,* p. 35.

[10] *Ibid.,* p. 34.

know of an unbroken divine love. Divine love is like a magnet with two poles. Man simply passes from the repulsive force of wrath to the attractive force of love. There is no "objective" change in God's attitude towards man, only a "subjective" change in man.[11] This is why Hofmann spoke only about the establishment of the new humanity. Christ's death is not a satisfaction of God's wrath, only a suffering of what he encounters due to the power of Satan.

The net result of Hofmann's construction, Philippi charged, was that there is no objective necessity for the atonement and thus it takes on the character of being purely accidental. It is only an accident that Jesus "comes upon bad times" in Jerusalem since there is no objective necessity for the atonement. Christianity is made to seem merely an institution based upon an accident, or at best upon divine arbitrariness.[12]

For our purposes, Philippi was the most important of Hofmann's opponents. There were others, as we shall see, who understood Hofmann better and were more sympathetic, but Philippi's attack demonstrated most clearly the clash between the two systems; he was the chief spokesman for the system Hofmann is opposing. This is quite evident in the last judgment which Philippi makes, the charge that for Hofmann the atonement is accidental. It is a revealing point, because it shows that when the rational framework demanded by the orthodox system has been denied, atonement is divested of the necessity which that framework gave it. Philippi can no longer make sense of the atonement when the system based on law is removed.

Hofmann's reply came in the first of four pamphlets he wrote defending his theology. Significantly, these pamphlets were entitled *Schutzschriften für eine neue Weise, alte Wahrheit zu lehren* (Defense for the Right to Teach Old Truth in a New Way),[13] a general defense of Hofmann's entire program. His attack on Philippi was sprinkled with caustic remarks about the kind of theology

---

[11] *Ibid.*, p. 44.

[12] *Ibid.*, p. 36.

[13] 4 parts (Nördlingen: C. H. Beck, 1856-58). Wapler, Hofmann's biographer, calls the *Schutzschriften* "one of the greatest polemical accomplishments in evangelical theology since Luthers' time. ... " *J. v. Hofmann*, p. 242.

which refuses to move in new directions. It is, he said, "A pharisaic orthodoxy . . . whose theology strains out the tiny seeds and throws the important ones away," [14] a theology which is ". . . sentenced to that anxiety which adheres to the legalistic position both in its scientific disciplines and in its life." [15]

To the charge that he has taught contrary to the Lutheran Confessions and ecumenical Catholic doctrine, Hofmann replied that he knew of no Lutheran theologian or any historian of dogma who would maintain that the doctrine of vicarious satisfaction belongs to the essential teaching of the church.[16] Nevertheless, he realized that Philippi's charges could not be taken lightly since they represented the thinking of an entire theological era. The charge of "subjectivism" had to be met. Hence, Hofmann said that it is not correct to say that in his system the divine righteousness is satisfied merely by a subjective change of attitude in man. It is God's *relationship* to man which has changed in the atonement, and it is changed *objectively*, if one must use such terms, in and through what is accomplished *by God* in Christ. In acting this way through Christ, God has not exercised his will to love mankind without at the same time exercising his hatred of sin.[17] What has occurred is a change in dispensation, a real and "objective" change in the "times" which changes man's relationship to God. Of course, the change has not occurred "objectively" in the sense that the old dispensation has been obliterated. One can participate in the new only through faith. This is why it is difficult, if not impossible, to use such terms as "subjective" and "objective." God does not give himself to man apart from "subjective" participation in that giving. Nevertheless, the action which brings about the transition from the old to the new is God's, and not merely a change in man's attitude.

It is against this background also that the question of the relationship between wrath and love must be seen. Hofmann insisted that it is not the case that God's wrath and holiness must *first* be satisfied before he can be loving. Rather, God's activity in Christ is

---

[14] Hofmann, *Schutzschriften*, I, p. 2.

[15] *Ibid.*, I, pp. 2-3.

[16] *Ibid.*, I, pp. 5-6.

[17] *Ibid.*, I, p. 12.

at one and the same time the manifestation of his love *and* his hatred of sin. This means that the new relationship *could not* be established without at the same time bringing about the end of the old, or in other words, that Christ could not be the originator of a new humanity without accomplishing an expiation *(Sühnung)* [18] of sin. Christ, insofar as he enters into the mankind which has become the object of the divine wrath, does suffer under that wrath himself in the form of the antagonism of Satan. Furthermore, such suffering was *necessary* in order to defeat the power of Satan and establish the new relationship—to realize the will of God.

Thus Hofmann insisted that the charge that the atonement becomes accidental is unwarranted. There is a *necessity* for the atonement, rooted in God's will, but it is a *heilsgeschichtliche* necessity, not a legal necessity. Christ *must suffer* under the power of sin in order to bring that power to an end. Christ must suffer because of the will of God to reconcile, to create a new beginning for man. It is because God does not want to be wrathful eternally that he sent Christ. The necessity for atonement is grounded, therefore, in love and not in wrath.[19]

But this raises the question of just what it is that Christ's death accomplishes. Here Hofmann went more deeply into the term he had used all along, the idea of *Sühnung.*[20] By this Hofmann meant that atonement is not something less but something *more* than vicarious satisfaction. The vicarious satisfaction terminology is inadequate because it is too narrow to convey what really happens. It is too narrow because it does not take into account that Christ dies not just *instead of man,* but dies the death that he *himself* must die as a mediator, as eternal Son and man together. It is *his own death* which he must die to bring in the new age. There is no system of righteousness in the old age which can bring this about, either through substitution or otherwise. Vicarious satisfaction is inadequate because it assumes that there is a system according to

---

[18] *Ibid.,* I, p. 17.

[19] "So it cannot be a question of necessity for God, by whose will and through whom all things are. But the fact that he allows Jesus to die and to go the way of sorrows to glory can be rooted only in his intention to be gracious." *Der Schriftbeweis* (1st ed.), II a, p. 272.

[20] Hofmann, *Schutzschriften,* I, p. 19.

which God can be "bought off." But Christ's death is an expiation
(*Sühnung*). This was something quite different from vicarious satisfaction for Hofmann. It was not a substitution but an active and
positive accomplishment which literally "makes amends" for sin by
repairing the damage:

> . . . The maintenance of his obedience under all the results
> of sin or the suffering of all the results of sin as the mainte-
> nance of his obedience is the accomplishment in action and in
> suffering of antagonism through which that which was begun
> with his conception is perfected, i.e., the propitiation (*Süh-
> nung*) corresponding and antithetical to sin. For propitiation
> (*Sühnung*) is in its essence a making amends for sin and not a
> substitute for punishment. It is not for our punishment that
> Christ has satisfied, but rather for our sins.[21]

Sühnung is an action which God has taken in order that sin in man
might cease to be a cause for making man the object of divine wrath.

> The proper concept of propitiation (*Sühnung*), therefore, is
> that it is a making amends for sin. It is a positive accomplish-
> ment corresponding antithetically to sin by virtue of which
> sin ceases to be the justified cause of the wrath of the one
> against whom it is committed towards those who committed
> it. Such propitiation God has provided. It is not that for legal
> reasons he can no longer punish because the punishment has
> been completed, but rather that because he wanted to forgive
> he gave man a righteousness which does not come from man-
> kind but which comes to be in mankind. This righteousness
> does not consist in the fact that something was merely suffered,
> nor merely that something was done, but in the person of the
> incarnate Son of God with his eternal holiness maintained under
> all the results of sin, a holiness which is now also a human
> holiness.[22]

What happens is not that according to a legal scheme God has
gotten his "pound of flesh" so that now he *must forgive*, but rather

---

[21] Hofmann, *Schutzschriften*, I, p. 19. He expresses dependence here upon a
concept of *Sühnung* taken from Julius Stahl's *Rechtsphilosophie* (II, 1, No. 56-59)
which states that a wrong can be dealt with either by punishment or by making
amends (*Sühnung*) which makes punishment unnecessary. Punishment is
merely negative and annihilates the wrongdoer. *Sühnung* is positive in that
it aims at a reconciliation of the parties in question.

[22] *Ibid.*, II, pp. 105-106.

that *because he willed to forgive* he created a new situation by establishing a new righteousness in Christ.

From this it follows that Christ's work cannot be described as a substitution. Christ, one might say, is *the* true man, not a substitute. He did not suffer alongside of man, as one man instead of another, but *in* mankind. *In* him, not merely *through* him, man becomes the object of the divine love.[23]

Man is righteous, therefore, only *in* Christ. There is no confusion here, Hofmann maintained, between the Christ for us and the Christ in us. It is only because he is first and foremost Christ for us that he can be Christ in us. Justification is and remains *sola gratia.*

After this reply in the first *Schutzschrift*, Philippi never entered the debate publically again except to state that he was not convinced by Hofmann's arguments.[24] Further debate was taken up by men closer and more sympathetic to Hofmann. For the most part, the debate tended to become repetitious, so in following it we shall attempt to concentrate only on those aspects where there is further clarification or where the argument is substantially advanced.

Gottfried Thomasius, one of Hofmann's colleagues at Erlangen, entered the debate in a pamphlet entitled *Das Bekenntnis der lutherischen Kirche von der Versöhnung und die Versöhnungslehre D. Chr. K. v. Hofmanns,*[25] to which another colleague, Theodosius Harnack, added a *Nachwort.* Thomasius was disturbed by Hofmann's rather cavalier treatment of the tradition of the Lutheran Church. Like Philippi, he felt that one could not make such an easy distinction between form and substance in the matter of the atonement. He too insisted that the doctrine of vicarious satisfaction is the necessary presupposition for the doctrine of justification; on this basis he was willing to assert that vicarious satisfaction had to be considered a fundamental article of the confessions, that is, that it belongs to the substance of faith and not merely to the form.[26]

---

[23] *Ibid.,* III, p. 28.
[24] F. A. Philippi, "Erklärung," *Evangelische Kirchenzeitung* 62 (August 20, 1856), p. 638.
[25] (Erlangen: Theodore Bläsing, 1857). Cited hereafter as *Das Bekenntnis.*
[26] Thomasius, *Das Bekenntnis,* pp. 20-21.

To buttress his position, Thomasius argued that it was necessary to go back into the thought of the men behind the confessional statements, especially Luther and Melanchthon. This was a fateful step, for especially in the case of Luther it was an invitation to a more fundamental research into the question of Luther's "orthodoxy" on this point, an invitation which Hofmann did not fail to accept. Thomasius admitted that he had found no doctrinaire development of the idea of atonement in Luther, but instead a richness of views including even the revival of the old idea of the deception of Satan. Nevertheless, Thomasius maintained that Luther in essence supported vicarious satisfaction because it was the necessary presupposition for his doctrine of justification.[27] In Melanchthon and later teachers Thomasius found the doctrine more unambiguously stated and supported. It was then worked out more fully in orthodoxy. But orthodoxy, in Thomasius' view, only spelled out what was implicit in the beginnings. He did admit, however, that one could perhaps blame the 17th century dogmaticians for making Christ's sufferings appear much too quantitative and external, especially when, like Quenstedt and Hollaz, one begins to calculate the equivalence between the infinite worth of Christ's suffering and eternal punishment.[28]

Nevertheless, Thomasius held to the concept of vicarious satisfaction. Like Philippi, he argued that it has its basis in the experience of guilt, not in abstract reasoning.[29] He recognized the fact that Hofmann was trying to work with a different "form" but he felt that this form did not do justice to the Christian experience. He had no doubt that Hofmann ascribed a real mediatorial role to Christ and that neglected views such as the conquest of Satan once again received their due, but he simply did not feel that the traditional church doctrine was done adequate justice.[30]

Thomasius objected to Hofmann's denial of substitutionary punishment and to his treatment of divine wrath. In Hofmann's teaching, Thomasius said, Christ suffered the most extreme opposition of

[27] *Ibid.*, p. 22.
[28] *Ibid.*, pp. 90-91.
[29] *Ibid.*, p. 94.
[30] *Ibid.*, pp. 97-98.

Satan as a result of sin. But this is not quite what the church doctrine meant, because it would mean that Christ all the while was
conscious of the divine love, so that the wrathful judgment did not
actually strike *him* personally.[31] Christ suffered, to be sure, but he
did not himself experience this as the judgment of wrath because
he was always conscious of his calling, conscious of the divine love-
will. And this precisely, Thomasius says, is the point of the doctrine of vicarious satisfaction—that Christ himself experienced and
bore the judgment of wrath instead of us.[32] In denying this, Hofmann rejects not only a temporary doctrinal form but something
essential. For this means that Christ's suffering is merely a fate
which befalls him because of his calling. He suffers in the same way
that a completely saintly person suffers in the community determined by sin. There is no *qualitative* difference between Christ's
suffering and the suffering of the righteous, for there is no causal
relationship between God's wrath and Christ's suffering.[33]

Thus the question of the necessity of the atonement was raised
once again. By raising it in this form, however, Thomasius went an
important step farther; he raised the question about the necessity
for suffering the divine wrath *in the consciousness of Jesus himself*.
He pointed out that if Jesus suffered merely in the consciousness
of his calling, then wrath was not really a problem for him personally but only a fate which he knows he must suffer. For Jesus
himself, suffering and death would then lose their ultimate seriousness. Here Thomasius raised an important question to which we
shall have to return later.

In his "Nachwort" Theodosius Harnack expressed substantial
agreement with Thomasius. He was, if anything, even more dogmatic on the form-substance question. He insisted that the doctrine of justification would allow no other view of the atonement
than that of the dogmatics of the 16th and 17th centuries. He was
adamant about the necessity for satisfaction of divine wrath. He
took outright objection to Hofmann's view that atonement had to
mean a real breaking or removal of the power of sin rather than a

---

[31] *Ibid.*, p. 100.

[32] *Ibid.*, pp. 102-105.

[33] *Ibid.*, p. 100.

juridical satisfaction of guilt. He was even willing to go so far as to say that the primary thing in atonement is the juridical aspect (Versöhnung) rather than the redemptive (Erlösung). Necessity for the atonement lies in the fact of man's guilt before God and not in his need for release from the power of sin or death.[34]

Resistance to Hofmann thus crystallized chiefly around the question of the necessity of the atonement. Wherein lies this necessity? Is it rooted in the righteousness or holiness of God which must express itself as wrath until it is satisfied? Or does it root rather in the loving will of a God who cannot rest until this will is realized? Or are those really legitimate alternatives? The debate seems to reach a kind of stalemate before these alternatives. There is certainly legitimacy in Hofmann's objections to the orthodox doctrine. On the other hand, there is no doubt validity to the orthodox objections as well, especially when Thomasius points out that in Hofmann Christ himself did not really experience divine judgment in his suffering.[35]

This last objection undoubtedly exposed an element of docetism in Hofmann's Christology. But could not the same thing be said of the orthodox view as well? If Christ is the divine-human mediator who comes to make satisfaction, does he not know that he is in fact making satisfaction for someone else and that when payment is made the "game" will be over? Here a failure common to *both* sides has been exposed which indicates, no doubt, an underlying similarity in approach in spite of differences. The question of the consciousness of Jesus in the atonement is, of course, an extremely tricky one which can be turned against either side. To this we shall have to return later.

The debate reached something of a stalemate, no doubt, because of the failure of both sides to see the problem in terms of the wider perspective of opposing *systems.* They could not get beyond the problem of necessity and all that that problem entails. Hofmann

---

[34] *Ibid.,* p. 138.

[35] It is no doubt somewhat misleading to align Thomasius with the orthodox on this point. Thomasius makes his objections about the consciousness of Jesus from the standpoint of his *Kenosis* Christology which is equally critical of orthodoxy. A discussion of the significance of *kenosis* for the doctrine of the atonement at this point, however, would take us beyond the scope of this book.

saw quite clearly the problem in the orthodox system, but he was apparently unable to persuade his opponents that his view took seriously enough the necessity for Christ's death as an atoning sacrifice.

The first to attempt to see the problem in terms of the wider perspective of opposing systems, to my knowledge, was Johannes Ebrard [36] in his *Die Lehre von der Stellvertretende Genugthuung in der heiligen Schrift begründet.*[37] In the question of the necessity of the atonement, he said, we are faced with the old theological question of the divine freedom.[38] Is God's essence the result of his self-determination or is his self-determination derived from his essence? These alternatives give rise to different systems, and either will lead to absurdities if pressed too far. The only solution that Ebrard could offer, however, was the suggestion that each must have its justification over against the other. He was favorably disposed to Hofmann's attempt because, he said, after dogmatics has been dominated by the scholastic concept of necessity for such a long time it was refreshing to be shown the reverse side.[39] Thus Ebrard tried to understand Hofmann in terms of the idea of divine freedom. He tried to establish a correspondence between Hofmann and the old Arminians, especially Limborch. This is somewhat questionable, however [40]; the only thing Hofmann had in common with the Arminians is the denial of the necessity for satisfaction before God can be gracious. Hofmann did not derive this denial from the idea of freedom, however, but from a concept of divine love. Hofmann did not seem to be concerned about an abstract idea of freedom as such.

Ebrard also noted that one of the difficulties in the debate was due to differing concepts of law. Orthodoxy, he said, understood by law not only the laws revealed in history through Moses in the

[36] Also an Erlangen theologian, but at the time *Konsistorialrat* in Speyer.

[37] (Königsberg: A. W. Unzer, 1857). Cited hereafter as *Stellvertretende Genugthuung.*

[38] *Ibid.*, pp. 18 ff.

[39] *Ibid.*, p. 19.

[40] See Carl Weizsäcker, "Um was handelt es sich in dem Streit über die Versöhnungslehre," *Jahrbücher für Deutsche Theologie,* Vol. 3, No. 1 (1858), pp. 174-175.

form of external commandments and propositions, but also the *lex naturalis Dei,* the eternal will of God for man as such, rooted both in the essence of God and in the essence of man. Hofmann, on the other hand, placed himself only in history. He avoided or ignored any speculative or abstract concept of the eternal demand of the divine will. He understood law as something historically given to man who is already a sinner, the revealed or literal law demanding that he, a sinner, must become holy.[41]

In spite of these rather promising beginnings, Ebrard's analysis did not lead any closer to a systematic solution. The two systems based on necessity and freedom were simply left in a kind of polar relationship as mutual correctives, and he did not extend his insight into the problem of law, which could have been helpful. His main interest, as the title of his article indicates, was to probe the scriptural authority for Hofmann's view. Despite a few reservations, Ebrard decided finally for the orthodox view because it represented more adequately to him the biblical view of Christ vicariously bearing the wrathful judgment of God. Even though the orthodox view is not explicit in scripture, he said, it is implicit. Thus Hofmann's view was opposed by conservative theologians both systematically and exegetically.[42]

Hofmann's reply to these critics came in his second and third *Schutzschriften.* He remained unconvinced by the arguments of Thomasius and Harnack that vicarious satisfaction belongs to the essential content and not just the temporary form of the church's doctrine. If it is possible, Hofmann asserted, to maintain a doctrine of justification *sola gratia* without the doctrine of vicarious satisfaction, then it cannot be held that vicarious satisfaction is *essential* to the reformation faith. Since Thomasius and Harnack did not attack Hofmann on the doctrine of justification, it would seem that they would have to concede Hofmann this point at least. Here Philippi was more consistent.

But by far the most important aspect of the second *Schutzschrift* for the subsequent history of the debate was the attention given to

---

[41] Ebrard, *Stellvertretende Genugthuung,* pp. 26-27.

[42] *Ibid.,* p. 68.

Luther.[43] Hofmann, taking up Thomasius' challenge, was concerned to demonstrate that Luther cannot unambiguously be associated with the doctrine of vicarious satisfaction. Quoting Luther at great length, Hofmann challenged Thomasius' rather cavalier treatment of the evidence, especially the assertion that for Luther the idea of the conquest of Satan was not of any great moment. He cited several passages to show that Luther really understands the death of Christ as the result of the onslaught of Satan. This, Hofmann insisted, is not a process of punishment which would have devolved on us, "but the fate of a suffering in which Christ resists the devil in order to gain a victory over him for us." [44]

For Luther, Hofmann said, Christ entered into our nature so that in this nature—under the suffering of everything that Satan could do to us—he could battle Satan and win the victory for all mankind. Furthermore, contrary to Thomasius, it is of the greatest importance if it can be shown not only that Luther taught this view, but that it is basically incompatible with the orthodox view. Hofmann felt that this is true, for if Christ suffered punishment for sin vicariously, then this would be an arrangement between God and Christ in which Satan would have no place. The prominence of Satan in Luther's doctrine of the atonement demands something different from the orthodox view.[45]

Hofmann had certainly revived one of the main motifs of Luther's thought on the atonement,[46] a motif which proponents of the orthodox view found quite embarrassing. Like Thomasius, they most often treated it as an interesting curiosity with no real systematic import. Hofmann was certainly justified in rejecting such cavalier treatment of a major theme in Luther's thought. But the really difficult problem for subsequent research is that Hofmann claimed Luther's use of the "victory motif" indicated a view of the atonement which is *basically incompatible* with the orthodox view of vicarious satisfaction. Hofmann raised a question which was to occupy Luther researchers for decades to come.

---

[43] Hofmann, *Schutzschriften*, II, pp. 23-83.
[44] *Ibid.*, II, p. 64.
[45] *Ibid.*, II, p. 63.
[46] See Gustaf Aulén, *Christus Victor*, trans. A. G. Hebert (London: SPCK, 1931). Hofmann anticipates Aulén's research on this aspect of Luther's thought.

For the moment, however, the importance of Hofmann's appeal to Luther lies in the fact that his orthodox opponents had held that the concept of justification in Luther necessarily demands a doctrine of vicarious satisfaction. Hofmann quite justifiably doubted this, and for proof he needed only to point to the fact that Luther could, on occasion, expound the doctrine of justification without once referring to vicarious satisfaction.[47] In his argument for the possibility of a different form for the doctrine of the atonement this is really all he had to do, but it is obvious that he was not satisfied with this alone. By insisting as he did that the two forms are mutually exclusive, he was contending for the *removal* of the opposing view. And this, indeed, was his aim.

The fact that Hofmann set Luther against orthodoxy on the question of atonement was in itself vitally important not only for the subsequent history of the debate but for the history of modern theology as well. It meant that the argument about the atonement would become inextricably involved with the argument about Luther's theology. It meant also that for the first time Luther research was given a *Problemstellung* which could make it fruitful. This controversy over the atonement, then, is one of the important starting points for modern Luther research.[48] Furthermore, the appeal to Luther is further reason why subsequent debate would have to become increasingly concerned with the problem of law and gospel.

Beyond the appeal to Luther, Hofmann attempted further defense and clarification of his own view. As we have seen, his orthodox opponents had sought to defend vicarious satisfaction from the charge of "abstract reasoning" by claiming that it was necessary to meet the demands of a guilty conscience. Hofmann refused to

---

[47] Hofmann, *Schutzschriften*, II, pp. 35-39.

[48] "For the first time a theologian sets Luther against Lutheranism on a basic problem. This assertion of Hofmann's became the starting point for the entire Luther research of the 19th and 20th centuries. It is not, to be sure, that Luther was not already the object of historical investigation in the first half of the 19th century with its awakening strong historical interest. But in order to become fruitful, historical research needs a point of view which allows one to look at the object with questioning eyes. This had hitherto been missing in Luther research." Hirsch, *Geschichte der neueren evangelischen Theologie*, V. p. 427.

allow this kind of argument, because for him it is too subjective!
It commits the very kind of error which Hofmann had insisted all
along lay at the root of the orthodox view: it attempts to prescribe
what God must do to atone on man's terms.

> But cannot conscience also err? Should we determine what God
> must have done according to our easily misunderstood needs,
> or console ourselves with our own thoughts about what he has
> done? For one must take care here that one does not identify
> the God who speaks in the conscience with one's own
> thoughts. We should not measure God's righteousness by what
> we call human righteousness nor bargain with him when he is
> wrathful nor prescribe how he may be gracious. "That which is
> presumed about God according to law, measure and limit does
> not hit the mark," says Luther.[49]

Hofmann insisted that methodologically one cannot proceed in this
manner, for one will only end by making his own thoughts about
how God *must* atone for man's sin.

On the question of the necessity of atonement, Hofmann could
only amplify what he had said previously. One cannot present the
matter as though God was enabled to forgive only in the course of
time. But there is in the second *Schutzschrift* a fuller explanation
of what Hofmann means by the working of divine wrath. God
cannot show his love without concurrently exercising his hatred of
sin.[50] It is in this fact that the "necessity" for Christ's suffering is
rooted. He entered into a mankind which stood under the divine
wrath because of sin, and as a part of mankind he had to bear the
working of this wrath. He bore it, however, not just in the moment
of sacrifice on the cross, but throughout his whole life. All the evil
suffered in the world is the result of the working of the divine
wrath, so that all suffering is the suffering of that wrath. It is because of God's wrath against sin that Israel was placed under the
law and for the same reason that Christ lived under the law. God's
wrath against Israel brought the people to misery, and Christ himself suffered that misery. It is also because of the divine wrath that
the righteous must suffer at the hands of the unrighteous so that

---

[49] Hofmann, *Schutzschriften,* II, p. 91.

[50] *Ibid.,* p. 99.

the unrighteous fill the measure of their sin and come into judgment. This same wrath gives Christ over to his enemies in order that enmity against God may come into its *ultimate* judgment. Thus God's wrath expresses itself in that it does not cease without the work of Christ. In Christ the resistance of those antagonists to the divine will is raised to the point where they fall into their final judgment. Christ suffers to the utmost the wrath of God against sin in the form of the antagonism of Satan.[51]

Against those who base the comfort of the sinner on sufferings of Christ, Hofmann asserted that true comfort can come only as the result of Christ's victory; the certainty for this lies in the resurrection, not in the equivalence of payment and debt.

> Human sin is propitiated, we insist, through that which results from Christ's divine-human righteousness. Forgiveness is as certain as this accomplishment; forgiveness is certain as surely as Christ is resurrected.[52]

For Hofmann, the certainty of forgiveness roots in the experience of the new humanity, not in the working out of an equivalence between debt and payment.

Hofmann was adamant in his assertion that atonement results because Christ suffers in obedience to his calling. He suffers for man's good, but not as man's substitute. Hofmann insisted on Christ's consciousness of his calling even to the point of denying that Christ suffered eternal damnation and the torments of hell. Eternal damnation and the torments of hell would mean absolute separation from God, the torments of an unrequited conscience. Since Jesus suffered in faithfulness of his calling he could not have suffered these things. These involve one in a system of quantitative reckoning which comes from the point of view which has been rejected.[53] Christ's death cannot mean anything more than that it was the realization of the divine love-will and a translation to the newer life of unconditioned communion with the Father. This does not mean, however, that Christ suffers *less* than man. On the con-

---

[51] *Ibid.*, II, p. 95.
[52] *Ibid.*, III, p. 23.
[53] *Ibid.*, I, p. 18.

trary, since he is conscious of his calling he feels the antagonism of sin *more* acutely in his own being.[54] He suffers more severely than man could suffer to realize the divine will.

The question which remains is whether all that Hofmann has said necessarily rules out the vicariousness of Christ's work. Is there not still a sense in which Christ's work is vicarious, namely that in entering into mankind Christ entered man's "place" and therefore suffered "in man's place"? Here is the point at which Hofmann probably overstated his case in order to pose the problem and bring it to debate. In the third *Schutzschrift* he finally admits that there is a sense in which he could accept the term "vicarious" *(Stellvertretung)*:

> The Son accomplished over against the Father what was possible only for the eternal holiness and suffered the Father's wrath against mankind as the eternally beloved alone could suffer it. Herein he takes up the cause of mankind and accomplishes over against the Father what was impossible for mankind to accomplish for itself. In this sense, but only in this sense, can his work be called vicarious.[55]

One can say that for Hofmann Christ did battle and suffered for man "in man's place" *(an unserer Statt)* by virtue of the fact that he is *true man,* but he did not suffer thereby what man was supposed to suffer instead of man *(statt unser)*. It is a subtle distinction, but everything that Hofmann wanted to say depends upon it. Had he used the traditional terminology, the entire point of his reconstruction would have been missed. Therefore he saw no other alternative than to conduct the debate as a polemic against the doctrine of vicarious satisfaction. It was not so much the term that he rejected (if it had been properly understood); rather it was the *structure* of the theology which lay behind the term that he wanted to destroy. The only way to get at the theological structure was by way of a frontal attack on a formula crucial to that structure.

This brings us to the end of our treatment of the atonement controversy. There are other writings which arise out of the debate

---

[54] *Ibid.,* III, pp. 15-16.
[55] *Ibid.,* III, p. 28.

in Hofmann's time, but they are more or less redundant. They represent a rather weary repetition of arguments already stated. No doubt there is good reason for this. The debate simply reached a stalemate; the two systems stood opposed to each other and neither could entirely controvert the other. This indicates a failure on the part of both sides to locate the critical issues which could solve the problem. This failure gave rise to a continuing discussion which eventually comes to grips with the problem at the heart of the matter: the problem of law and gospel. Before turning to this discussion, however, we must attempt in our next chapter briefly to assess the critical problem as it emerged from the atonement controversy.

CHAPTER V

THE CRITICAL PROBLEM:
THE PLACE OF LAW IN
THE THEOLOGICAL SYSTEM

The 19th century controversy over the atonement was inconclusive. We have suggested that this was so because both parties failed to locate the critical problem in the debate. Here we must seek briefly to spell out this contention before turning to an account of the manner in which the debate continued.

The critical problem is the manner in which one conceives the place of law in the theological system. Is law, as the orthodox system implied, the structure through which man is related to God, the expression of the eternal will of God for man, or is it, as Hofmann has said, only a part of a historical dispensation, so that man's relationship to God must be understood more in terms of the historical realization of the divine will to love? This is the question which we must examine more closely.

Hofmann was quite astute in exposing the difficulties in the orthodox view. For when one assumes that the law is the eternal standard governing man's relationship to God one can hardly avoid a number of problems. These problems are all reflected in the perennial problem of the relationship between wrath and love in God. When law is the standard, one can hardly avoid the implication that "before" the atonement God is wrathful and only "after" being satisfied does his attitude change to love. By this, of course, the orthodox intended to give real significance to the historical event of atonement itself. It brought about a real and "objective" change in God's attitude towards man and, supposedly, established justification as an *actus forensis* (declarative act) on a solid basis.

The difficulties in this scheme are manifest, though, as Hofmann was quick to point out. They can be summed up by saying that it becomes difficult, in such a view, to give systematic expression to the divine love. There is, of course, the old question: If God was simply wrathful "before" the atonement why was Christ sent? Further, there is the equally perennial question: If God's wrath has been "bought off," how can one call it an act of mercy? And when, in seeking to explain how such "payment" could take place, one is drawn into a computation of the equivalence between the payment due and the "infinite worth" of the God-man's sufferings, the problems are only compounded and the legalistic web is spun even tighter at the expense of the divine love.

Hofmann's opponents, as we have seen, generally attempted to disassociate themselves from such computation; they took refuge instead in the idea that it was not abstract reckoning that demanded payment but the sinner's experience of guilt. But this simply substantiated Hofmann's charge that the whole doctrine was a *theory* constructed according to *man's* ideas about what God *must* do to atone for sin, and does nothing to alleviate the difficulties of the system. In general, it can be said that since the question of God's eternal attitude has been preempted by law, it becomes exceedingly difficult to give systematic expression to the divine love. Wrath tends to become the primary category and love always comes off second best. And this leads in turn to the legalistic attitude toward scripture and revelation which we noted at the outset.[1]

Hofmann, on the other hand, wanted to give the primary place in the system to the divine love-will. He asserted that God was eternal love even "before" the event of the atonement. The event itself is the *realization* of the eternal love-will. This makes Hofmann the object of orthodox criticism because he seems to make the

---

[1] Above, pp. 7-8.

historical event a mere *demonstration* of an eternal truth and he is hard pressed to explain why the sufferings and death of the God-man are really necessary. But Hofmann's view, of course, is not that simple. That God is love is not a *general* truth; rather it is a conclusion reached only by "thinking in" the new situation "after" one has experienced the benefits of the cross. His system was supposed to be strictly the result of *ex post facto* reasoning.

This is where the difficulty of comparing Hofmann's system with the orthodox system arises. It raises the difficult question of whether in fact one can really reason in this manner and still give the historical event of atonement crucial significance—a question with which subsequent debate will become increasingly involved. The orthodox theologian argues on the basis of a more or less natural logic of law and retribution common to everyday experience available to everyone. Hofmann, however, wants to argue on the basis of a special *heilsgeschichtliche* logic available, supposedly, only to the man of faith. Thinking in the situation of faith leads, in Hofmann's view, to the demand for a continuous historical scheme describing the progressive self-realization of the divine love.

It was the orthodox inability really to cope with the problem posed by Hofmann's type of reasoning that lay at the root of the difficulties introduced by the atonement controversy. Hofmann actually proposed that by "thinking in" the situation of being a Christian one can penetrate behind the events of history into the divine intent in such a way as to deduce therefrom the whole sweep of the process. When this is judged to be possible, one can simply put law in its proper place in the historical scheme. The law is something which comes "between the times" and pertains only to a particular stage in the process. This means that a theory of history—a historical continuum—has displaced the law as the "system" for understanding the atonement.

The orthodox objection at this point was that such a view does not take law and wrath in its ultimate seriousness. There was a certain legitimacy to this objection, but the real difficulty is in the system which Hofmann proposed. For Hofmann, just as much as the orthodox, could insist that it is only in the historical event that the law was "fulfilled." But when in theologizing about that event he reasoned *behind* the event so as to make it seem that the fulfillment of the law was from the outset a foregone conclusion, that Jesus by his very nature could not do otherwise, then he had assimilated law into a scheme in which it is easily disposed of. And this means that the real threat of the law has been removed by a theological construction. The "theory" to which the Christian is privy has depotentiated the law.

This means, in effect, that the wrath of God has been "seen through." Even though he asserted the place of wrath in no uncertain terms, Hofmann fit it into a scheme in which it is no longer very terrifying. He had "figured God out." When Hofmann reasoned behind the cross to set up his historical scheme he ran the risk of making the divine wrath seem fictive. It is because he did this that his system in turn threatened to rob the historical event of atonement of its decisiveness. Hofmann's Jesus suffered as he has said, in consciousness of and faithfulness to his calling. This means that Jesus himself is all the while privy to the divine plan, that he knows its outcome, and that since at all times he preserves his relationship to God he cannot suffer "what man should have suffered"—the desolation of ultimate defeat and despair. The atonement then appears as the working out of the divine plan which was from the outset a foregone conclusion. The historical event threatens to become mere demonstration, in spite of all the insistence upon "history." An element of docetism comes to the surface for, when all is said and done, Hofmann's Jesus is "protected" from the full reality of historical death, despair, and defeat. The "system" which Hofmann proposed demanded a Jesus who at all times preserved his *Berufstreue* and whose suffering had to be a *Berufsleiden*.

In effect, Hofmann's Jesus died the death of a good *heilsgeschichtliche* theologian. He knew what the eventual outcome would be and thus he was protected from its ultimate seriousness. This, really, is the point at which Thomasius' objection that in Hofmann Jesus never experienced wrath *personally* receives its due. And it is hardly to the point for Hofmann to defend himself by saying that a Jesus who suffers in consciousness of his calling does not suffer *less* but *more* than man, for then he is indulging in the same kind of *quantitative* speculation for which he has castigated his opponents. It does nothing to rescue the fact that by means of the system the wrath of God had been "seen through."

Orthodox criticism of Hofmann was therefore in a certain sense justified. Nevertheless, the difficulty in the controversy lay in the fact that the orthodox attack on Hofmann was based upon a set of assumptions which were equally as vulnerable. They too assumed that it was possible to reason behind the cross into the divine mind; they did it, however, on the basis of law and righteousness rather than a historical scheme. They too had "figured God out" in their own way and could develop a theory about the atonement as the satisfaction of the divine wrath. Even though the scheme was different the results were similar, for a wrath which can and in fact has been "bought off" can hardly be taken very seriously. A forgiveness which has been "earned" and a divine "love" which could stage such a "show" is not very persuasive. Furthermore, the objection raised against Hofmann that Jesus did not *personally* suffer the divine wrath could with equal justice be made against the orthodox view. For the orthodox Jesus too must be one who suffered with full knowledge of the end which such suffering would accomplish. He knew that he was the God-man and that his suffering would satisfy the divine wrath; he knew, therefore, that it would all "come out well" in the end. If Hofmann's Jesus died the death of a good *heilsgeschichtliche* theologian, the orthodox Jesus dies the death of a good orthodox theologian. In either case the outcome was assured by the system, and Jesus was protected from the full consequences of death and defeat. The orthodox structure too is one which threatens the real historical nature of the cross event. The theologizing about the event leads one to focus attention on a theory or doctrine *about* the event rather than to trust *in* the event itself.

Thus the underlying similarity of the two systems is exposed in spite of differences. *Both* attempted to understand the atonement in terms of a *theory* which threatened to rob the event of the cross and resurrection of its historical actuality. The orthodox operated with a theory about an eternal law whose demands could be vicariously satisfied by proper payment. Hofmann operated with a theory about a divine love-will which realized itself in a historical process—a view of history borrowed from German Idealism.[2] In the one instance, law provided the eternal standard for understanding the atonement; in the other law is simply replaced by a historical scheme. But in *either* case one ends up with a system which robs the cross of its historical actuality. This is demonstrated by the inescapable element of docetism that remains in both views. Jesus is "protected" from the full consequences of his death because he "knows the system."

We have reached a point here where something of the complexity of the problem of the place of law in the theological system is revealed. If our analysis to this point is correct, some conclusions can be drawn.

On the one hand, law cannot be understood merely in a static-ontological sense, as a *lex aeterna* according to which God can be "bought off." On the other hand, law cannot be treated merely as though it were part of a historical dispensation superseded by a dispensation of love. For in either case one runs into difficulties and detracts from the seriousness of the cross event itself. One draws attention away from the event to a speculative scheme "behind" the event.

But what then is to be the place of law in the theological system? How is one to think theologically about law? This is a question which we are not yet prepared to answer, for it is the subject of the discussion which continued after Hofmann's time. Perhaps we can just say in anticipation that it must be a view of law—and of wrath—which is more existentially real than either the orthodox or Hofmann could admit, so that the event of the cross becomes for the believer a real deliverance. It must be so conceived that faith for the believer is not merely belief in a theory *about* the cross, but a real *participation* in the event of deliverance itself.

This is a subtle and elusive distinction but nevertheless an exceedingly important one for the understanding of law. Perhaps I can illustrate what I mean with the problems which we have discovered in both views of the atonement, the significance of

---

[2] See E. W. Wendebourg, "Die Heilsgeschichtliche Theologie J. C. K. v. Hofmanns in ihrem Verhältnis zur romantischen Weltanschauung," *Zeitschrift für Theologie und Kirche,* Vol. 52, No. 1 (1955), pp. 64-104.

Christ's death for himself. If when they came to that point they could have said that Christ actually suffered defeat, that he met his *end*, suffering under all the consequences of sin that historical man encounters *including* the agony of despair and utter desolation, then the full gravity of the event would have become apparent. For this means that *even in his own consciousness* Jesus would see nothing but dereliction. Then the resurrection would appear in all its eschatological newness as an absolutely new act, not as a foregone conclusion on the basis of the "system." Then there would be no *theory* to lessen the gravity of the event by providing for some kind of continuous transition from death to life, but only the event itself. Resurrection would be an entirely new event, actually snatching victory from defeat.

In this understanding the real significance of the death of Christ as an actual event is intensified because even for Jesus himself there would have been no way around the full consequences of the cross, no protection from real suffering and death, no theory or system to provide an escape. The death of Jesus Christ itself would then have been the ultimate proclamation of "the law." Christ's death is then the final proclamation that there is for the sinner no convenient alternative of "believing a system" but only the person of Christ himself and the event of death and resurrection.

Such a view of law could result in an ultimate and existential conviction, for if the sinner wanted to inherit the hope of the resurrection, he would have to "die with Christ in order to be raised with him." He could not merely accept a theory about the cross, for in such a view there is no theory about the event which could remove the necessity of participation in the event. In other words, the paradigm for faith is not an act of cognition, the acceptance of a theory, but death and resurrection, participation in the event itself. The life of faith is a life of participation, a life in the "body of Christ."

Such a view of the atonement demands a thinking about law which is much more existential and actual than that of either orthodoxy or Hofmann. It is a type of thinking which seeks to protect and convey more accurately the nature of the cross and resurrection event as an absolute end and a new beginning. It is a type of thinking which confronts the sinner with a theology *of* the cross and not merely a theory *about* the cross. Such thinking presents theology, no doubt, with a subtle and elusive problem, but the subsequent history of the debate shows quite evidently that nothing less than such thinking is demanded by the nature of the case; indeed, the continuing discussion after the atonement controversy can be seen as the struggle to reach that goal.

Before we turn to that discussion, however, it would be well to assess Hofmann's significance in the history of the debate. Does Hofmann's theology represent an advance or a retreat? In a recent study, Robert Schultz judged that Hofmann's attack on the concept of vicarious satisfaction was basically destructive for Lutheran theology.[3] What was at stake, he argued, was the problem of law and gospel; in this he is certainly correct. But he maintains that Hofmann's reconstruction in terms of salvation history brought about a neglect of this problem which left Lutheran theology ill-prepared to cope with subsequent developments such as Ritschlianism and historicism.

There is no doubt some truth to this charge. Insofar as Hofmann sought to solve the problem of law and gospel by shifting the emphasis to history he is responsible for some of the confusion which resulted. But Schultz does not seem to appreciate the nature of the difficulty which confronted Lutheran theology at this time. The attack against legalism was open and widespread, and the demand for a reorientation persistent. Orthodoxy could protect itself against Hofmann only by returning to a concept of wrath and law which was beset with difficulties. As long as Lutheranism remained bound to this scheme it would be doomed to theological insignificance. Hofmann's great importance lies in the fact that he challenged this system and criticized it cogently. Because of this challenge he presented a severe crisis for orthodox Lutheran theology, a crisis which had to come if there was to be any advance beyond a covert repristination of 17th century theology. It may be true that not everything which resulted from this crisis was en-

---

[3] Robert Schultz, *Gesetz und Evangelium in der Lutherischen Theologie des 19. Jahrhunderts* (Berlin: Lutherisches Verlagshaus, 1958), p. 110. I am indebted to Schultz's book for many helpful suggestions and insights but find myself in some disagreement over final conclusions.

tirely fortunate, but it was only because of Hofmann's kind of attack that discussion over law and gospel could begin anew. This is apparent from the subsequent history of the debate. It is not, after all, simply accidental that theology today has returned to a discussion of the problem of law and gospel; it is a result of the discussions set in motion by the attack which Hofmann made.

In spite of the criticisms we have made of Hofmann's theology, there are many points at which he made contributions of great value. His was a creative attempt to restate the theology of the Reformation in terms of the emerging historical world-view. His project of "thinking in" the situation of faith may have led him to overstep somewhat the boundaries of such thinking, but nevertheless he directed our attention to the proper starting point for theological reflection. His battle against all forms of legalism, especially in theological thinking and doctrinal form, can only be applauded. His reassertion of the concept of divine love as the deepest creative ground in God rescued a fundamental theological insight from its relative oblivion in the orthodox scheme. His attempt to understand the atonement as the victory of this divine love placed him considerably ahead of his time. Both in his Luther research and in his own thinking he anticipated present-day views.

Perhaps Hofmann's most important contribution, however, is his concept of the new humanity in Christ. His view of the church as the new humanity is an attempt to overcome both the individualism and the subjectivism of earlier views. As such this attempt to think in terms of the new was an attempt to find a real theological place for the "new age" in the theological system. Instead of thinking only in terms of a static ontological scheme, Hofmann introduced the concept of a transition from the old to the new. Due to his *heilsgeschichtliche* scheme the nature of this transition remained somewhat problematical, but in introducing this "two age" scheme he had returned to a fundamental biblical motif. Eschatology is no longer just the "doctrine of the last things" as it was for orthodoxy, but it now permeates the entire system.

Nevertheless, despite those fruitful beginnings Hofmann bequeathed to subsequent generations a complex problem. In effect he substituted an idea of historical progress for the static-ontological concept of law as the main structure of his system. This meant that he attempted to understand the Christ event in terms of a more or less continuous process, the self-realization of the divine love. According to the important study on *Heilsgeschichte* by Gustav Weth, this is the point at which the basic difficulty of every *Heilsgeschichte* intrudes.[4] In the shift from the legalistic scheme of orthodoxy to a scheme based on historical process, the continuity or idea of progress accomplishes the same function as law in the system of orthodoxy— it provides the structure for understanding the Christ event. But when the event is understood as part of a continuous scheme, it is inevitably robbed of its newness. It does not represent a radical break, an end and a beginning in man's history. It is simply a part of a necessary process. In other words, the eschatological nature of the event itself is threatened. *Heilsgeschichte* as a system obscures the eschatological newness of the Christ event just as the old system of law had done. As we shall see, it took subsequent generations considerable time to sort out the problems involved in Hofmann's reconstruction. Perhaps the most immediate effect of it all was that in shifting from the system of law to the system of the realization of the divine love-will, Hofmann changed the emphasis in the theological system from wrath to love. Consequently it was in this form—the argument about wrath and love—that the debate about law and gospel was prosecuted in the years after Hofmann's work.

---

[4] Gustav Weth, *Die Heilsgeschichte* (München: Chr. Kaiser Verlag, 1931), pp. 134 ff.

Part Two

THE
CONTINUING
DISCUSSION:

Wrath
Versus
Love

CHAPTER VI

THEODOSIUS HARNACK

Hofmann's systematic reconstruction was largely forgotten by subsequent generations. There are no doubt several reasons for this. It was not generally accepted in his own circles, and in its dependence upon Idealism it was dated. Most important, however, is the fact that it was soon to be overshadowed by Ritschlianism, in which many of its concerns were taken up and presented in an apparently more palatable form. Even though Hofmann's system was forgotten, however, the discussion of the issues surrounding law and gospel was just beginning, and in this discussion, Hofmann's influence has remained a "silently active ferment"[1] until the present day.

The basic nature of the discussion is best seen by looking at two major reactions to Hofmann's theology in the work of Theodosius Harnack and Albrecht Ritschl. These two men take opposite poles in the debate, and the positions which they take are determinative for subsequent discussions even though these positions are modified considerably by their respective followers.

In the debate the interpretation of Luther becomes almost the dominant theme. This is a result of the fact that Hofmann had claimed support for his view in Luther. Thus Hofmann shaped, to a large degree, the main problem for the growing Luther research,

---

[1] Paul Bachmann, *J. Chr. K. v. Hofmanns Versöhnungslehre* (Gütersloh: C. Bertelsmann, 1910), p. 61.

which was largely a continuation of the controversy over wrath and love in the doctrine of the atonement. It should not be forgotten, therefore, that research into Luther's theology was carried out against this background, and that it always had a degree of systematic intent.

Theodosius Harnack pioneered in the research into Luther's theology. We have already encountered Harnack in the atonement controversy in opposition to Hofmann; he crowned this opposition with his two-volume study of Luther's theology.[2] Harnack's study was largely an attempt to dispute the right of Hofmann and those who agreed with him to claim Luther for their cause.[3] More than 20 years elapsed between the appearance of the first and second volumes; in the meantime the work of Albrecht Ritschl had appeared, so it was actually Ritschl who became the main object of attack in the second volume. Even so, Hofmann was still prominently mentioned.

As Harnack's stand in the atonement controversy indicated, he did not believe that Luther's theology could be used to support Hofmann's point of view. In his preface to the first volume of his Luther study he repeated this conviction; he affirmed that the essential content of Luther's theology found expression in the Lutheran confessional writings and that there is a more genuine understanding of Luther in orthodox dogmatics than is generally believed. Harnack did admit, however, that there is in Luther a rich treasury of profound and original thought which had not received the attention it deserved,[4] but in general he attempted to reclaim Luther for the orthodox side.

The task which Harnack set himself was not that of an exposition of Luther's entire theology, but rather—significantly—of the "mid-

---

[2]Theodosius Harnack, *Luthers Theologie* (Neue Ausgabe: 2 vols.: München: Chr. Kaiser Verlag, 1927). Harnack's work has gained considerable vogue among contemporary theologians (Brunner, Elert, etc.), but little attention has been given to the polemical context in which it arose. No doubt it is the polemical character which gives the work much of its value for the contemporary situation. Nevertheless, it should be read with care. The crucial question is whether the polemical situation has not influenced the interpretation at decisive points.

[3] See Harnack, *Luthers Theologie*, pp. 10-11.

[4] Harnack, *Luthers Theologie*, Vol. I, p. viii.

point of his faith and doctrine, namely the doctrine of atonement and redemption" and "all those basic theological viewpoints . . . which are necessary for the basic and many-sided understanding of that doctrine." [5] Harnack chose a systematic rather than a historical method, seeking to expound the central doctrine at issue in the light of the whole of Luther's theology rather than attempting to trace a historical development. Such a method presupposes, he said, that the reformer, in spite of discernible development, remained unchanged in "certain basic doctrines." It also places upon the researcher the condition that he attempt neither to impose a system on Luther nor to construct a scholastic system out of Luther. Luther, Harnack says, was not a "system man" even though his view does have organic consistency. [6]

Many people have doubted, however, that Harnack was able completely to carry out his expressed intentions. Otto Wolff, in his study of basic types of Luther interpretation, [7] pointed out that there were several factors which inhibited Harnack's desire for objectivity. Harnack's commitment to the confessions, which made him read Luther through the orthodox tradition, limited the freedom from systematizing that he desired. His systematic method, which does not take sufficient note of historical development, could be quite dangerous, as more recent research has shown. Also, Harnack did not have the benefit of recent critical editions of Luther's works. The edition which he used was the Walch edition, so that some of his citations reflected the vocabulary and views of Luther's students and translators as well as Luther's own views. In some instances quite crucial issues were at stake, as we shall see. [8]

Harnack's basic concern—quite natural in the light of the atonement controversy—was to present Luther's teaching on the wrath of God in all its forcefulness in order to offset the tendency towards the sentimental and undialectical concept of divine love

---

[5] *Luthers Theologie*, p. ix.

[6] *Ibid.*, pp. 9 ff.

[7] Otto Wolff, *Die Haupttypen der neueren Lutherdeutung*, Stuttgart: W. Kohlhammer, 1958.

[8] Emanuel Hirsch, in his review of the new edition, remarks that if every critically suspect passage was marked the book would resemble a "graveyard of crosses." Quoted in Wolff, *Die Haupttypen*, p. 67.

which he saw in Hofmann and in the 19th century in general. Luther understood the wrath of God, Harnack said, as an eternal and objective reality,[9] rooted in the divine essence itself. It is not subjective, rooted merely in the imagination of the frightened human conscience, but objectively real in God's relation to fallen men.

But how is this to be squared with the concept of divine love? Harnack found the answer in Luther's distinction between God "in Christ" and God "outside of" Christ *(ausser Christo)*. This is an objectively real double relationship of God to the world which was of fundamental significance for Luther's entire theology.[10] It was the *principium movens* of his theological dialectic of faith,[11] the "main motor nerve of his theology." [12]

This distinction gives us the basic key to Harnack's understanding of Luther. A glance at the table of contents of his study is sufficient to verify this. After a discussion of general presuppositions, Harnack's first major section deals with *"Gott und die Welt ausser Christo,"* the second section with *"Gott und die Welt in Christo,"* and the final section with law and Gospel. Harnack's Luther is an uncompromising dialectician. God stands in a double relationship to the world; both these relationships are essentially, objectively real and stand in material tension with each other. They are to be maintained in all their full reality in a simultaneous dialectic as contrary (though valid and real) relations, rooted in the depths of the divine being itself.[13]

According to Harnack's interpretation of Luther, this distinction between God "in Christ" and "outside of Christ" is a result of the double attitude God must take to the fallen world. God in his "creator relationship" or "world relationship" is the God of the active and retributive righteousness *(iustitia activa et retributiva)* who rewards good and punishes evil, the God of threatening majesty and jealous will, the God of terrifying wrath, self-identical

[9] Harnack, *Luthers Theologie*, I, p. 221.

[10] *Ibid.*, p. 84.

[11] *Ibid.*, p. 104.

[12] *Ibid.*, p. 336.

[13] *Ibid.*, p. 226.

righteousness, and holiness. God as redeemer, however, stands apart from this. "In Christ" God has established a second order of pure grace, a soteriological order over against the cosmological order. This second order is the "realization of the innermost divine nature according to its pure aseity, the seeking love, pure forgiving grace, in contrast to the other order where the divine self-integrity reacts in wrath and punishment against a world which has taken the way of sin." [14]

Harnack understood Luther in terms of a dialectic between these two types of relationships. Otto Wolff has termed this a "two-spheres" type of Luther interpretation.[15] From the methodological point of view the important thing is that these two spheres rest ultimately on a concept of a twofold knowledge of God.[16] There is a knowledge of God available outside of Christ and a knowledge available in Christ. This does not mean, Harnack was careful to point out, that Luther taught that there are two sources from which equally valid propositional truths about the ultimate nature of the divine being can be derived, so that the two types of knowledge could then be synthesized. Nor does it mean one complements the other in a quantitative manner. That would be a kind of scholastic *cognitio dei generalis et specialis*. What Luther saw was a twofold knowledge of God in a more practical or directly theological sense. What was involved for Luther is a knowledge of God as it impinges directly on the conscience—two ways of apprehending God in his concrete relationship to men which seem to be contradictory and mutually exclusive, which cannot be joined by an abstract speculative synthesis. These two types of knowledge of God have objective reality because as a result of sin God can relate to the world only in this twofold manner. The twofold knowledge of God is determined by this antithesis of sin and grace.[17] This corresponds exactly to the dialectic between God "in Christ" and God "outside of Christ."

On the basis of this dialectic, Harnack found justification in Lu-

---

[14] Wolff, *Die Haupttypen*, p. 68.

[15] *Ibid.*, pp. 63-120.

[16] Harnack, *Luthers Theologie*, I, p. 69 ff.

[17] *Ibid.*, p. 72.

ther for speaking of a "natural knowledge of God," a knowledge of
God "outside of Christ." The source of this knowledge is the "law
written in the heart," the "voice of the conscience," the natural moral
reason. But Harnack said further that even though this knowledge
is objectively correct and valid insofar as it pertains to the real
situation of knowing God outside of Christ, still it does not stand
on the same level with the knowledge gained "in Christ." It is
"correct" in its own way, but nevertheless it is not the ultimate
truth about God because it does not bring salvation.

The "natural knowledge" of God is not in this sense "true" knowledge, because sin inevitably falsifies and misuses it.[18] By nature
man knows that God is and the difference between right and wrong.
This knowledge of God according to the law is "correct." But it is
not "true" knowledge of God because it does not know God in his
innermost essence as pure self-giving love. Consequently it is misused by sinful man as a means for attaining self-righteousness,
which is the fundamental perversion of its intent. The knowledge
of God which comes through the gospel is not a mere completion
or even purification or transformation of the natural knowledge,
but something absolutely new, something unattainable by reason
altogether. This "new knowledge" is "true" because it is saving.
It is the knowledge of the inmost essence of God himself.

Harnack sets the two types of knowledge against each other,
but the difficult problem is the question of how the two are to be
related. Harnack, it must be remembered, wanted to establish that
Luther taught the wrath of God as an "objective" reality." This
knowledge of God as wrathful is established as a knowledge of God
"outside of Christ." But how is this related to the knowledge of
God "in Christ"? Luther, Harnack said, held that the knowledge
of God derived through the law—God as wrathful—is "correct" in
its own way, but is not the "ultimate" or "true" knowledge of God.
Such knowledge is given only "in Christ" to faith.

Harnack is wrestling here with a difficult problem in Luther's
theology. It arises from the fact that Luther could alternately
praise and damn the knowledge of God given through the law.

---

[18] *Ibid.*, p. 72.

He could say on the one hand that it is good and true, and on the other that it is *idolatria, idolum* and *falsum figmentium*,[19] that the only true knowledge comes in the gospel. The difficulty is in keeping these apparently contradictory statements together without destroying the dialectic.

Otto Wolff maintains that Harnack did not succeed in capturing Luther's true intent at this point; he feels that here Harnack may have been too much influenced by the polemical situation. Because of his opposition to Hofmann, Harnack wanted to assert the objective validity of the divine wrath in the strongest possible terms. And he could, as he demonstrated, find ample justification in Luther for such a view, but the difficulty arises in understanding the relationship between wrath and love in Luther. For if wrath and love are equally valid, then the structure threatens to collapse into a *dualism* of love and wrath in God. Wolff feels that Harnack was unable to follow Luther's dialectic at this point, that he compromised by relativizing the antithesis. Thus Harnack said that the knowledge of God as wrath gained through the law is objectively valid, but "only conditionally and not of the same stature" as the knowledge of God gained through the gospel.[20] Therefore Wolff claims that the relationship between the "two-spheres" is a "relativized conjunction or coexistence." [21]

We need not decide at this point on the correctness of Wolff's judgment. I point it out, however, because it will be of importance in later discussion.

To avoid confusion I should perhaps make clear at this point that I am interested in Harnack's interpretation of Luther solely for its contribution to the controversy over the atonement. The question will inevitably arise as to whether Harnack's interpretation is correct, but this question need not concern us now. Later interpreters will, in turn, take issue with Harnack in the continuing discussion. We are interested here only in Harnack's interpretation within the context of the controversy as a particular view

---

[19] Cf. Wolff, *Die Haupttypen,* p. 88, and also Ernst Wolf, *Peregrinatio* (München: Chr. Kaiser Verlag, 1954), pp. 13-15.

[20] Harnack, *Luthers Theologie,* I, p. 84.

[21] Wolff, *Die Haupttypen,* p. 74.

of the atonement. Whether the logic behind that view was ultimately Luther's or Harnack's is a question we can leave for later
interpreters to answer in the course of the discussion.

In the context of the atonement controversy, the most important
feature of Harnack's interpretation of Luther was his use of the
concept of the natural knowledge of God as the basis for the doctrine of wrath. Such natural knowledge helps to secure the dialectic of wrath and love. Hofmann, it is to be remembered, rejected
all thought of a natural knowledge of God; he claimed that it was
on the basis of such knowledge that a faulty doctrine of the atonement was constructed. Harnack, on the contrary, claimed that there
is such a thing as a natural knowledge of God in Luther, and that
such knowledge forms a necessary part of his theology.

Most significant, however, was Harnack's insistence that on the
basis of this natural knowledge of God through the law, Luther
taught a doctrine of vicarious satisfaction. Harnack believed that
for Luther the law was an independent and objectively valid expression of the divine will for man, and that as such its demands
had to be satisfied if man were to be released from the threat of punishment and death. The concept of the natural knowledge of God
is, according to Harnack, the basis for Luther's teaching on the law,
and consequently the basis for the doctrine of vicarious satisfaction.[22]

Here Harnack encountered a certain difficulty. He was well aware
that Luther could alternately praise and damn the law.[23] The problem for Harnack lay in determining how Luther's ambiguous attitude toward the law corresponded with the idea that the law is
an expression of God's eternal will, a "way" of salvation which can
serve as the structure for the doctrine of vicarious satisfaction.
How can the law be both a benefactor and at the same time placed
among the despicable tyrants that assail man? Harnack answered
that Luther made a basic distinction in the doctrine of law "between "essence" and "office" (Wesen und Amt).[24] The law in its
essence is eternal, irrevocable, and good. In the office it has to carry

---

[22] Harnack, Luthers Theologie, I, pp. 365-368.
[23] Ibid., pp. 368-383.
[24] Ibid., pp. 368-401.

out among sinful men, however, it is the instrument of wrath, an accusing tyrant which destroys. By means of this basic distinction, Harnack claimed, Luther left the law intact as an objective juridical scheme in "essence," while the "office" it performs against sin is overcome through the atonement. Because of this interpretation of the law, Luther could both praise the law as good, see it as providing the necessity for a doctrine of vicarious satisfaction, and also condemn it as a tyrant whose power must be overcome.[25]

But even when the problem of law is thus "settled" there are further difficulties in connection with Luther's view of the atonement. Harnack is well aware that Luther expressly rejected any "theological apriorism" which constructed a doctrine of God from rational premises in order constantly to determine what God must do to redeem the world.[26] Here we face again the question of the necessity for the atonement. In a section entitled "The relative necessity for the sacrifice of the Son" Harnack pointed out that Luther held no thought of an absolute necessity from God's point of view.[27] Love was not first made possible by a vicarious satisfaction. Harnack even quoted those passages in which Luther suggested that perhaps God could have given the Son in a different manner. But Harnack was inclined to regard these as vestiges of nominalism which had not been fully overcome.[28] Harnack insisted that even if Luther rejected the idea of necessity, he also rejected the concept of an arbitrary God. Luther, Harnack said, placed himself solely under the revelation in the Word; from that vantage point for Luther the atonement "must" happen in the way it did happen. Thus the atonement in this form was "relatively necessary." It was not an absolute necessity for God, but given the situation it was the neces-

---

[25] Harnack's interpretation of the "essence"-"office" distinction has been questioned, partly because one of the main passages Harnack uses to support his case is critically suspect. Robert Schultz points out that one of the passages Harnack uses does not clearly bear Harnack's interpretation and the other is a faulty translation of Luther's original statement. Schultz further contends that the essence-office distinction is one which Harnack got from his earlier teachers and imposed upon his Luther study. Robert Schultz, *Gesetz und Evangelium in der Lutherischen Theologie des 19. Jahrhunderts,* p. 142.

[26] Harnack, *Luthers Theologie,* II, p. 82.

[27] *Ibid.,* pp. 75-85.

[28] Harnack, *Luthers Theologie,* II, p. 83.

sary form for the manifestation and realization of his love among men. It was, one might say, the necessary sign and seal of the divine love; as such it was the actual realization of that love and not merely a proclamation of a love that could be taken for granted.

Here there could be no thought of an abstract *a priori* system which set up a scheme according to which the necessity of the atonement could be developed. God did not need to be atoned before he could be loving. He is loving *in* Christ, and one is not faced with the "before" or "after" alternative. Harnack's interpretation, though, became considerably more confused when he followed this section with a section entitled "The absolute necessity of atoning God." [29] Before he came to this section Harnack had given considerable attention to Luther's "dramatic-dualistic" imagery in treating the atonement. Harnack did not obscure the fact that Luther put a great deal of his emphasis upon such imagery. He admitted that orthodoxy had not creatively developed this aspect of Luther's thought. But Harnack seemed to regard this simply as an evidence of the "richness" and "profundity" of Luther's spirituality. Luther, he said, was not content to expound atonement merely in external and theoretical terms, but described it in terms of its "full, profound and immeasurable ethical significance." For Luther there had to be an actual redemption of the subject from the tyrannical forces (flesh, world, death, devil, and hell); this could come about only through redemption from a bad conscience.[30] The dramatic-dualistic element was therefore interpreted in terms of its relation to the release of the individual subject from the tyranny of a bad conscience. But, said Harnack, there is a fundamental distinction between this redemption (*Erlösung*) and objective atonement (*Versöhnung*). Redemption is the release of the captive in the present, but such a redemption is possible only insofar as it is based upon the atonement accomplished once for all in the past. Redemption releases one from the *dominion* of Satan, but this is possible because he has lost his *rights* in the atonement. The rights which he possessed under the sanction of the divine wrath had to be "bought off." This could only have come about by a vicarious

[29] *Ibid.*, pp. 241-250.
[30] Harnack, *Luthers Theologie*, II, p. 250.

satisfaction for man's guilt. God's wrath had to be stilled and his righteousness satisfied. The dualistic-dramatic element in Luther's thought thus did not exclude for Harnack the doctrine of vicarious satisfaction, but rather *required* it.

Thus the stage was set for a return to the basic orthodox doctrine of the atonement. Harnack claimed to find in Luther the idea of "an absolute inner-divine necessity for the sacrifice of the Son." [31] The concept of vicarious satisfaction, Harnack held, was the heart of Luther's view of the atonement.[32] This in turn rested upon an interpretation of law in which a distinction was made between essence and office. One is redeemed from the "office" of the law because the "essential" demand has been satisfied vicariously.

So we have in Harnack's Luther a "relative" and an "absolute" necessity for the sacrifice of the Son. It is difficult to see how these two could be held together. What Harnack seemed to be saying was that for Luther the sacrifice of the Son was not an abstract *a priori* necessity in order for God to be loving, but rather an inner-divine necessity for the divine love to be actually realized among men. God did not have to atone, and no one could dictate from man's point of view the manner in which he would have had to send the Son. But if the love of God was to be realized among men as love, then it must have occurred in the manner in which it did occur. This seems to be the gist of Harnack's interpretation of Luther.

The view of the atonement which Harnack derived from Luther presented a rather confusing picture. Its most distinctive feature was its doctrine of wrath derived from a natural knowledge of God and the law. This knowledge is dialectically opposed to the knowledge of God which comes through the gospel. So there is to be a real dialectic between wrath and love, law and gospel, but how is this dialectic to be conceived? If both wrath and love are of equal status, then one is threatened with a dualism in God. The solution, in this view, was given, apparently, in faith. In faith one learns that natural knowledge does not yield the ultimate truth about God. It is true that God is wrathful towards sinful men, but this is God

---

[31] Harnack, *Luthers Theologie,* II, p. 242.
[32] *Ibid.,* p. 250.

as he is only "outside of Christ." "In Christ" and for faith he is different; there he is a God of love. This is the ultimate truth about God.

But what is the nature of this knowledge gained by faith and how does it relate to the natural knowledge? Faith, apparently, is the acceptance of objective atonement, the acceptance that the demands of the law have been satisfied. It seems therefore to be a propositional truth of the same type that one derives from the natural knowledge. But the propositions "God is wrathful" and "God is loving" cannot both be equally true. One must therefore be relativized. One is *more true* than the other. Wrath, though it is asserted in no uncertain terms, must be relativized if love is to be maintained.

There was an inner connection for Harnack between the doctrine of the atonement and the manner in which the wrath-love dialectic was stated. Because the atonement was an "objective" vicarious satisfaction, the dialectic ultimately had to be relativized. For then the "knowledge of faith" is a doctrine, a propositional truth which must either compete or be synthesized with the natural knowledge. Both could not be equally true if they contradicted each other, so that one had to be relativized at the expense of the other.

By way of anticipation, it can be asked if there is not another way of understanding the problem. If, for instance, faith is something else, if it consists solely in participation in the death of Christ, then there would be no reason to relativize the divine wrath. If one could say that wrath in its full force is the historical power under which man must meet his end—God's judgment of man—then the atonement could be interpreted as the event in which Christ suffered that end and won the victory. Wrath would be *conquered* in him but not relativized. It would still be in force as the judgment that unless man dies with Christ he shall not be raised with him. Faith would then be understood as participation, not merely as the reception of truths about an "objective" transaction. And there would be no reason for a "knowledge of faith" to compete on the same level with a natural knowledge. In such a view it could even be said that the knowledge of faith was the "true" knowledge of God, whereas natural knowledge is not ultimate truth; but in doing so one would be saying it in a different setting and it would mean something quite different. In such a view it could be said that knowledge of God derived from the law leads only to *idolatria* and that it was a *falsum figmentum*, or the devil's instrument. This would not mean that one was relativizing it but only *exposing its terrible power*. In short, in such a view all of the same terminology could be used, but it would mean something quite different; the atonement would be understood against the background of an entirely different systematic structure, and some of Harnack's inadequacies could be avoided.

The view of the atonement which Harnack derived from Luther had the same shortcomings that we found in the orthodox view and in Hofmann's view. Whether Harnack's interpretation was true to Luther is an open question. One can hardly avoid the impression that there was a real "tug-of-war" in Harnack's interpretation between Luther's view and the orthodox view. Harnack himself pointed out that Luther often polemicized against the concept of satisfaction because he felt it "too weak, not descriptive enough or comprehensive enough, and too easily leading to a superficial juridical view." [33] It is difficult to see how Luther could make such criticism and at the same time hold that a juridical view of vicarious satisfaction was the most basic interpretation of the atonement.

Nevertheless, Harnack made some important contributions to the continuing discussion. He showed, certainly, that there is more to Luther's view than Hofmann was willing to realize. He demonstrated that there was a place in Luther's thought for such a thing as a "natural knowledge of God" and that such natural knowledge was intimately connected with Luther's understanding of law and wrath. Harnack also showed that Luther used the terminology of the vicarious satisfaction view side by side with the dramatic-dualistic terminology, and that Luther did not seem to be aware of any contradiction between them.

Perhaps Harnack's greatest contribution, however, was his discovery of Luther's dialectical concept of God. This stood in sharp contrast to the monistic tendencies in Hofmann and Ritschl and the

---

[33] Harnack, *Luthers Theologie*, II, p. 270.

entire 19th century. It is for this reason that Harnack's work still enjoys popularity today. The dialectic between God "in Christ" and God "outside of Christ" injected new possibilities into the discussion of the atonement. Whether Harnack himself fully understood and accurately reproduced Luther's own thought on all these matters, however, will also be a part of the continuing discussion.

For our purposes, though, Harnack's work is important as one extreme in the field of the various reactions to Hofmann. The important fact is that he tried to establish a more dialectical understanding of God in relation to man and that he did this by insisting on a "natural knowledge" as the dialectical opposite of revealed knowledge. He maintained the dialectic by holding law, wrath, and hiddenness *outside* of Christ in a strict separation. Law remained outside the revelation in Christ and provided eventually a structure for understanding the atonement. The construction is faulty, however, because to avoid a dualism Harnack had to relativize one pole; this led ultimately to the same sort of speculative synthesis between wrath and love which was present in orthodoxy. Clearly the idea of a natural knowledge which is equated with law and wrath needed closer attention.

Thus the controversy which began as a debate over the doctrine of the atonement came to focus increasingly on the issues of law, wrath, and love—the problem of the doctrine of God. For this reason, direct debate about the atonement receded into the background for some time; it came to the fore again only in later Luther studies. Since atonement ceased to occupy a central position in the discussion, we shall attempt in what follows to trace the debate as it developed and then return to the question of atonement when it is raised again.

Looking forward to the contemporary debate, it is significant to note that Harnack has exercised some influence on present-day theologians.[34] Emil Brunner, for instance, admits to having been influenced quite heavily by Harnack's Luther study in his understanding of divine wrath. Since for Harnack divine wrath was connected with a natural knowledge, this admission sheds some light

---

[34] Wolff, *Die Haupttypen*, pp. 112-120.

on Brunner's argument with Barth. Gogarten has used Harnack's interpretation as support for a divine and natural law in the form of a *Volksnomos* with its fateful implications for the German church situation under Hitler. Wolff also sees strong echoes of this "two-spheres" type of Luther interpretation in men like Elert, Bohlin, Runestam, and Stange.

Harnack's interpretation of Luther has therefore had some fateful consequences. It arose from a polemical situation and sought to establish certain points about Luther in opposition to the interpretations of Hofmann and Ritschl, but it has often been taken out of this context and used to establish points which were perhaps quite different. Had more attention been given to the polemical context Harnack might have been read with more care.

CHAPTER VII

ALBRECHT RITSCHL

Albrecht Ritschl provided a reaction to Hofmann quite opposed to Harnack's. Ritschl serves therefore as the opposing prototype in the continuing discussion. Ritschl and Hofmann apparently never met personally even though they were academic contemporaries for 37 years (1840-1877). The theological relationship between them is not difficult to establish, however, especially in the case of Ritschl's dependence upon Hofmann.[1] Ritschl often refers to Hofmann's work, both favorably and unfavorably. Little is known, however, about how Hofmann regarded Ritschl. He refers to Ritschl's work only twice [2]; even when Ritschl criticized Hofmann's method,[3] Hofmann did not reply. In view of his acid replies to other critics this is quite strange. Perhaps it is an indication that he was not nearly as antipathetic to the more "liberal" Ritschl as he was to the more conservative theologians in his own midst.

Apart from a criticism of Hofmann's method, there is every indication that Ritschl held Hofmann in high esteem, especially as an exegete.[4] As we shall see, it is quite possible that Ritschl received

---

[1] See Bernhard Steffen, *Hofmanns und Ritschls Lehren über die Heilsbedeutung des Todes Jesu* (Gütersloh: C. Bertelsmann, 1910), pp. 38 ff. Cited hereafter as *Hofmanns und Ritschls Lehren.*

[2] Hofmann, *Der Schriftbeweis*, 2nd ed., Vol. I, pp. 296 and 340.

[3] Albrecht Ritschl, "Über die methodischen Prinzipien der Theologie des Herrn Dr. v. Hofmann," *Allgemeinen Kirchenzeitung*, Vol. 1, No. 12, 1858, pp. 353-364.

[4] Steffen, *Hofmanns und Ritschls Lehren*, pp. 38, 43.

much of the impetus for his major work from his interest in the atonement controversy. So in spite of differences there is a definite positive relationship between the two theologians. Reinhold Seeberg goes so far as to claim that Hofmann was the only theologian of the time other than Schleiermacher upon whom Ritschl really depended.[5] Certainly Hofmann and Ritschl shared many common concerns, principally their rejection of the entire legalistic structure of orthodoxy and the concept of vicarious satisfaction which accompanied it.

The most convenient place to begin the discussion of Ritschl's relationship to Hofmann is with Ritschl's criticism of Hofmann's theological method. In criticizing Hofmann's method Ritschl said that it was his aim not to destroy but to remain true to and to establish more firmly Hofmann's own intention and results.[6] Ritschl asserted that for all his significance as an exegete, Hofmann was quite immature as a systematic theologian.[7] In Ritschl's view Hofmann did not define his terms carefully and systematically enough and did not arrive at a satisfactory scientific definition of the task of theology.

The main object of Ritschl's attack was Hofmann's method of "thinking in" and unfolding the content of the experience of Christianity. Ritschl held that this was too subjective and too imprecise. To say that the task of the theologian is to unfold the content of his experience does not distinguish systematic theology from other types of Christian expression in hymnody, art, etc.

Ritschl was also unable to accept Hofmann's insistence upon the independence of a theology based on this methodology. He said he could not understand what this could mean other than that one should attempt to transpose oneself by means of imagination into the manner of thinking inherent in the revelation itself and thus simply reproduce it under its own conditions. But this, for Ritschl,

---

[5] Reinhold Seeberg, *Die Kirche Deutschlands im 19. Jahrhundert* (2nd ed.: Leipzig: A. Deichert, 1904), p. 259. See also Steffen, *Hofmanns und Ritschls Lehren*, pp. 7ff., and Wolff, *Die Haupttypen*, p. 210.

[6] Albrecht Ritschl, *Rechtfertigung und Versöhnung* (3rd ed.; 3 vols.; Bonn: Adolph Marcus, 1889), Vol. I, p. 623.

[7] Otto Ritschl, *Albrecht Ritschls Leben* (Freiburg: J. C. B. Mohr, 1892), Vol. I, p. 307.

was biblical rather than systematic theology, and he remarked that Hofmann never really got beyond a type of biblical thinking.[8] True systematic theology, Ritschl said, involves a thinking *about*, not merely *in* the experience of Christianity. It involves a thinking about Christianity because systematic theology works with general concepts which have arisen outside of Christianity, so that one must employ the general rules of thought available to everyone in clarifying the special nature of Christianity. In this way Christianity strives for an exposition of Christianity which is logically consistent, generally intelligible, and not limited by a pietistic isolation.

It was therefore wrong, in Ritschl's view, for Hofmann to hold that systematic theology unfolds the content of subjective experience. Instead, theology is concerned with the objective historical revelation in Scripture. Its task is the "ordered reproduction of the thought-circle *(Gedankenkreis)* of Christ,"[9] and the subsequent comparison of the results of this reproduction with the various types and stages of other religions. Only in this comparison can the uniqueness of Christianity be recognized and its peculiar place be established.

Ritschl went on from this point to establish, with the aid of his interpretation of Kant, the case for Christianity as the highest religion—the perfect spiritual and ethical religion. In the first edition of *Rechtfertigung und Versöhnung*, there are, as well, attempts at a general "scientific proof" for the reasonableness and truth of Christianity.[10]

On this basis Ritschl criticized Hofmann for his exclusivism and his refusal of every scientific question about the connection between revelation and a general concept of God, the world, and history. Ritschl stated in the first edition of *Rechtfertigung und Versöhnung*

---

[8] Ritschl, *Rechtfertigung und Versöhnung*, I, 1st ed., p. 571. Ritschl's criticism of Hofmann's method first appeared in the article in the *Allgemeinen Kirchenzeitung* (above p. 96, note 3). I have not been able to obtain this article. Its contents are summarized, however, in Steffen, *Hofmanns und Ritschls Lehren* (above, p. 96, note 1) and in O. Ritschl, *A. Ritschls Leben* (above, p. 97, note 7). Virtually the same criticism is repeated in *Rechtfertigung und Versöhnung*, Vol. I, 1st ed., pp. 569-570, and in a slightly though significantly altered form in the 3rd ed., pp. 614-615.

[9] Ritschl, *Rechtfertigung und Versöhnung*, 1st ed., Vol. III, p. 4.

[10] *Ibid.*, p. 14.

that he was convinced that the science of systematic theology, however much it may be bound to biblical material, could develop only out of such general questions. One must think *about* the truth and necessity of Christianity in the light of the general questions about man and God arising out of man's situation.[11]

Thus Ritschl's initial criticism of Hofmann arose from the charge of subjectivism which we have encountered previously, but it was augmented by an attempt to establish the place of Christianity on the basis of a Kantian analysis of religion. In Ritschl, therefore, Hofmann's attempt to establish an independent theological method was rejected in favor of an analysis of religion in general.

Ritschl, however, later altered this initial criticism of Hofmann. In the first place, he withdrew the charge of subjectivism in his review of Hofmann's book on ethics when it became clear to him that Hofmann held that the theologian unfolds the content of *the* Christian experience and not his own subjective experience.[12] Ritschl claimed that Hofmann had changed his position on this point, but the retraction was really due to his misreading of Hofmann's earlier statements; Hofmann's viewpoint remained essentially the same throughout his career.

In the second place, Ritschl altered his own position on the use of general proofs in validating Christianity. In the third edition of *Rechtfertigung und Versöhnung*, all references to such an attempt were removed. Ritschl began to say instead that theology can provide neither a direct nor an indirect proof for the truth of revelation. The only proof possible is in actual participation as in John 7:17: "If any man's will is to do his will, he shall know whether the teaching is from God . . . "[13] It is interesting to note that the criticism made of Hofmann for refusing all reference to the general question about God was removed from the third edition.[14]

After he removed the charge of subjectivism and rejected general proofs, Ritschl himself moved more and more in Hofmann's direc-

---

[11] *Ibid.*, p. 571.

[12] Albrecht Ritschl, Review of *Theologische Ethik* by J. v. Hofmann, *Theologische Literaturzeitung*, 3 (Oct. 12, 1878), No. 21, pp. 514-516.

[13] Ritschl, *Rechtfertigung und Versöhnung*, 3rd ed., Vol. III, p. 24.

[14] *Ibid.*, I, p. 615.

tion. There remained, however, one essential difference. Whereas Hofmann understood the Christian experience more in terms of the direct relationship of the risen Christ to the individual as something prior to the historical community as such, Ritschl thought more strictly in terms of actual mediation through the historical community—what has been termed his "revelational positivism." [15] For Hofmann, one might say, the experience had mystical and pietistic overtones, whereas for Ritschl it had to be more concrete and historical. For Ritschl the object of theological science was not the religious consciousness but revelation as objectively given and mediated in and through the historical community.

This difference was the basis for the final distinction between "thinking in" and "thinking about." For Hofmann the Christian "thinks in" a situation which is absolutely new and independent in its own right, a situation which only subsequently can be compared with the other expression in the community. For Ritschl the object of theology is the faith of the community "about" which the theologian thinks and brings to conceptual clarity.

This methodological difference accounted for the basic difference in the respective systems of the two men. Hofmann thought "behind" the revelation to a trinitarian scheme of *Heilsgeschichte*. Ritschl concentrated his attention on the meaning of the historically given. Hofmann's method allowed him "independence" both from the claims of historical criticism and "religion in general." Ritschl, however, by rejecting Hofmann's method, was all the more dependent upon the historical itself, and so had to provide a conceptual scheme for understanding the historical revelation. Thus in the third edition of *Rechtfertigung und Versöhnung*, the task of theology was still defined as the "ordered reproduction of the thought circle of Christ and the apostles" which is then "fixed through comparison with the other types and stages of religion." [16]

The conceptual scheme which Ritschl used to understand the historical revelation was his own particular synthesis of Luther and

---

[15] Wolff, *Die Haupttypen*, p. 125.

[16] Vol. III, pp. 8-9.

Kant. He used this synthesis to displace the orthodox system and its legalism.[17]

From Kant Ritschl took an interpretation of the nature of religion, the rejection of traditional metaphysics, the distinction between nature and spirit, and the distinction between the theoretical and practical reason. Ritschl held that religion should be concerned with the establishment and maintenance of the freedom of the spirit against the restrictions and inhibitions of nature and natural causality. The freedom of the spirit is achieved when one acts freely out of love, independent of natural necessity or reward. Christianity is the perfect moral and spiritual religion because through the redemption in Christ men are called into the freedom of God's children to act solely out of love. To be so called is to be taken up into the divine *telos*, into the kingdom of God. This religion of the spirit brought with it for Ritschl a necessary rejection of all metaphysics derived from nature through theoretical reason. God could not be known through such metaphysics, but only through the historical revelation in Christ mediated by the historical community.

From Luther Ritschl took the concept of justification by faith and what he believed to be Luther's understanding of faith as trust. Ritschl believed that in his reconstruction he was faithfully carrying out Luther's intention. His aim was to renew theology on the basis of a return to Luther,[18] and to repair those places where he believed Luther was not systematically consistent.

The aspect of Luther's theology which seemed to attract Ritschl most was Luther's strong emphasis upon the *pro me* in matters theological. This tied in quite nicely with Ritschl's rejection of the theoretical and with his strong emphasis upon what was practical and ethical.

Luther and Kant come together in Ritschl's mind. The knowledge of God given in revelation cannot be understood merely as theoretical knowledge, or as Luther would say, as a mere *fides historica*.

---

[17] Otto Wolff in *Die Haupttypen* characterizes Ritschl's interpretation of Luther as a "synthesis of reformation and idealism." p. 121.

[18] Wolff, *Die Haupttypen*, p. 137. Cf. also Walther v. Löwenich, *Luther und der Neuprotestantismus* (Witten: Luther-Verlag, 1963), p. 93.

The knowledge of God, for Ritschl, had to be practical. It is given in and through the community and communicated only through participation in the community. It is a knowledge of God which comes only through the divine action and which has real ethical renewal as its consequence.[19] This excludes the possibility of a knowledge in which one is not personally involved. Ritschl believed therefore that the distinction between theoretical and practical reason would allow him to reassert Luther's view that faith is essentially trust and not the acceptance of theoretical truth.[20]

From this rejection of theoretical reason comes also the idea that religious knowledge consists of "independent value judgments." This was often attacked as subjectivism on Ritschl's part—the ego supposedly acknowledges God only insofar as he is "valuable"—but Ritschl clearly sought to avoid this. He affirmed that value judgments of faith are *independent,* that is, not derived from a subjective or theoretical value system but arising solely from the revelation itself.[21] What Ritschl sought to establish was that one cannot know God theoretically. Only in practical involvement can he be known. One cannot discuss revelation as a detached observer, but only as a participant in the community of faith. This was the way Ritschl understood Melanchthon's "to know Christ is to know his benefits" and Luther's explanation of the First Commandment in the Large Catechism, "To have a God is nothing other than to trust and believe him from the whole heart. . . . These two, faith and God, are inseparably conjoined." [22]

Ritschl's purpose in his marriage of Luther and Kant, then, was to overcome the use of metaphysics and the place of intellectualism in theology by reasserting Luther's *pro me* in theology. This was the weapon Ritschl hoped to use to destroy once and for all the orthodox system. The distinction between theoretical and practical reason, between nature and spirit, and even between theology (as a theoretical science) and religion (as practical and ethical involvement) allowed Ritschl to reject all abstract speculation, which he

---

[19] Ritschl, *Rechtfertigung und Versöhnung,* 3rd ed., Vol. III, p. 7.

[20] *Ibid.,* p. 97.

[21] Löwenich, *Luther und der Neuprotestantismus,* pp. 95-97.

[22] Ritschl, *Rechtfertigung und Versöhnung,* 3rd ed., Vol. III, p. 201.

felt did not have immediate bearing on the religious life. Thus Ritschl's attack on legalism had systematic force much greater than it had in Hofmann. Ritschl eventually brought all of this systematic power to bear upon the doctrines of justification and the atonement.

Ritschl's interest in these particular doctrines seems to have derived at least partially from the atonement controversy. He was asked by I. Dorner to write a critique of the controversy for the *Jahrbücher für Deutsche Theologie,* and he reported that he found a particular fascination in entering the matter. However, he also found that the preliminary historical work necessary for an adequate evaluation of the matter was so great that it was impossible immediately to comply with Dorner's request. Ritschl offered instead an article on "Die Rechtfertigungslehre des Andrias Osiander," which was published in the 1857 issue.[23]

This article is significant because in it Ritschl declared that he believed that an ambiguity in the doctrine of justification lay at the root of the trouble between Hofmann and Philippi, and that this same ambiguity was reflected already in the dispute over Osiander's theology.[24] In the article Ritschl traced the source of the difficulty to the fact that Luther had never arrived at a theologically viable formulation of the relationship between justification and rebirth. Luther, Ritschl says, worked within the already existing community of faith. Hence his question about the subjective religious assurance of justification arose within an already given context of rebirth and faith. Faith and rebirth were already assumed by Luther; he was concerned only with the problem of assurance in justification. But for those who came afterwards, for the *epigoni* like Osiander, the context of faith and rebirth could no longer be assumed. This is where the problem arose. Rebirth must be thought of as the *result* of justification, and yet faith must be presupposed *for* justification.

The question was whether rebirth precedes justification or vice versa. For Ritschl this ultimately resolved into the question of the relationship between the objective and the subjective aspects of

---

[23] *Jahrbücher für deutsche Theologie,* Vol. II (Stuttgart: 1857), No. 4, pp. 785-830.
[24] Ritschl, *A. Ritschls Leben,* Vol. I, pp. 294 ff.

the work of Christ.[25] Did Christ's work atone for man so that justification is an objective, forensic act which precedes rebirth, or must some subjective alteration take place before justification can be said to be valid? The orthodox took the former alternative. For Osiander this was an "empty" faith, a legal fiction, so he made justification contingent upon the coincident indwelling of Christ in the believer—a real "making just" on the basis of the *Christus in nobis.*[26] Justification could occur then only in conjunction with subjective faith in the present. But this questioned the objective sufficiency of the cross, so Osiander made a distinction between justification in the present and redemption in the past. Redemption is the past objective act of atonement—Christ's work over against God—but justification is the present subjective realization—Christ's work over against man.[27]

When Ritschl analyzed Osiander's theology, he focused on just this problem of atonement and history. The problem was that there is an "abyss" between the past "objective" act and the present "subjective" reception of that act. Ritschl himself posed the question which became determinative for all his subsequent work:

> How can . . . the justification and redemption through the activity and suffering of Christ be objectively expressed, when those who are the objects of that activity are in their personal existence infinitely removed from the time of Christ's suffering?[28]

Ritschl's problem was made even more acute because of his rejection of theoretical reasoning and metaphysics. If one attempted to formulate a doctrine of the atonement as a once-for-all objective act in the past upon which a purely forensic justification is based, then one has succumbed, according to Ritschl, to abstract metaphysical categories which are theoretical in nature and have no direct bearing on present religious and moral life. If one, on

---

[25] Ritschl, *Jahrbücher für deutsche Theologie,* II, No. 4, pp. 788-789.

[26] *Ibid.,* pp. 803-806.

[27] It is interesting to note that Ritschl finds the same sort of distinction between objective past act and subjective realization in Osiander that Harnack finds in Luther, only the terminology is reversed. For Luther, according to Harnack, redemption is subjective, not vice versa.

[28] Ritschl, *Jahrbücher für deutsche Theologie,* II, No. 4, p. 807.

the other hand, had recourse like Osiander to some mystical-substantial concept of the "Christ in us" then one has made justification dependent upon subjective experience. Ritschl could not accept either alternative, and he was faced with his dilemma: To state the atonement in once-for-all objective terms is to succumb to abstraction and theory, so that atonement simply recedes into the past. On the other hand, to speak of a "Christ in us" becomes mystical and subjective and loses the objectivity of the justifying act of God.

Ritschl saw only one way out of the problem:

> The unity in time between the objective justification and the subjective consciousness of it which has its place *in religious experience* must be surrendered *in the theological view* of the matter.[29]

This is an exceedingly important statement because it defined the direction of Ritschl's entire subsequent work on history and atonement. In making a distinction between religious experience and theological exposition, Ritschl gave up the attempt to define *theologically* the simultaneity of objective justification and subjective consciousness. The simultaneity is given in religious experience but cannot be expressed in a theological system. Any attempt to define atonement theoretically had to be surrendered in order to realize the religious significance of Christ in the present.

Ritschl said further that one can understand justification only as an "attribute of the historical work of Christ"[30] and "the consciousness of being justified by Christ as the necessary attribute of the state of regeneration."[31] So Ritschl wanted to solve the time problem by describing Christ's work solely in terms of its actual historical significance in the community rather than in terms of some objective past transaction; in this way the act of justification will always occur simultaneously with the subjective experience of rebirth.

From this starting point, Ritschl's view of the atonement followed quite naturally. Justification as an "attribute of the historical work of Christ" can be realized only as the work of the historical

---

[29] *Ibid.*, p. 828. (Italicizing mine.)
[30] *Ibid.*, p. 828. (Italicizing mine.)
[31] *Ibid.*, p. 829.

community which Christ founded. Ritschl's relationship to Hofmann, both in similarity and dissimilarity, is apparent. Hofmann, Ritschl says, correctly determined the religious significance of the atonement because he established the intimate connection between Christ's death in faithfulness to his calling and the new community.[32] Here, Ritschl declared, a Lutheran had finally broken the hold of the Melanchthonian tradition of vicarious satisfaction and risen above the indolence which always hindered the proper formulation of the problem.[33] The formation of the historical community was the decisive factor for Ritschl in the reconstruction of the atonement doctrine. Christ, by being faithful to his calling unto death, established the historical community in which the actual work of atonement is carried forward.

But how is this to be understood? Christ was conscious in his own life of the love of God and consequently of the divine *telos*, the kingdom of God. Realizing the divine *telos* therefore defined his calling. In faithfulness and obedience he maintained his communion of love towards God unto the end, under all the conditions of suffering and death. His purpose in so doing was to bring about the atonement of God with man. But how? Not, of course, by making a vicarious satisfaction. Ritschl rejected that theory as a remnant of Hellenistic and naturalistic thinking.[34] The obvious alternative then would seem to be a kind of Socinian general prophetic announcement of forgiveness on Jesus' authority, but Ritschl rejected this as well. The idea of a general prophetic announcement is *theoretical* rather than religious; it also turns the church into a school.[35] Nor could atonement be understood in the Enlightenment sense of a love of God which is self-evidently derived from the divine nature. Ritschl is often misunderstood in this way, but he clearly rejected such a view. The Enlightenment view, he said, was merely the result of becoming accustomed to the Christian concept of God under conditions in which philosophical naturalism and moralistic individualism had crippled the traditional dog-

---

[32] Ritschl, *Rechtfertigung und Versöhnung*, 3rd ed., Vol. I, p. 620.
[33] *Ibid.*, p. 621.
[34] *Ibid.*, III, p. 444.
[35] *Ibid.*, III, p. 506.

matic.[36] Both Socinianism and the Enlightenment, though they may have been right in rejecting vicarious satisfaction, nevertheless did not understand the *religious* nature of atonement. They both committed the error of individualism, relating forgiveness and moral order only to the life of the individual in a *theoretical* manner.[37] For these schools of thought justification was merely a matter of information.

Ritschl affirmed with the tradition of the church that atonement had to be related to the person of Jesus and his actual historical work, including his death. But against the metaphysical view of orthodoxy and the theoretical view of Socinianism, Ritschl insisted that atonement could be understood only in its positive *religious* sense, which is carried solely in and through the historical community. Jesus, in faithfulness to his calling, did not allow any circumstance, either the antipathy of the authorities or any "natural" inhibitions, to alter his course. He died in faithfulness to his calling, in absolute trust in the love and providence of the Father. His was, one might say, the victory of the spirit over nature.

By his faithfulness, Jesus established a community. He took men into this positive religious sphere of faith and trust. The importance of the work of Jesus lies in the fact that he founded a religious community through his own personal and religious influence, and that only under this religious influence in the community can atonement between God and man be realized. It is only in the community that true knowledge of God is possible.

In his death, therefore, Jesus did not atone or satisfy God. Such a thought could arise only because of the intrusion of non-Christian naturalistic metaphysics. God is revealed in the community as a God of love; here it can be known that justification is not contingent upon satisfaction of the divine wrath but rather stems from God's absolutely free judgment.[38] Atonement is the intended goal of God's free judgment.[39] Man is to be reunited with the divine

---

[36] *Ibid.*, 3rd ed., p. 509.

[37] *Ibid.*, p. 509.

[38] Albrecht Ritschl, *Unterricht in der Christlichen Religion* (2nd ed.; Bonn: Adolph Marcus, 1881), pp. 32-33. Cited hereafter as *Unterricht*.

[39] *Ibid.*, p. 33.

telos, the kingdom of God, through the religious influence of Jesus in the historical community. This occurs when through the realization of forgiveness one is enabled to overcome his enmity toward God and to approach him in faith and trust. Sin forms a barrier to man's approach to God, but not in the sense of "natural" inherited guilt; rather sin is a moral and religious inhibition. Because of the feeling of guilt one's approach to God is inhibited. One is at enmity with God. Sin is a "kingdom" which perpetuates itself in opposition to the kingdom of God.

Christ's work, then broke down the moral and religious barriers of sin. His death was analogous to sacrifice in the Old Testament, where the important thing was not the substitutionary slaying or outpouring of the victim's blood but the drawing near to God of the separated sinner through the priestly act within the context of the covenant—within the established community. Christ as priestly representative "drew near" to God by carrying out his calling unto death and thereby established a community of mutual love and trust between God and men. In this community men are enabled to approach God in trust in spite of their sin.

Of the connection between forgiveness and the work of Christ nothing more can be said than that the awareness of forgiveness comes through the influence of the life and death of Christ and its peculiar working in the community throughout all ages. No necessary rules can be established. Faith comes about only according to the laws of freedom,[40] so that faith cannot be the object of scientific theological investigation. The community is based upon the fact that the remembrance of the completed work of Christ remains present in it and that his personal impetus works unceasingly in all similar efforts of the members.[41]

Atonement and forgiveness, therefore, are dependent upon Christ, not in the old orthodox "objective" sense but in the sense of the "religious" atonement in the present in and through the community. Ritschl rejected all attempts at objective formulations because they could only be abstract theorizing with no direct religious significance.

---

[40] Ritschl, *Rechtfertigung und Versöhnung,* 3rd ed., Vol. III, pp. 545, 573.
[41] Ritschl, *Unterricht,* p. 23.

In this development the movement from Hofmann to Ritschl can be clearly seen. The basic concept of Christ's faithfulness to his calling was common to both men; it was the key concept in opposing the orthodox as well as the Socinian view. There were, of course, differences. Hofmann interpreted Christ's faithfulness to his calling in the context of a trinitarian *Heilsgeschichte*. Christ suffered by entering into humanity under wrath and subject to demonic forces; he was faithful by suffering the utmost possible. The demonic forces exhaust themselves in Christ, and through his resurrection he won the final victory and established a new transfigured humanity. Ritschl, on the other hand, interpreted Christ's faithfulness to his calling in the context of an interpretation of religion. Christ faithfully suffered under the conditions of human life and maintained his love to God despite every threat. He established a new community in which man, under his influence, can rise above the world in spiritual freedom. In Hofmann a *new humanity* was objectively established by Christ's victory. In Ritschl a *new community* was founded whose *telos* is the moral kingdom of God; the kingdom is established only through actual subjective participation, in the historical community. Nevertheless, Ritschl says, since the historical community is not yet perfected, one may not simply *identify* it with the kingdom.

The main difference is that Ritschl did not use the objective victory motif which dominates Hofmann's work. In his critique of Hofmann's doctrine of the atonement,[42] Ritschl admitted that he could not make sense of the victory motif; he said he could not understand how God's hatred of sin could express itself in Christ's suffering. Nor could he understand how Hofmann could say that the forces of evil exhausted themselves in attacking Christ, for the history of the church shows that rather than being defeated, they were aroused to greater activity.[43] For Ritschl, the "victory" of the Christian is that through Christ's influence he is able to trust

---

[42] Ritschl, *Rechtfertigung und Versöhnung*, 3rd ed., Vol. I, pp. 618 ff.

[43] It is interesting and significant that Ritschl had to admit to being in the odd position of agreeing with Philippi. It was not as much of a coincidence as Ritschl thinks, though, for in the last analysis neither the "orthodox" nor the "liberal" could digest the victory motif. Their common rejection of the victory motif suggests an underlying agreement of which they were not aware.

in the providence of God *whatever* "nature" or "the world" imposes upon him. There is no "objective" victory over the world as such, for to affirm this would be to slip back into the danger of theoretical thinking.

It is not difficult to see Ritschl's intention in this development. He was concerned to foster actual ethical renewal in the present through the concrete practical effect of Jesus' influence. Because of this goal his entire interest was centered upon the historical community as the focus of Christ's influence. He was interested in actual atonement rather than "theoretical" atonement.

This is also the reason for his theological exclusivism; it was extremely difficult for him to state his position without letting it relapse into "theory" and "metaphysics." He must very carefully separate himself from all types of "natural" theology and cosmological thinking. Everything had to be discussed within the confines of the concept of religion and of community which he defined, for outside this sphere, he said, there is no proper knowledge of God.

Ritschl's aims led him to the corollary that outside the sphere of religion and community man is in ignorance. Sin, therefore, could not be judged ultimately as revolt against God but only as ignorance *(Unwissenheit)*.[44] Indeed, sin itself cannot really be known outside the community.[45] Though it may exist as a general feeling of guilt, it is only in the experience of redemption that it is both magnified and pardoned. Sin, then, does not form a barrier to one's approach to God. Moreover, it is only within the community that one can gain true knowledge of sin. Knowledge of things religious is given only within the community—only in the practical experience of Christianity. Ritschl insisted upon this kind of exclusivism because his whole reconstruction depended upon it.

It is of prime importance to see that Ritschl's construction involved a thoroughgoing rejection of the traditional doctrine of law and gospel. The idea that knowledge of sin comes only within the community was also quite contrary to Harnack's interpretation of Luther in which he insisted that knowledge of sin and guilt comes

---

[44] Ritschl, *Rechtfertigung und Versöhnung*, 3rd ed., Vol. III, p. 363.
[45] Ritschl, *Unterricht*, pp. 24-25.

through knowledge of the law "outside of Christ." Ritschl maintained that the trouble with the traditional doctrine of law was that it conceived of God in analogy with an earthly ruler administrating his kingdom under external laws (a *Rechtsordnung*)[46]; it was this concept of law which made the orthodox doctrine of the atonement possible. Ritschl, in contrast, insisted that the kingdom of God is not a kingdom of law but of love. This kingdom of love is God's self-determined *telos;* when men are united with this *telos* they are at once free and in harmony with God. God's "law" therefore is not an *external* order of justice but an *internal* moral law *(Sittengesetz).* For Ritschl, then, law is a reality *within* the kingdom of God which applies only to those who through divine pardon have been led to trust in divine love.[47] Law has to do with internal disposition *(Gesinnung);* it is the law of love, the basic order and moral imperative of the kingdom of God. Thus Ritschl arrived at a synthesis or perhaps even identification of law and gospel as a result of his understanding of religion and the kingdom of God.

Ritschl's understanding of law stems from the Kantian interpretation of the moral law. Kant had held that the true law of virtue is internal and non-coercive, that indeed it is the basis for man's freedom. In the *Critique of Pure Reason* Kant reached the conclusion that as far as *theoretical* reason was concerned, man is completely determined by the laws of nature. In the *Critique of Practical Reason,* however, Kant drew from man's experience of moral obligation the conclusion that man is morally free. Man can act as a free and morally responsible being because practical reason tells him that he "ought" to do so. The imperative, moreover, is categorical and not hypothetical; practical reason drives us to the idea of obedience to the moral law *for its own sake,* not for the sake of sensuous or other external motives.[48]

Man is able to envisage and cherish this ideal, Kant held, because of his rational nature. The moral law is *spontaneously* imposed upon man by his own reason, not heteronomously imposed by empirical

[46] Ritschl, *Rechtfertigung und Versöhnung,* 3rd ed., Vol. III, p. 233.

[47] *Ibid.,* p. 304.

[47] Immanuel Kant, *Kant Selections,* ed. T. M. Greene (New York: Charles Scribner's Sons, 1929), pp. 296-300.

or extraneous forces. It is because of the experience of the "ought" within that man knows he is free and not determined by external forces. The moral law is therefore the basis for man's self-motivation or freedom (autonomy). Man is *auto-nomos,* a law unto himself. True moral law, the law of virtue, is therefore *internal and spontaneous,* not external or coercive.

According to Kant, therefore, it is this ought within, the categorical imperative, which must govern man's action if man is to be truly moral. But what does this imperative demand? It demands, according to Kant, that man's internal will in determining the course of its actions be properly motivated. The internal rules of action—what Kant calls *maxims of action*—must be pure.[49]

The problem is, however, that the will is motivated always by material objects; man is led to act because of sensuous pleasure. Hence man is dependent in his moral activity upon natural desires. Insofar as the will is so motivated, however, it is not autonomous, because it is determined by something external to it.

In order to reach a true principle of morals, the maxims must be purified; they must be relieved of their limitations and enlarged into the form of universal laws.[50] Only those are to be adopted as motives which can be made universal laws of reason. Kant himself saw three forms in which the categorical imperative can be stated:

> I. Act only on that maxim through which you can at the same time will that it should become a universal law.[51]
>
> II. So act as to use humanity, both in your own person and in the person of every other, always at the same time as an end, never simply as a means.[52]
>
> III. So act that your will can regard itself at the same time as making universal law through its maxim.[53]

In *Religion Within the Limits of Reason Alone,* Kant expanded his view into the religious dimension. Man inevitably perverts his

---

[49] *Ibid.,* p. 306.
[50] *Ibid.,* p. 305.
[51] H. J. Paton, *The Categorical Imperative* (London: Hutchinson Publishing Group Ltd., 1948), p. 133.
[52] *Ibid.,* p. 165.
[53] *Ibid.,* p. 180.

maxims by making his obedience conditional upon sensuous incentives. There is a natural propensity in man to do this—a "radical evil." This can be extirpated only by a moral revolution, a "change of heart" in which purely moral motives are again placed above sensuous motives.[54]

We need not go into Kant's idea of how such a revolution comes about. The important point for our understanding of Ritschl is that through such a revolution of his motives man is freely joined to what Kant calls an ethical commonwealth, the "kingdom of God," existing under "ethical laws." These ethical laws are the "laws of virtue," which are internal and non-coercive. The kingdom of God, for Kant, is a "Community banded together by laws of virtue" *(Verbindung der Menschen durch Tugendgesetze")*.[55]

Ritschl's concept of law must be understood against this Kantian background. The distinction between external and internal law which Ritschl used came from his adaptation of Kant's distinction between a political commonwealth with its external juridical laws and an ethical commonwealth with its internal laws of virtue. Insofar as man acts in accordance with the moral law he is free, that is, not determined by external attractions and natural desires. When man is transformed internally, the desired goal is reached. For Ritschl, then, redemption involved a change in disposition or mind *(Sinnesänderung)*.[56] It was this adaptation of Kant which allowed Ritschl to take law within the kingdom and unite it with the gospel. There is no dialectic of law and gospel, rather a synthesis in the kingdom of God.

This synthesis is most evident, perhaps, in Ritschl's position on the relationship between law and gospel in repentance.[57] He maintained that if repentance is to be distinguished from the hypocritical *contritio* of the Roman Catholic doctrine of penance, it must arise from the love of the good. Consequently, it must *follow* faith and arise from the gospel rather than the law.

---

[54] Immanuel Kant, *Religion Within the Limits of Reason Alone,* tr. T. M. Greene and H. H. Hudson (New York: Harper Torchbooks, Harper and Brothers, 1960), p. 43.

[55] Ritschl, *Rechtfertigung und Versöhnung,* 3rd ed., Vol. III, p. 11.

[56] *Ibid.,* II, p. 37.

[57] *Ibid.,* I, pp. 198-201.

On logical, theological, and psychological grounds, faith as a condition is indispensable to a due apprehension of the *contritio* that is to be gained from the law. The negation of sin by the will can be decisive and effectual only when it follows upon an affirmation of the value of goodness, its opposite. . . . The transition from repudiation of sin to appropriation of God's grace is logical only when the spirit in contrition has already felt itself drawn by that power which is to be recognized as the only saving power.[58]

Ritschl's understanding of the kingdom of God as the "highest good" led him to reverse the normal order of law and gospel.

There is no doubt a great deal to be said for Ritschl's contention at this point, especially when compared to orthodox theology. Ritschl's affirmation that one cannot make an abstract logical and material distinction between law and gospel located one of the difficulties of the older structure. But whether Ritschl himself correctly determined the relationship between law and gospel is another question.

It is significant that it was at this point that Ritschl (despite his claim to have based himself on Luther), found it necessary to criticize Luther's thought. Luther's statements to the effect that repentance and despair of self are worked by the law are well known. In order to justify his claim to represent Luther faithfully, Ritschl used the idea of a decisive difference between the young and old Luther.[59] This was Ritschl's answer to Harnack's interpretation of Luther. According to Ritschl the decisive and epoch-making discovery of the young Luther was that true repentance comes from the love of righteousness and not from the fear of the law. The old Luther, who spoke of the law working repentance, must then at some time have given up his early view and relapsed into a legalistic position on penance.

Ritschl, however, was not very precise about when such a change took place. He made at least three suggestions at different

---

[58] Albrecht Ritschl, *A Critical History of the Christian Doctrine of Justification and Reconciliation,* tr. John S. Black (Edinburgh: Edmonston and Douglas, 1872), p. 181.

[59] Ritschl's use of this distinction gave it considerable vogue among Luther interpreters—a vogue which has not diminished to the present. See Schultz, *Gesetz und Evangelium,* pp. 168-170.

times: after the outbreak of the indulgence controversy (1517-1518); in the conflict with the Zwickau prophets (1520-1522); and after Melanchthon's visitation articles and the ensuing argument with Agricola (1527). Generally, Ritschl seems to believe that the influence of Melanchthon was decisive in the shift.[60] His difficulty in dating the shift was one of the indicators that it is a risky venture to posit such a sudden and radical shift in Luther's thought. There may well have been change and development, but it seems fanciful to suggest that *the* decisive evangelical discovery of the young Luther could be surrendered without hesitation by the old Luther. Once again it would seem that Luther had been forced into an alien mold.

Ritschl's criticism of Luther on the question of repentance was only an indication, however, of a larger difference which affected his interpretation of Luther. In Ritschl's view Luther, although he made a breakthrough to an evangelical understanding in his *religion,* did not secure and carry through this breakthrough in his *theology.* The picture which Ritschl painted of Luther was one which has become quite familiar: Luther the religious genius but systematic bungler.[61]

Specifically, Ritschl said that Luther made the discovery of the unity of justification and rebirth in his own religious experience, but that he did not possess the proper tools to express this experience systematically. Indeed, Luther's intensely practical interest constantly hindered him from doing so.[62] For this reason Lutheranism easily succumbed to the influence of Melanchthon and relapsed into adaptations of medieval views.

Luther's theology itself was full of medieval remainders. Evidence for this, Ritschl said, is the fact that Luther never reached a unified concept of God because of his stand on the bondage of the will and his concept of the divine wrath. Ritschl applauded Luther's insistence upon divine love as the highest principle in God,

---

[60] See R. A. Lipsius, "Luthers Lehre von der Busse," *Jahrbücher für Protestantische Theologie,* XVIII (Apr. 1892), No. 2, pp. 168-170.

[61] Ritschl, *Rechtfertigung und Versöhnung,* 3rd ed., Vol. I, p. 187.

[62] Ritschl, *Jahrbücher für deutsche Theologie,* II, No. 4, p. 796.

but he said that this was never systematically secured.[63] Ritschl also classified Luther's understanding of Christ's victory over wrath and the tyrants as a medieval remnant.

As one might suspect, Ritschl's criticism became even more pointed when he took up the question of the moral life.[64] He said that Luther did not establish the necessary connection between justification and ethics. The idea that good works are the "automatic" result of justification simply avoids the problem. Thus Ritschl saw his own task as that of providing a more systematic foundation for Luther's original impulses. He believed he had done this in the concept of the kingdom of God as a uniting of mankind under the laws of virtue.

The picture of Luther which emerged from Ritschl's writings is one which became quite common in the late 19th and early 20th centuries. In this portrait Luther was the man of faith whose systematic views were too heavily influenced by medieval scholasticism and nominalism to secure that Reformation against relapse into a new type of scholasticism. Ritschl tried to rescue and use Luther by separating his "practical religion" from his theology. To accomplish this he also attempted to separate the young from the old Luther.

It is hardly necessary to point out that this picture has not been accepted without severe qualification by subsequent research. The change in the concept of repentance simply cannot be substantiated.[65] Furthermore, there was considerable ambiguity in Ritschl's understanding of the relationship between Luther and the medieval view of repentance. It was common to medieval thology that true repentance is worked by grace. This is somewhat similar to Ritschl's own view that repentance comes by faith—that is, a change in disposition, a *Sinnesänderung* brought about by the love of the good. In view of the similarity between Ritschl's own view and the medieval view, it is doubtful that this could be understood as *the* decisive evangelical discovery.

---

[63] Wolff, *Die Haupttypen*, p. 210.

[64] Ritschl, *Rechtfertigung und Versöhnung*, 3rd ed., Vol. I, pp. 190-200.

[65] Lipsius, *Jahrbücher für Protestantische Theologie*, XVIII, No. 2, pp. 170-177. Cf. Schultz, *Gesetz und Evangelium*, p. 171.

There is also difficulty fitting the argument about wrath and love to the young-old scheme in Luther. Whereas it was supposed to be the young Luther who made the basic evangelical discovery, which he later supposedly forgot, it seems also to be this same young Luther who emphasized the concept of divine wrath to which Ritschl objected, while the old Luther, who was supposed to be more "unevangelical," turned more unambiguously to the concent of divine love. The same is true with respect to the bondage of the will. It was the old Luther who more and more left these problems behind. These facts indicate that the problem of interpreting Luther is considerably more complicated than Ritschl was willing to admit.

Yet there is something essentially correct about Ritschl's main concern—the concern for actual atonement in the present, actual ethical renewal here and now, rather than theoretical atonement in the dim past. Here Ritschl had in fact understood Luther better than his orthodox opponents, and his work does represent a genuine attempt to renew Luther's concerns.

Ritschl's problem, however, was that he could not bridge the historical gap between atonement as a completed past transaction and one's present experience. He sought to solve the problem by surrendering altogether the attempt to describe Christ's work as an objective, wholly past transaction against the background of a metaphysical structure. He sought instead to define the work of Christ in terms of its actual influence in the ongoing historical community.

But this attempt had at least two fateful consequences. First, it meant that Ritschl's entire case stood or fell with his conception of the historical Jesus. His theology was dependent entirely upon the picture of a Jesus conscious of and faithful to his "calling" to establish a kingdom of God consonant with Ritschlian ideas. This led ultimately to the search for the historical Jesus—the cul-de-sac of later theology. Second, since Ritschl refused to define an objective, once-for-all atonement, he was dependent upon an interpretation of religion for understanding Christ's significance. His emphasis fell almost exclusively therefore on the actual historical realization of the kingdom. Ritschl was thus bound to understand the kingdom as a realization of possibilities inherent in "this age." To be sure, they are not "natural" possibilities, but rather "spiritual" or "religious" possibilities. Nevertheless, they are the possibilities limited to "this age." This makes it difficult to avoid falling eventually into a kind of moralistic utopianism. That is, religion is virtually equated with moral and social improvement. Jesus becomes the founder of a religion, and that religion becomes a moralism.

It is not necessary to recount here the fate of this theology in the light of more recent findings in exegesis and systematic theology. What was missing was a proper definition of the eschatological dimension. It was because there is no eschatological dialectic that Ritschl's religion was limited to the present age and that he had difficulty escaping the charge of moralism. Ritschl's greatest asset —his passion for actuality—became a liability within his system because it in turn was threatened by a new type of unreality: moralistic utopianism.

This criticism means that his attempted synthesis of law and gospel must also be questioned. The close connection between eschatology and the problem of law and gospel becomes increasingly evident here. The loss of the eschatological dimension led Ritschl into moralism and toward a religion purely of law. This, of course, was the opposite of what Ritschl wanted, for he had intended to assert the love of God in the strongest possible manner against law, legalism, and the concept of wrath.

The fate of Ritschl's intention is particularly instructive for our problem. A theology must do more than *assert* the love of God as a general truth. Ritschl was well aware of this, so he tried to protect this assertion of divine love by making a distinction between theoretical and practical reason. He sought to serve the concept of love by simply rejecting the undesirable concepts of law and wrath. He attributed them to the influence of theoretical reason, to a mistaken application of political and metaphysical ideas in the sphere of religion. He tried, in effect, to make a theological *tour de force.*

What Ritschl did not see was that he had made his constructions fully as theoretical as those of his opponents. One simply cannot remove the law with an "eraser"; to do this is to be fully as theoretical as the theory of the atonement which holds that the demands of the law have been objectively satisfied and hence removed. Ritschl removed the threat of the law simply by maintaining that it has been "misunderstood," and that the way out was through proper understanding. His teaching, consequently, was a theory which competed with other theories. Its similarity with orthodoxy was exposed by its presupposing an underlying continuity in the concept of law and in the nature of religion. There was no radical break in the structure into which the new, eschatological dimension could be interjected.

Ritschl's attempt therefore illustrates the fact that when one seeks to get rid of the law by means of a theory, the law always comes back in a different form. The true actuality of the gospel— no doubt that which Ritschl himself sought—is established only when it is recognized that no *theology* as such, however cleverly constructed, can set one free from the law. That is something which Christ alone can do; theology, if it is to be "actual" and not "theoretical," must freely acknowledge that fact. The difficulty is to construct a theology which serves the divine act in Christ instead of attempting to replace it. Only then can the proper relationship between law and gospel come into focus.

CHAPTER VIII

THE LINKS TO
THE PRESENT

The debate over Hofmann's doctrine of the atonement thus issued in opposing views of the relationship between law and gospel. Harnack, opposing Hofmann's interpretation of Luther, found a view of law based on a natural knowledge of God "outside of Christ." This concept of law, he insisted, is the basis for a real dialectic between wrath and love. Ritschl, on the other hand, believed it necessary to eliminate all "natural knowledge" because it distorts the purely spiritual religion of love and freedom. In Harnack's development, law still remains as an unchangeable eternal order which must be reckoned with in atonement. For Ritschl law in the Christian sense is sharply distinguished from the eternal order of nature; the moral law of love frees one from mere "nature" and is virtually synonymous with the gospel.

We have found both these concepts wanting; indeed, all such doctrines of law suffer from the same difficulty. They are attempts to remove the threat of law theoretically by means of a systematic construction. Hofmann did it with a historical dispensationalism, Harnack by returning to an orthodox concept of juridical atonement and Ritschl by a Kantian interpretation of the kingdom of God. Each position had suggestive and helpful elements, but none, ultimately, did justice to the nature of the divine act as it is related to law and gospel.

From this perspective there is no really decisive difference between the orthodox, the *heilsgeschichtliche,* and the liberal theologian. Neither the acceptance of some view of natural law (as in orthodoxy), nor the rejection of such a view (as in Ritschl), nor placing law in a historical scheme (as in Hofmann) is a guarantee of theological success.

Theological success in this question depends much more upon one's concept of the divine act in Christ and its relationship to the law; that is, upon one's concept of the gospel. None of the types of theology in question succeeds in properly capturing the eschatological newness of the gospel. Hofmann approached it in this concept of the new humanity in Christ, but this was weakened by his view of historical continuity. Harnack made a valuable contribution in his discovery of Luther's dialectic of wrath and love, but he returned to orthodox continuity in his concept of law. Ritschl tried to realize the newness in his view of an actual atonement in the present through the community, but the absence of the eschatological meant a return to moralism—equating religion with continuous moral improvement. It is evident from these attempts that the place of law had not been adequately determined.

These three types of theology can serve, though, as a background to the contemporary discussion. There were, however, some further developments which form connecting links to the present and modify some of the positions taken. These connecting links are to be found in the men who followed Ritschl both in systematic development and in historical investigation (especially the investigation of Luther's theology). Wilhelm Herrmann was such a systematic link to the present, and men like Kattenbusch and Holl provided continuity in the investigation of Luther's view.

Wilhelm Herrmann continued Ritschl's program, but not without some modification. He intensified Ritschl's polemic against legalism. He maintained that by making the task of dogmatics just describing the content of faith as found in Scripture, Ritschl made Scripture into a doctrinal law.[1] In this sense, Herrmann said, Ritschl was actually the "last great representative of orthodox dog-

[1] Wilhelm Herrmann, *Gesammelte Aufsätze* (Tübingen: J. C. B. Mohr (Paul Siebeck, 1923), p. 118. Cited hereafter as *Aufsätze.*

matics." Further, this meant that Ritschl did not solve the historical problem, for he did not say how faith could be produced by a past historical record,[2] nor did he adequately protect faith from historical criticism.

Herrmann looked for the answers to these difficulties by locating the source and basis of faith in the inner life of Jesus. The inner life of Jesus is the "saving fact."[3] This inner life of Jesus is the rule of God in the heart which Jesus brings to men (the kingdom of God) insofar as they experience it personally. This personal experience is mediated through history by the community, by men who have experienced it.[4] When one experiences this himself, and only in this way (not as "teaching" or "doctrine") he is set free from the mediation. He experiences the power and influence of the inner life of Jesus in his own life. Thus he need not depend upon the historical records as such.[5] Communion with God is established through the influence and power of the inner life of Jesus. This is beyond the reach of historical criticism.

This, briefly, is the solution which Herrmann offered to the historical problem. He forced the Ritschlian concentration on the historical to take refuge entirely in the consciousness, the "inner life," of Jesus. "The one question of absolute importance is whether Jesus gains a power over us through His personal life."[6] This is the end of the road which began with Hofmann's interpretation of Jesus' faithfulness to his calling.

In general Herrmann continued the basic Ritschlian position on atonement, law, and gospel, and the interpretation of Luther. He understood law in the Kantian sense of the moral law in sharp contrast to the laws of nature. Law is wholly within the kingdom of God.[7] He retained the Ritschlian view of repentance; true re-

---

[2] *Ibid.*, p. 116.

[3] Karl Barth, *Theology and Church*, tr. L. P. Smith (London: SCM Press, 1962), p. 249.

[4] Wilhelm Herrmann, *The Communion of the Christian With God*, tr. J. S. Stanton (New York: G. P. Putnam's Sons, 1906), p. 73. Cited hereafter as *Communion.*

[5] *Ibid.*, p. 74.

[6] *Ibid.*, p. 129.

[7] Wilhelm Herrmann, *Ethik* (2nd ed.; Tübingen: J. C. B. Mohr (Paul Siebeck), 1901), p. 43.

pentance grows out of love for the good and not from the law. According to Herrmann, this original view of Luther's was obscured by later developments, especially Melanchthon's Visitation Articles.[8] Herrmann also made the Rischlian distinction between Luther's religion and his theology: "If then, Luther is to be our guide, we must distinguish between Luther's Christianity and Luther's theology; for the latter is built on the assumptions of Roman Catholicism."[9]

Herrmann's concentration upon the experience of the Christian and the manner in which it occurs, however, already pointed in a direction which weakened the Ritschlian monism of love. Herrmann introduced an element of movement and struggle which is absent in Ritschl. Christian experience, he said, can by no means be taken for granted. No one attains it without "great shaking of soul."[10] One must be "overwhelmed," "grasped" by its irresistible "power."[11] Faith can by no means be understood as merely acceptance of facts; rather it is the result of a man being grasped by the spiritual power of Jesus himself.

The idea of struggle is reflected both in Herrmann's concept of God[12] and in his view of the atonement. Herrmann criticized both Hofmann and Ritschl for their monistic tendencies in the concept of divine love.

> That idea of love which Hofmann and Ritschl wish—justifiably, to be sure—to take seriously, is nevertheless really religious only when it comes as a victory in an internal struggle. As soon as it is driven beyond the limits of such living moments and expanded into a systematic principle which dominates everything, it loses its power. It threatens then to become a triviality from which men who find themselves in the serious battles of religion flee in horror.[13]

---

[8] Herrmann, *Aufsätze*, p. 33.

[9] Herrmann, *Communion*, p. 51.

[10] *Ibid.*, p. 237.

[11] Herrmann, *Aufsätze*, p. 148.

[12] Wolff, *Die Haupttypen*, p. 229.

[13] Wilhelm Herrmann, "Christlich-Protestantische Dogmatik," *Kultur der Gegenwart*, ed., P. Hinneberg, Part I, Sec. IV 2, (2nd ed.; Berlin: B. G. Tübner, 1909), p. 172.

In his view of the atonement, Herrmann tried to see the value of the orthodox doctrine of satisfaction. It stands, he says, for the religious truth that the love of God cannot simply be taken for granted and that the realization of this love is dependent upon the life and death of Jesus.[14] Forgiveness cannot be assumed; it is an act of "unfathomable goodness." [15] Furthermore, Herrmann developed more expicitly the idea that it is precisely in the revelation that one is confronted with a mystery which both fosters repentance and comforts:

> It must stand before us as an incomprehensible reality that the same fact that increased our grief for our unfaithfulness and weakness of will nevertheless is also perceptible to us as a word of God convincing us that he has reached down to us.[16]

The point of view represented in this statement will become quite important in subsequent development.

There was, therefore, a direction in Herrmann's thought which pointed beyond Ritschl. But because of his Kantian bias and his insistence upon describing the Christian experience in terms of the historical influence of the community, Herrmann could not give his development any firm systematic structure. It remained simply an assertion with no structural basis. Herrmann does not succeed, therefore, in breaking out of the Ritschlian mold. It is, if anything, even more difficult to base a theology on the "inner life" of Jesus; this is only a surrogate for a real facing of the issue.

More important for approaching the present-day discussion were the modifications of the picture of Luther under the influence of continued research. These modifications have been discussed in a number of works,[17] so we need here only to point out what is most significant for our problem. Of most interest are the developments in the concepts of hiddenness and revealedness and love and wrath.

Harnack saw the dialectic of hiddenness and revealedness in

---

[14] Herrmann, *Communion*, pp. 129 ff.

[15] *Ibid.*, p. 131.

[16] *Ibid.*, p. 141.

[17] See for instance, John Dillenberger, *God Hidden and Revealed* (Philadelphia: Muhlenberg Press, 1953); Wolff, *Die Haupttypen;* Edgar Carlson, *The Reinterpretation of Luther* (Philadelphia: The Westminster Press, 1948).

Luther, but the threat of dualism between love and wrath forced him to return to the orthodox point of view. The Ritschlians could abide neither the Lutheran dualism nor the orthodox synthesis; they sought to solve the difficulty by excluding one side of the dialectic—the side of wrath. What follows in the discussion can perhaps best be described as a modification of both these extremes under the pressure of Luther's own thought.

F. Kattenbusch showed that in Luther's thought hiddenness does not apply simply to God apart from revelation, that is, not only to God "outside of Christ" as Harnack thought, but also most profoundly to the revelation itself, to God "in Christ." [18] God revealed in the flesh is at the same time the *deus absconditus*. This meant that Harnack's conception of the dialectic between a knowledge of God "outside" and "in" Christ had to be altered. For if it is true that revelation in Christ does not come apart from hiddenness but rather in and through it, then it cannot be true that knowledge of God apart from Christ, knowledge according to law, alone comprises that hiddenness. In Luther's view, Kattenbusch said, God is more profoundly hidden "in Christ" than he is "outside of" Christ. God is hidden in Christ because in the incarnation he comes in the form of a servant, in humility and weakness, and dies on a cross. Hiddenness, to be sure, does apply to God in nature, but this hiddenness is intensified in Christ.

It is evident from this that Luther's dialectic, however it may eventually be construed, could not be identified with a simple dialectic between natural and revealed knowledge. To do this only creates greater confusion. The hidden-revealed dialectic is quite different from a "natural-revealed" or a "reason-revelation" dialectic. For hiddenness means that "natural reason," even when it is given the fact of Christ, cannot penetrate the mystery, cannot make "sense" of it by incorporating it into one of its "systems."

This also raises further question about the understanding of the law. Harnack had seen that law and hiddenness were closely related, but he had said that knowledge of God derived from the

---

[18] Ferdinand Kattenbusch, "Deus Absconditus bei Luther," *Westgabe für Julius Kaften* (Tübingen: J. C. B. Mohr (Paul Siebeck), 1920), pp. 170-173. Cf. Dillenberger, *God Hidden and Revealed*, pp. 26-35.

law came out of the hiddenness "apart from Christ." But if the hiddenness is *in* revelation, *in* Christ, then what happens to the doctrine of law? If God is hidden in Christ, and "the hidden God" is the God of law, would it not seem that Christ is also a revelation of law? In other words, if God in Christ is both hidden and revealed, is he also both law and gospel?

This was the next question which arose. Kattenbusch had helped to clarify the question of hiddenness and revealedness, but he did not apply it toward a solution of the structural systematic problem at the root of the discussion: the problem of law and gospel. The reinterpretation of the hidden-revealed dialectic called for a reinterpretation of the law-gospel dialectic as well. Since he made no such reinterpretation, Kattenbusch's contribution was only a potential source of greater confusion.

Kattenbusch's view, however, also undercut the Ritschlian theology. It is apparent that the idea of hiddenness gives at least partial support both to the Ritschlian contention that repentance arises from the same divine action that creates faith and to Herrmann's statement that "the same fact that increases our grief . . . is also perceptible to us as a word of God convincing us that he has reached down to us." [19] The Ritschlians had intuitively seen that it is through the revelation itself that repentance is worked and that the kind of schematic and material distinction between law and gospel which orthodoxy made was impossible. But at the same time the question of how law and gospel are to be related remained unanswered. The Ritschlian was unable to answer this because he could not really cope systematically with the reinterpretation of hiddenness and revealedness. Whereas on the one hand the hidden-revealed dialectic gave some support to the Ritschlian view of repentance, on the other hand it created considerable systematic difficulty. It meant that revelation is not so simple and univocal as the Ritschlian had thought. For a Ritschlian, revelation brings the practical knowledge of the love of God. He sought to protect this from misunderstanding by making a distinction between theoretical and practical reason and a corresponding distinction between nature and spirit.

---

[19] Above, p. 124.

But if hiddenness reintroduces the concept of nature—God is hidden in nature as well as being hidden in Christ—then the Ritschlian would have to give up his systematic distinction between nature and spirit—at least in the form in which he has made it. For in the hidden-revealed dialectic the decisive distinction is not between a natural or theoretical knowledge and a spiritual or practical knowledge, but between cross and resurrection, between death and life. Even the distinction between theoretical and practical reason cannot penetrate the hiddenness of God in Christ.

The Ritschlian system finally could not bear the hidden-revealed dialectic because this dialectic did not correspond to the nature-spirit distinction upon which Ritschl built. Kattenbusch himself is an example; he remained essentially Ritschlian when he said that the dialectic of hiddenness and revealedness refers merely to the mystery of God as "the incomprehensible" *(der Ungreifbare)*, the mystery of the divine love.[20] Here he hardly said any more than Herrmann said in referring to the "incomprehensible reality" of the divine action.[21]

The systematic difficulty of the Ritschlian system became even more apparent in the subsequent development of the problem of wrath and love. Further research made it apparent that the concept of divine wrath played a vital part in Luther's theology and could not simply be explained away as a vestige of medievalism. The concept of wrath is maintained in Luther in all its seriousness, up to and including the idea of eternal damnation. Luther even said on occasion that wrath is eternal, belonging to God's essence.[22] This of course countered the oversimplified Ritschlian interpretation of Luther and in turn reinforced many of Harnack's contentions.

Luther, however, did not make the problem easy; he also said on occasion that God is pure love and that the idea of God as wrathful is "false and vain speculation" and the work of the devil.[23]

---

[20] Dillenberger, *God Hidden and Revealed*, p. 32.

[21] Above, p. 124.

[22] Gerhard Rost, "Der Zorn Gottes in Luthers Theologie," *Lutherischer Rundblick*, Vol 9, No. 1 (1961), p. 24.

[23] *Ibid.*, p. 9.

Both wrath and love are spoken of as belonging to God's eternal essence. The problem is how to hold together these elements in Luther's doctrine of God and give each its full force without allowing it to collapse into a dualism.

Karl Holl attempted to find a solution in Luther which would both reproduce Luther's true intent and avoid the kind of relapse into orthodoxy found in Harnack. Holl recognized the paradox between wrath and love in Luther, and he insisted that no speculative synthesis could be made between them:

> Over against the idea of the holy, unrelenting, demanding God is set the other, that God is full of marvelous goodness. The one is to be maintained as sharply and completely as the other, without attempting an internal compromise. But this paradox is nothing other than the essence of the Christian faith.[24]

But this leaves the question of the relation of wrath and love unanswered. Is there no unity behind the paradox? In Holl's own view, an unresolved paradox goes contrary to the nature of religion,[25] but since a speculative resolution between wrath and love is impossible, the unity must be sought on some other level. Luther, Holl maintained, found the unity behind the antithesis in his conception of the relation between God's alien and proper activity. Wrath, God's alien work, ultimately serves the purpose of the divine will which is determined by love, the proper work. The unity in the antithesis is one which must be *experienced* in becoming the object of the divine activity in the process of justification. One experiences the wrath of God which exposes sin as selfishness, unbelief, and ingratitude. One cannot "theologize" this wrath away. One must accept the judgment of wrath and acknowledge God's own righteousness. When this is done, faith is born, and in faith one perceives the unity between wrath and love:

> . . . The one aspiring to faith . . . recognizes the love of God which seeks his soul precisely in the unrelenting truthfulness with which God holds his judgment over him. He knows it was

---

[24] Karl Holl, *Gesammelte Aufsätze* (3 vols.; Tübingen: J. C. B. Mohr (Paul Siebeck), 1928), III, p. 566.

[25] Wolff, *Die Haupttypen*, pp. 340-342.

God's intention therewith to heal him from his self-seeking. Only insofar as he thus surrenders himself does he know that God "forgives" him.[26]

The unity behind the paradox consists in the fact that wrath ultimately serves love. Otto Wolff characterizes Holl's Luther interpretation as one which holds a "paradoxical unity of opposites."[27] Faith, in Holl's Luther interpretation, stands before the paradox of the divine love for the sinner. As a constant miracle and yet without rationalizing the mystery, faith can *believe* and *experience* a unity between wrath and love which cannot be captured by "the system."

Holl's work was an important advance towards an understanding of the problem, yet it has raised several questions. The concept of a wrath which serves entirely the purpose of love has not been accepted by all interpreters.[28] Luther maintained that the divine wrath could lead to despair and damnation. Could this be done in the service of the divine love? Holl was apparently aware of this concept of wrath in Luther, but he could not find any place for it in his "paradoxical unity of opposites." Holl referred to this type of wrath as a "stringent wrath" *(Zorn der Strenge)*, a wrath revealed at the last judgment and one which is active wherever God rejects that which is completely useless. But it did not fit Holl's idea that wrath serves only the divine love, so he largely ignored it and concentrated his attention on the "merciful wrath" *(Zorn des Erbarmens)*.[29]

Perhaps this can be taken as an indication that Holl, the Ritschlian historian, was still not ready to accept the full consequences of Luther's theology. The original Ritschlian position had been considerably modified under the pressure of the new Luther research, but Holl was still within the Ritschlian view of religious experience. Further evidence for this is Holl's interpretation of Luther's "religion." Luther's religion rooted, for Holl, in his consciousness of the imperative. It is clear that "the feeling of an imperative

---

[26] Holl, *Gesammelte Aufsätze*, 7th ed., 1948, I, p. 76.

[27] Wolff, *Die Haupttypen*, p. 343.

[28] Cf. Rost, *Lutherischer Rundblick*, IX, No. 1, p. 5.

[29] Holl, *Gesammelte Aufsätze*, I, p. 42.

forms the basis for all of his piety and that the duty to God appeared to him to be the first among all duties." [30]

Luther's religion was to Holl, a "religion of conscience" (Gewissensreligion) in the strictest sense of the word.[31] Man owes God the duty of religion. This imperative, of course, is not a legalistic imperative but rather the imperative which stems from being grasped by the divine love.[32] The command which confronts man is in its basic content nothing other than the gospel. The word of the First Commandment, "I am the Lord thy God," is in its content the same as the gospel.[33] As we shall see, there is perhaps some justification for saying this, but it is difficult to escape the impression that we are still hearing the Ritschlian concept of law. This is the point at which Holl's interpretation of Luther has most consistently been criticized; in the basic structure of his thought, Holl had not escaped the Ritschlian moralism.[34]

In spite of certain advances, then, Luther was still understood in terms of a Kantian view of religion. This perspective had been broadened to include a concept of wrath which rejected a presumptuous and egoistic approach to God, but in the end this wrath was unified with the divine love in what Wolff called an "ethical rationalization." Wrath serves merely to place judgment on man's self-seeking and thus to reinforce the moral imperative. In many respects, Holl stood at the end of the line for the Ritschlian point of view. The pressure exerted by the attempt to take Luther into the system had strained it to the breaking point. If Luther was to be accepted entirely, a fundamental reorientation of the system would be necessary.

Kattenbusch and Holl illustrated the need for this reorientation in their interpretation of Luther, especially in their confusion about the law and gospel. Ritschlian theology began with an outright rejection of the orthodox concepts of law, wrath, and righteousness, but Ritschlianism itself was largely responsible for the renewed

---

[30] Ibid., pp. 73-74.

[31] Ibid., p. 35.

[32] Wolff, Die Haupttypen, p .332.

[33] Hoff, Gesammelte Aufsätze, III, p. 248.

[34] Wolff, Die Haupttypen, p. 344.

interest in Luther as a part of its defense against orthodoxy. The renewed interest in Luther, it turns out, bore fruit which was fully as bitter to the Ritschlian as it had been to the orthodox. It became evident that wrath, law, hiddenness, atonement, etc., in Luther were not merely leftovers from medieval scholasticism, but vital parts of a distinctive theology. The question the Ritschlian had to answer was how these concepts were to be understood if Luther was to be taken at all seriously. The Ritschlian historians made attempts at integrating such concepts as wrath, hiddenness, and alien work with their view of religion, but they were always left with elements of Luther's thought which did not fit their scheme.

Most troublesome for the Ritschlians from the systematic point of view was the concept of law. Hiddenness and wrath are in themselves somewhat indefinite terms which can be adapted to fit almost any system, as the preceding development demonstrates. This is not so with law. It has usually enjoyed a specific place, one which is determinative for the whole structure of the system. If the concepts of wrath, hiddenness, righteousness, *opus alienum* and *proprium*, etc., are to be reclaimed, what is to happen to the concept of law? Is it to be understood as the standard by which divine wrath measures its retribution, as in orthodoxy? Is it a part of the historical dispensation, as Hofmann said? Is it the Ritschlian moral imperative? How are law and wrath or law and hiddenness related? These are the questions which arise from the discussion at this point.

Thus the whole problem comes to focus on the theological place of law. For orthodoxy law was really the main structural component of the system; with the aid of their doctrine of law they attempted to understand the nature of the divine act in Christ in terms of an equivalence between wrath and love. We have seen how unsuccessful this attempt was. But at the same time we have also seen several attempts to displace law in the system, and these attempts have also been unsuccessful. Hofmann attempted to replace law with a scheme of *Heilsgeschichte;* this resulted in a view of history which obscured the eschatological newness of the gospel. Ritschl attempted it with an interpretation of religion influenced by Kant, and the result was the same—a loss of the eschatological nature of the gospel. It is an ironic fact that *both* the systematic *inclusion* of law as the structural backbone of the system as in orthodoxy and the systematic *exclusion* of the law by those who react against orthodoxy had the same result. This indicates that law can be neither the sole determining factor in the system, nor can it simply be dismissed. Clearly there was need for a more careful consideration of the place of law.

Before turning to the contemporary discussion it would perhaps be helpful to summarize the most important features brought out so far. Hofmann rightly challenged the orthodox concept of law and atonement. His main positive contribution to a more viable position was the idea that Christ's death should be understood as a victory over the forces which tyrannize man and that by this victory Christ established a new humanity. Hofmann's problem, however, was that because of his method he was led to understand this victory as part of a historical process of divine self-realization, and the newness of the victory was threatened. Law was made part of a historical dispensation; Christ, though he suffers under law and wrath, was conscious of his place in the scheme of the self-realization of divine love, so that he did not really suffer as man suffers. Because of the scheme, law and wrath are no longer a real threat, love tends to become self-evident and sentimentalized, and the eschatological dimension loses its radical nature.

Theodosius Harnack's important contribution was his discovery in Luther of a dialectic between wrath and love, law and gospel, which resisted Hofmann's tendency toward a sentimental view of divine love. Harnack's problem, in the light of subsequent investigation of Luther, was that he did not discover the true nature of this dialectic. His concept of a dialectic between a natural knowledge "apart from Christ" and a revealed knowledge "in Christ" did not do justice to Luther's understanding of hiddenness and revealedness. Because of this failure, Harnack did not evaluate correctly Luther's use of the victory motif in the interpretation of the atonement. Instead, on the basis of the doctrine of law and with the aid of a dubious distinction between the essence and the office of the law, Harnack returned to the basic orthodox view of the atonement.

Ritschl's positive contribution to the development was his attempt to understand atonement as actual atonement in the present—real ethical renewal—rather than mere "theoretical" atonement in the past. This attempt brought with it a genuine appreciation of the place and function of the historical community in the work of atonement which was somewhat akin to Hofmann's idea of the new humanity. Ritschl's difficulty, however, was that in order to give systematic expression to this actual renewal in the present, he adopted a Kantian view of religion and attempted to solve all systematic problems within that view. This produced a reinterpretation of law in which law and gospel are virtually identified in the concept of the "kingdom of God." The result is a loss of the seriousness of the divine wrath and consequently a loss of the eschatological newness of the divine act of love.

Throughout the discussion the interpretation of Luther played an important part. Hofmann began by claiming Luther's victory motif for his side in the debate. Harnack countered by insisting on Luther's "orthodoxy." Ritschl maintained that both the victory motif and the orthodox elements were left-overs from medieval views. Interpreters like Holl and Kattenbusch, however, indicate that no one in the debate can lay full claim to Luther. Luther's views, elusive as they are, do not fit into any of the "systems" presented. The constant sources of difficulty are the seemingly contradictory statements in Luther on many of the central issues in the debate, especially on law and wrath and the many diverse descriptions of the nature of atonement.

Nevertheless, important progress had been made. Kattenbusch's discovery of the nature of hiddenness pointed to a dialectic which modified Harnack's orthodox interpretation and suggested a need for further investigation of Luther's view of law. Holl's development of Luther's teaching on the *opus alienum* and the *opus proprium* assisted in understanding the dialectic between wrath and love. But until the dialectic of law and gospel was further clarified, those gains would remain insecure. Also, it was not yet clear how Luther had apparently held together both a view of vicarious satisfaction and a victory motif in the doctrine of the atonement.

The basic problem of the dialectic between law and gospel, therefore, had not yet been settled. What is the proper definition of law and what is its position in the system relative to the gospel? If my analysis up to this point is correct, several possibilities must be excluded. Law cannot be regarded as the eternal "framework" of the system. Nor can law be "gotten rid of" by relegating it to a minor role in the system. It cannot be understood simply as a part of a historical dispensation which has been superseded by a later dispensation. It cannot be "erased" by a theological tour de force. Whenever any of these alternatives are attempted it is the gospel that eventually suffers. The gospel loses its eschatological newness and power when its function is taken over by *the system;* the law simply comes back in a different form. The problem, therefore, is to define the place of the law in such a way that the eschatological newness and power of the gospel are not lost. Such a definition would be an attempt to appreciate and utilize the positive features of the discussion to this point. Hofmann's understanding of the newness of the Christian experience, Harnack's desire for a more dialectical understanding, Ritschl's insistence upon the need for actual atonement—all these elements would contribute to a better understanding of the nature of the gospel.

Part Three

THE
CONTEMPORARY
DEBATE:

*Gospel and Law
Versus
Law and Gospel*

CHAPTER IX

KARL BARTH

The contemporary debate over law and gospel began in earnest with the publication of Karl Barth's essay "Gospel and Law" in 1935.[1] Of course, much had happened theologically as well as politically and socially between the time of Herrmann, Kattenbusch, and Holl and the appearance of Barth's statement in 1935. The recovery of biblical eschatology and the rediscovery of Søren Kierkegaard, to mention only two factors, had had their effect upon the discussion. Politically and socially, one needs mention only the appearance of Hitler and the "German Christian" movement. It is not necessary for us to go into these developments specifically. Instead we shall turn directly to the debate over law and gospel and attempt to show how these developments have affected that debate. In this way we can demonstrate both the continuity of the contemporary debate with the older debate, and the alterations which the new situation brought about.

Karl Barth startled theologians, especially Lutherans, by suggesting a basic reorientation of the law-gospel dialectic. His essay was the first major attempt at a redefinition of the problem. What startled the Lutheran theologians was Barth's assertion that the traditional order should be reversed; instead of going from law to gospel, one must proceed from gospel to law.

---

[1] Karl Barth, "Gospel and Law," *Community, State and Church* (Anchor Books; Garden City: Doubleday and Company, 1960), pp. 71-100. Cited hereafter as "Gospel and Law."

In doing this, Barth was motivated, no doubt, by a twofold concern. First was his systematic concern to bring the law-gospel dialectic into line with his general theological program. Since true knowledge of the law of God can only follow the divine self-revelation, law must follow gospel.

> The nature of the case is such that anyone who really and ear-
> nestly would first say law and only then, presupposing this, say
> gospel would not, no matter how good his intention, be speak-
> ing of the law of *God* and therefore certainly not of *his* gospel.
> This usual way is, even in the most favorable case, enveloped in
> ambiguities of every sort.[2]

Second was Barth's ethical and political concern, which though not revealed in this essay can be readily seen from the historical situation in which it appeared. Some theologians, wedded to the older formulation in which law precedes gospel and is based on natural law, had used Luther's idea of the two realms to accommodate the concept of law to the national ethos, or *Volksnomos*. The law of God was compromised with the principles and practices of Nazism. Barth expressed the suspicion that the false concept of law and gospel inherited from Luther was in some measure responsible for the incapacity of the church to exercise its political responsibility. Since law came before Gospel, this led to the view that the whole realm of practical life was left to the political rulers and the church was content with a false evangelical inwardness.[3] By reversing the order of law and gospel Barth sought to guarantee that the law of which one speaks when one links gospel and law is really God's law and not man's.

The dialectic between law and gospel therefore had to be subordinated to Barth's concern that the Word of God not be confused with the words of men. This is a consistent Barthian theme dating back to the days of the *Römerbrief*. God's Word is not man's word, nor are the two to be confused in any way. However one distinguishes between law and gospel, one must see them both as God's address to man. This fact—that both law and gospel are God's address to

---

[2] Barth, "Gospel and Law," p. 71.
[3] Karl Barth, *Eine Schweizer Stimme* (Zellikon-Zürich: Evangelischer Verlag A. G., 1945), pp. 113, 122, 328.

man—determines their unity. For Barth law and gospel have their unity in the fact that they are both God's address, and as God's address their essential content is grace. The very fact that God speaks to us at all is in itself grace, and this is true whether he speaks through gospel or through law.

> The Word of God, when it is addressed to us and when we are allowed to hear it, demonstrates its unity in that it is always grace; i.e., it is free, non-obligatory, undeserved divine goodness, mercy, and condescension. A gospel or a law which we speak to ourselves, by virtue of our own ability, would as such, not be *God's* Word; it would not be his *Gospel* and it would not be his law. The *very fact that* God speaks to us, that, under all circumstances, is, in itself, grace.[4]

God's Word, for Barth, could be either law or gospel, but since it is God's Word it is always grace. This is true even though God's address to man can mean judgment and death.

How is this to be understood? In an attempt to clarify his meaning Barth introduced a distinction between form and content. God's Word to man, God's grace which is called Jesus Christ, is the manifest will of God. It is "not only uncertain and dangerous but perverse"[5] to want to understand the law on any other basis than that which is revealed in Christ. "From what God does *for* us, we infer what he wants *with* us and from us."[6] God's action in Christ, Barth says, does not end in itself, but always has its goal in our action. The publication of grace, therefore, *establishes the law* and is to be met by the obedience of faith. Grace cannot be given to men unless it means that it is translated into the future tense: "You shall be!" Consequently, Barth said, we may call the law the *form* of the gospel. It is the shape of existence which the gospel creates in this world.

> Thus, we can certainly make the general and comprehensive statement that the law is nothing else than the necessary *form* of the gospel, whose content is grace. Precisely this content de-

---

[4] Barth, "Gospel and Law," p. 72.

[5] *Ibid.*, p. 77.

[6] *Ibid.*, p. 78.

mands this form, the form which calls for its like, the law's form.[7]

The unity of law and gospel was defined by Barth as a unity of content and form. The law is in the gospel "as the tablets from Sinai were in the ark"[8]; the gospel is always in the law as that which is manifest and proclaimed. Because of this the law can be called holy and good. The law is "the work of God which makes room for the gospel in our human sphere and room for us men in the sphere of the gospel."[9] The law, in Barth's view, gives the gospel concrete shape and direction in the sphere of men. Even though the law and the gospel are not the same, without the law we could not have the gospel either.[10]

To sum up, the traditional distinction between gospel and law was subordinated to Barth's distinction between the Word of God and the word of man. Gospel and law must then be related to one another as content and form of the one Word of God which is always grace. On this basis Barth said that law, if it is really the expression of the will of God, must follow gospel.

But what then happens to the traditional formulation in which the law was defined as God's address to sinful man prior to repentance and faith? Barth discussed this question in the two final sections of his essay, where he asked what it means that the gospel as well as the law—or in our previous terms, the content and form of the gospel—have been put into our hands, into the hands of sinners.[11] Barth said that God gives his gift of gospel and law to us nevertheless, in spite of "the worse than questionable purity of our hands." This means, for Barth, something negative and something positive. The negative result of this *nevertheless* is considered under the concepts of *misuse* and *misinterpretation* of the law. Sin "uses the law as a springboard" to serve its own ends because by the law sin is deceived into attempting to establish its own righteousness. In so doing sin leads to a misuse and misinterpretation of the law,

---

[7] *Ibid.*, p. 80.
[8] *Ibid.*, p. 80.
[9] *Ibid.*, p. 81.
[10] *Ibid.*, p. 81.
[11] *Ibid.*, p. 84.

an *ignorance* which is also disobedience. As a result the gospel is also misunderstood and corrupted.

When the form is corrupted, so also is the content. Christ becomes merely "the indispensable companion, the useful lever arm, and finally and above all the stop-gap for all our efforts towards our own justification!" Jesus Christ becomes "the great creditor who again and again is just good enough to cover the cost of our own ventures in righteousness!" [12] Man in sin uses the law to establish his own righteousness and makes the gospel into a mere helper in the process.

But in this very fact man begins to see the real power of the law and the nature of sin. The law which man dishonors and empties remains God's law *nevertheless* and turns on man. In this turning man sees the power of the wrath of God in the law:

> This is the law which was later so gravely mentioned in the same breath with the whore, reason, with sin and death, in fact with the devil, so urgently depicted as the enemy of faith, love and hope, as *the* great antagonist of the gospel. This is the law of which it was said and must be said: either entirely the law and then death, or entirely the gospel and then life, there is no third possibility.[13]

The negative result of the *nevertheless* is that the law remains God's law even though it is misunderstood; it turns upon man, manifesting God's wrath.

The positive result of the *nevertheless* lies in the fact that the victory of God through the gospel operates "fully for the first time" as "the really glad tidings for real sinners" when it comes as a rescue from apparent condemnation under the misunderstood law.[14] This means that God vivifies through the gospel when he kills through the law (that is, the misunderstood law). In this sense, Barth said, the order law-gospel has a legitimate and meaningful place.[15] Just as resurrection follows death, so gospel follows law here. The order law-gospel is "characterized by its identity with the order death-

---

[12] *Ibid.*, p. 90.
[13] *Ibid.*, p. 94.
[14] *Ibid.*, p. 95.
[15] *Ibid.*, p. 96.

life." But that means, Barth said, "that it is entirely unintelligible to us as an order. It can only be event and fact and we of ourselves believe it only as the promise of what Jesus Christ does for us, and our belief will be a source of amazement to us." [16]

Barth wanted to unify gospel and law as the content and form of the one Word of God, making true knowledge of God's will follow only upon his self-revelation in Christ. Since, however, this Word of God is *nevertheless* spoken to sinners, that knowledge and use of the law by sinners is recognized by Barth only as a misuse, a misinterpretation. Even the misuse, however, does not negate the fact that it remains God's law and is the instrument of his wrath. It is therefore only this *misused* law which can come before the gospel. Yet it appears that such a misused law *must* come before the gospel because God's Word is spoken to sinners, and the knowledge of the gospel can come "fully" as the "really glad tidings" only after this "misuse."

It would seem in this instance as though Barth rather grudgingly admitted the necessity of the traditional formulation which placed law before gospel, but that he did not want to give it any real status in his system. He recognized that law, in a sense, must come before gospel just as death before life. But such law, he said, is a misused and misunderstood law, a law which is to be superseded and dispelled. The order law-gospel in this process is not, Barth said, intelligible as an order. Since it is only by virtue of the subsequent knowledge of faith that the prior misuse is recognized as a misuse, it cannot be seen as an order. The only legitimate use of the law is that in which it is seen as *God's* law, as the expression of God's will which follows the gospel.

In Barth's reconstruction it is not difficult to discern a definite continuity with Ritschl and Herrmann. In these two men's works, law was divorced from all "natural knowledge" and taken entirely within "the kingdom." But this was done under the auspices of a Kantian interpretation of religion, which divorced theoretical and practical reason, nature and spirit. This produced, as we have seen, the subsequent search for the historical Jesus as well as a loss of the

---

[16] *Ibid.*, p. 97.

eschatological dimension of faith. Barth's reconstruction can be seen, I think, as an attempt to overcome *from within* the problems inherent in Ritschl's construction by making it even more radical. Barth rejects not only "natural knowledge" and "natural law" but also the Kantian idea of religion. The result is that law is taken even more strictly within the confines of "revelation." Law is "the form of the gospel," which can have nothing to do with man's natural understanding and most certainly not with man's "natural" understanding of religion. All understanding of law prior to revelation must be labeled as misunderstanding and misuse, and these must eventually be overcome.

But what does this mean for "the system"? The Ritschlians used Kant's idea of religion as a conceptual framework for understanding and explicating the nature of Christianity. Barth rejects this. How then does he understand revelation? It is here that the discontinuity between Ritschl and Barth becomes apparent. Whereas for Ritschl and Herrmann "the kingdom" was understood in a Kantian sense and was therefore primarily of "this age," for Barth it has become quite radically eschatologized. The kingdom is that which "breaks in" through the Word. Law is the "form" in which this "eschatologically other" breaks in, "the work of God which makes room for the gospel in our human sphere." This means on the one hand that one cannot understand law as the Ritschlians did, as a general command of love, as the practical moral imperative at the root of religious life. It means on the other hand that Barth's concept of law is quite different from anything in previous tradition. This is made more evident in the *Church Dogmatics*, especially in the explications of the nature and use of the law. Since, for Barth, the only legitimate use of law is that which follows gospel, the so-called "third use" of the law would be the only proper use. In every other case we have to deal with a misunderstood and misused law.[17]

However, as Edmund Schlink has pointed out,[18] it is even some-

---

[17] Karl Barth, *Church Dogmatics*, ed. G. W. Bromiley and T. F. Torrance, trans. G. T. Thompson and H. Knight (4 vols.; New York: Scribners, 1956), I. 2. p. 384. Cited hereafter as *Church Dogmatics*.

[18] Edmund Schlink, *"Gesetz und Paraklese,"* *Antwort* (Zollikon-Zürich: Evangelischer Verlag A. G., 1956), p. 323.

what misleading to speak of this as a "third use" of the law. The law of which Barth speaks is no longer a general command which man perceives prior to the gospel which is now to be used in a "third" way. The law of which Barth speaks is the concrete and particular form in which revelation comes to men at a particular time. This law, Barth says, is not a general law available to and understandable by everyone, but the particular and concrete demand of the moment, which is also permission, given in the gift of grace. As such it radically excludes that former concept of law, the misunderstood law. Barth's "law" is not a general moral imperative, nor is it a general command of love or a "third" use in the traditional sense. It is the form of the eschatological address, *one* true use, over against which every other use is a misuse.

This means that for Barth law in its "true" sense needs a very specific definition. Since true law is the form of the gospel, it distinguishes itself from all other commands. It is *permission*—the granting of a very definite *freedom*.[19] Other commands in every respect are a "holding fast, a binding, a fettering"; they create and maintain a sphere of distrust and fear. The command of God, however, which has its basis in the claim made upon men by Jesus Christ, orders man to be free, and it secures obedience by in fact setting men free. The obligation which the law demands means permission, while at the same time the permission means obligation. Barth realizes that this special use of the term law, this two-sided conjunction of permission and obligation, is in principle incomprehensible. One can never reduce it to a set of ethical standards. To attempt to do so would mean to fall off the path on one side or the other, into either lawlessness or legalism. That is why the law of which Barth speaks can always be only the law *in* the gospel, the law of freedom which can be grasped only through faith.[20] Law is the very specific unity of authority and freedom which is given in Jesus Christ and apprehended only by faith.

Barth is perfectly aware, of course, that there are other "commands" which man encounters, other uses of the term law.[21] In

---

[19] Barth, *Church Dogmatics*, II, 2, p. 585.

[20] *Ibid.*, II, 2, p. 603.

[21] *Ibid.*, II, 2, pp. 583-584.

fact, every object in the natural and historical world contains and expresses a command simply to the extent that in its existence and essence it demands our attention, observation, consideration, investigation and understanding purely for its own sake. Even the axioms of mathematics and logic are commands. So also certain results of human knowledge, pictures of nature and history, etc. And there are commands which are even more closely related to the decisions of the human will—the compelling necessities of food and drink, of warmth and sleep, as well as the need to see that our life always has qualities of dignity and honor. There are commands of circumspection, foresight, and discretion which have been forced upon us by education or custom. There are "commands of the hour" which a man thinks he has discovered for himself and others, even for a whole nation. There are commands to do this and not do that promulgated by someone in authority. Man is placed under a plethora of commands. But these, Barth insists, are all different from God's command, and not to be confused with it. For all these commands bind, while God's command sets free.

It is, however, somewhat difficult to see just how these "other commands" are related to the command of God. On the one hand Barth insists that the command of God is to be distinguished from all other commands not just relatively but *absolutely*, with the distinction of heaven and earth.[22] Yet at the same time it appears that for Barth the command of God—"without prejudice to its particular form"—*always* wears the "garment" of another claim of this kind.[23]

> An object with its question, the compulsion of a necessity of thought, one of those hypotheses or conventions, a higher necessity of life and particularly a more primitive, a necessity which in itself seems to be that of a very human wish or very human cleverness, a summons coming from this or that quarter, a call which a man directs to himself—all these can actually be the command of God veiled in this form, and therefore genuinely participate in the corresponding authority and dignity.[24]

Apparently this means that Barth does not wish to *identify* the

---

[22] *Ibid.*, II, 2, p. 588.
[23] *Ibid.*, II, 2, p. 584.
[24] *Ibid.*, II, 2, pp. 584-585.

"true" law with any of man's systems of law as such, but he admits that at a given time God's command will always wear the "garment" of a seemingly "human" demand. Faith, apparently, will be able to recognize it as God's command in that it will bear the marks of freedom—the specific conjunction of obligation and permission. Thus God's command will always be a concrete command in a specific human context.

But what of the law apart from faith? Does Barth mean that apart from faith—in the context of these purely "human" laws—one does not have to do with God? Not at all. Here again we are thrown back upon the concept of the "misused" law. Apart from faith these human laws can only mean a state of servitude for man. The law is then a harmful thing. But this means that even apart from faith, under this law, man has to do with God.[25] But in this case it is the God who is not mocked, who inexorably causes a man to reap what he has sown. Man in his sin misuses the law, but the misused law does not become ineffective in this misuse. It is effective because "its message and revelation to us is that sin dwells in us," [26] so that we do what we do not want to do and never do what we really want to do. This law "tears us in two." Nevertheless, this law is "from God."

> It is from God the Creator of all things, and therefore from our legitimate Commander, that they derive their authority and force. But the form which they now take—corresponding to our severance from the gracious divine command which is their source and truth—is the disintegrated, dismembered and individually distorted form of the "elements of the universe" against whose rule and operation, which in the last resort are so utterly harmful, Paul tried to warn the Galatians. . . . [27]

And, furthermore, it is from this "law" that man must be liberated. The "law of the Spirit of life" must step into the place of this law and radically exclude it. How can this happen? It can only happen if the sinful man who "misuses" the law dies.[28] The "old man" must

---

[25] *Ibid.*, II, 2, p. 590.
[26] *Ibid.*, II, 2, p. 590.
[27] *Ibid.*, II, 2, p. 590.
[28] *Ibid.*, II, 2, p. 591.

be "killed" in and with the killing of Jesus Christ on Golgotha. Thus they are no longer subject to the law that ruled the old man. "The subject Adam . . . is eliminated. The subject Jesus Christ has replaced and excluded this subject." [29] And this means also the replacement and exclusion of the misused and distorted law so that the true law of God is revealed again in its proper substance as the law of grace.

Barth prefers for his definition of law such New Testament designations as "the law of liberty" or "the law of the spirit of life" or "the law of love." All other law is "misused" law and must be completely excluded. The misused law, even though it derives its authority and power from God and apparently is in some sense a revelation of sin to man,[30] is not a propaedeutic to the gospel; it is, for Barth, simply the law of sin and death. The law of God is something entirely different. It is not the sum and superlative of the "infernal assault" of the law of sin and death, nor is it even the "infinitely multiplied" intensity of this assault.[31] The assault of the law of sin and death leads to death, no doubt, but it does not produce the death which leads to life. Only the command of God does that. The command of God assaults and seizes man indeed, but it does this not like an enemy but rather like a friend. This assault is radical precisely because it is the command of our true, best friend.[32] It is radical because it is the law *in* the gospel. This is why man cannot withdraw from it into himself as he can in the face of all other commands. God's law calls man out of himself to the freedom —and obligation—of the gospel. The command of God, the "true" law, is the only command which leads to life, for it alone is the "law of the spirit of life."

Barth's concept of law is the result of his general theological program. It is the result of a radical eschatologizing of the line of development coming from Ritschl and Herrmann. Ritschl rejected Hofmann's "thinking in" the experience of Christianity for a "thinking about" historical revelation. In Ritschl, this meant that Chris-

[29] *Ibid.*, II, 2, p. 591.
[30] *Ibid.*, II, 2, p. 590.
[31] *Ibid.*, II, 2, p. 587.
[32] *Ibid.*, II, 2, p. 595.

tianity would be "thought about" and classified in terms of "practical religion." Law, therefore, had to be taken within the practical "kingdom of God" as the general law of love. Barth, under the influence of his radical distinction between the Word of God and the word of man, rejects Ritschl's method. This means that one can no longer speak of law in terms of "practical religion." But at the same time one cannot speak of law in the metaphysical sense, as the *lex aeterna* of the older orthodoxy. The question arises for Barth of how one can speak of law at all. There is apparently only one solution. Law must be taken *within* the Word of God as the "form" of the eschatological address.

This means that for Barth both the dialectical opposition and the unity of law and gospel must be given in revelation itself. Barth defines this dialectic as the dialectic of veiling and unveiling in the Word of God given to man. The veiling is the worldly form, the demand; the unveiling is the content, the gift.[33] The dialectic of wrath and love corresponds also to this.[34] What this means, for Barth, is that the Word of God is not given to man as something over which he can exercise subsequent control. The Word remains God's Word, even in his giving it to man.

Moreover, Barth says, we cannot remove the distinction between form and content, veiling and unveiling, nor can we entertain any thought of synthesis between them. Faith means recognizing that such a synthesis cannot be made,[35] and committing the answer to God, seeking and finding it in God.

> Faith is therefore invariably the recognition of our limits and the recognition of the mystery of the Word of God, the recognition that our hearing is bound to God Himself who wills to lead us now through form to content, and now through content back to form, and in both cases to Himself, who one way or the other does not give Himself into our hands, but keeps us in His hand.[36]

What this means is that without law one does not know what the

---

[33] Barth, *Church Dogmatics*, I, 1, p. 204.
[34] *Ibid.*, p. 205.
[35] *Ibid.*, p. 200.
[36] *Ibid.*, p. 201.

gospel is, and without the gospel one cannot know what the law is. The relationship of law to gospel, form to content, wrath to love, is a relationship of dialectical unity. Each is necessary to its opposite, yet the two are never to be synthesized.

Barth's reformulation is the result of his attempt to solve the problem of giving expression to the eschatological newness of the gospel and restoring the act character of the Word of God. In Barth, the Word of revelation is no longer a mere report about a past event, nor is it a timeless truth, but it is an eschatological address carrying in itself that which it has to give as demand and gift, form and content. Barth has attempted to restore the act character of the Word by making it more "exclusive," by removing the possibility of understanding it in terms of some system of "natural theology." The Word is the eschatological address which breaks in upon man.

The result of this for the doctrine of law is that we have reached the final step in a process of narrowing down and particularizing. At the beginning of the development, in the orthodox system, law was understood in a broad sense, easily associated and often identified with natural law. Then it was reduced to a historical dispensation. Next it was divorced from the natural and the political altogether and taken within the "kingdom" as the law of love. Finally, in order to protect the actuality of the Word of God, Barth reduced law to a mathematical point, the concrete form of the Word in the moment of revelation. Barth's theology represents the climax and, I think, the end of this process.

CHAPTER X

THE REPLY TO BARTH

Barth's reformulation of the law-gospel problem has given rise to a lively debate. The problem which has been implicit in the development we have been tracing has here, at last, come to explicit expression. Barth's reversal of the order of law and gospel has evoked a stormy reply. We must, therefore, look at some of Barth's opponents in this debate. We shall not treat all of these opponents—they are many—but only some of the more representative types.

Werner Elert has from the beginning been one of Barth's most outspoken opponents. The main target of Elert's attack has been Barth's assertion that the very fact that God speaks to us is itself grace, regardless of what God says. This Elert has called a "fundamental error" which could only result in a depotentiation of both the law and the gospel.[1] It means, for Elert, that the dialectic between law and gospel is no longer a real or material dialectic but merely a verbal dialectic. A real or material dialectic, Elert says, is one in which there are two opposed possibilities, represented in this case by two kinds of speaking or two types of revelation which though united dialectically are nevertheless exclusive, so that when one speaks the other must remain silent. In Barth, according to Elert, God's act is always one and the same and manifests itself only in a *twofold manner of speaking*. Elert believes that this is an

---

[1] Werner Elert, *Zwischen Gnade und Ungnade* (München: Evangelischer Presseverband für Bayern, 1948), p. 135.

unbiblical distinction. He points to many biblical examples in which stringent and even gruesome acts of divine judgment are carried out. Such acts, Elert says, could not possibly have had *grace* as their content.

Elert thinks Barth's formulation of the law-gospel problem is a result of the attempt in recent "dialectical theology" to restore the proper distance between God and man—the ontic distance between Creator and creature and the noetic distance between divine revelation and human receptivity. In this movement, the essential thing in revelation is not, strictly speaking, *what* God says, but rather the fact *that* God speaks, not *what* man hears, but *that* he hears. The distinction between law and gospel is not, therefore, of ultimate importance, but only the difference between divine speaking and human hearing.[2]

The problem, Elert feels, was only aggravated by the *Kirchenkampf* and no real advance was made. Instead of dealing with the real problem of the nature and the purity of law, which could have led to a proper understanding of the law-gospel dialectic, the debate was carried out over the concept of revelation under the slogan: true versus false, natural versus special or "Word-" revelation. On this basis, Eleft feels, the problem could never be settled.[3] Barth's view of the law as the form of the gospel was the product of this development and is an unsatisfactory attempt at a solution.

Elert also sees in Barth's theology a reinforcement of the Calvinist position which upholds law as the ultimate standard through which man's relation to God is regulated and to which the gospel comes only secondarily as that which serves to fulfill and make the law work. Calvin's gospel, says Elert, was not a way of salvation apart from law, but something which only reinforces that which was hidden in the law, which uncovers what was promised and embodies what was foreshadowed. Gospel differs from law, therefore, only in its clarity of manifestation. Barth's teaching that the law is the form of the gospel Elert finds to be in substantial agreement with this Calvinist point of view. The result is that man's relationship to God is regulated by the law, and the gospel comes off sec-

---

[2] *Ibid.*, p. 133.
[3] *Ibid.*, p. 133.

ond-best as that which makes the law work. The overall result, according to Elert, is a legalized gospel and a picture of the life of faith as a life of obedience rather than Christian freedom.

Elert insists that law and gospel, judgment and grace, and wrath and love must be kept quite separate as divergent and yet real possibilities for man. Faith arises only out of the dialectical opposition of these real possibilities. Each is total, and one is faced with an either-or in which the two possibilities cannot be mixed or subsumed under a higher principle. Under the law, man experiences God's wrath in its ultimate consequences, and no arbitrary or premature escape by means of a theoretical unifying of law and gospel can be permitted. Law and wrath lead to despair. Into this situation the gospel breaks as an absolutely new possibility. It is God's victory, God's act of deliverance. Accepting this deliverance does not mean just accepting a "theological truth" or having a psychological experience; it is made possible only by the creation of faith. And faith is born only when through the divine wrath and judgment all other avenues have been blocked. The law as the instrument of wrath kills; only then can the gospel make alive.[4]

Obviously such a view depends upon a strict separation of law and gospel; it insists that the law can come only *before* the gospel. The order death-life dictates the order law-gospel. Also, in such a view it would make no sense to reintroduce the law in some other use "after" the gospel. Hence Elert rejects a "third use of the law."

It seems quite evident that Elert's demand for a "real" dialectic of wrath and love and of law and gospel has descended from Theodosius Harnack's interpretation of Luther. He insisted, like Harnack, upon the reality of wrath as well as the reality of the gospel. Elert was obviously afraid that making the law merely the form of the gospel unites them in such a way that both lose their reality. For Elert, that would mean that it is not God who acts in this double manner but man who either "misunderstands" or "understands" God's *one* way of acting, his address to man.

I shall not at this point question Elert's interpretation of either Barth or Calvin. It should be pointed out, however, that there seems

---

[4] Werner Elert, *The Structure of Lutheranism*, trans. W. A. Hansen (St. Louis: Concordia Publishing House, 1962), pp. 17-28.

to be considerable confusion surrounding especially the place and definition of law in the "system." Elert had, in effect, accused Barth of the very things which Barth had sought to avoid. Barth has said that it is precisely because law is placed before the gospel that it is misunderstood and made into a legalistic standard to which the gospel comes second. Only when the order is reversed can the law be freed from this misunderstanding. Obviously there is a confusion here which is not cleared up by the opposing formulations.

Elert's own position, certainly, seems extreme and rigid. Helmut Gollwitzer maintains that Elert starts from the false presupposition that wrath, judgment, and punishment must have an eternal law of retribution as their basis in order to have any validity. This would mean that God is wrathful because he is a God of law, and if this is followed to its logical conclusion it would have to mean that the law of retribution is the fundamental standard by which man's relationship to God is regulated, and that it was given before and not after the fall as the original form of man's relationship to God. But this would mean that the original relationship between God and man was not one of love, and therefore that the gospel could not be the reestablishment of that original relationship.[5] But this, in turn, is the very position against which Elert claimed he was fighting. So at this point the argument simply goes in circles; the need for more careful definition is evident.

Helmut Thielicke has also been one of Barth's most outspoken critics.[6] In answer to Barth, Thielicke holds that the sharp distinction between law and gospel must be maintained for several reasons. First, in order to preserve the miracle of the gospel, in which God himself overcomes sin and by his love rescues man from the threat of his holiness and wrath. Second, in order to preserve the historicity *(Geschichtlichkeit)* of the revelation, for without the miracle of the gospel as a contingent act in time, revelation threatens

---

[5] Helmut Gollwitzer, "Zur Einheit von Gesetz und Evangelium," *Antwort,* p. 303.

[6] For what follows see Helmut Thielicke, "Zur Frage Gesetz und Evangelium, eine Auseinandersetzung mit Karl Barth," *Auf dem Grunde der Apostel und Propheten* (Stuttgart: Quell-Verlag der Evang. Gesellschaft, 1948), pp. 173-197. Cited hereafter as *Zur Frage Gesetz und Evangelium.*

to be dissolved into a timeless idea and thus to become a general world-view. Third, because when the attempt is made to order law and gospel under a higher principle or to construct a teleological relationship between holiness and love, both are depotentiated and robbed of their essential nature. Law is depotentiated because it no longer brings total judgment, but is ordered under the *telos* of the gospel; the gospel is depotentiated because it no longer is that which awakes from the dead, since no total judgment has been pronounced. The gospel is only bound in various ways to the fulfillment of the law, in which it either furnishes the necessary power to fulfill the law or gives as a gift the task which man finds impossible to fulfill.

Thielicke's view is that only a strict separation of law and gospel can provide a conceptual scheme which preserves all these things. The miracle of the gospel—its character as pure grace—is lost by confusing law and gospel, because either the law will be understood as gospel or the gospel as law. Law is understood as gospel when one sees in the fact of the law itself the possibility of its being fulfilled; the law then becomes a system which leads to a false security. The gospel in this case becomes merely a means to an end —a help toward fulfilling the law. The gospel, in turn, is made into a law when it is understood as a *form* to be imitated—an *imitatio Christi* to which one *must* adhere. The example of Christ then becomes the *form* for the Christian life. This can only lead to a type of despair, which means that the gospel has lost its character as the miracle of grace. Law and gospel must be kept separate even if this gives the appearance of a dualism, because this conceptual form is necessary to preserve the nature of God as wrath and as love. If the tension between wrath and love is not allowed to stand but is rather resolved in a speculative system, then a type of optimism results, with "der liebe Gott" as the highest value whose "business" it is to forgive.

The same point is expressed in another way, Thielicke says, when one treats the problem in terms of history. If law and gospel are united so that, as Barth says, their content is always grace and nothing but grace, this leads ultimately to an optimistic *Weltanschauung* in which the true historical character of revelation as an event and its relationship to faith is in danger of being lost. For if God's Word has only one content a twofold outcome of the *Heilsgeschichte* is impossible from the start; the one content of the Word of God takes on the aspect of an eternal and timeless truth which possesses validity in and of itself apart from the relationship to the believer. God's action loses its double character as judgment and grace; with this loss, faith and justification become something other than the act of the living and present Christ, who alone through the Spirit brings about the transition from judgment to salvation. The tendency, here, Thielicke says, is toward a monism which obscures the significance of God's act *in history* through Jesus Christ.

Thielicke believes that this danger is at hand in Barth's unification of law and gospel. Ignoring the essential unity in content in law and gospel, Barth obscures the distinction between the Old and New Testament; he unites both under a common principle and thereby loses the real historicity of God's act in Christ.

Thielicke finds this Barthian tendency worked out in its logical consequences in studies like Wilhelm Vischer's *Das Christuszeugnis des Alten Testaments* and Hans Hellbardt's *Abrahams Lüge*. These works maintain, Thielicke says, that the Old Testament can be considered as a source of revelation only if it is a revelation of Jesus Christ (since revelation can have only one content). This means that the difference between the two Testaments is obscured, so that we must read Christ into the Old Testament at the expense of real historical scholarship. The Christ event in the New Testament consequently cannot be an event which brings something really new, a real crisis, a turning point in history, but merely one which reinforces or clarifies what was already present in the Old Testament.

To illustrate his argument, Thielicke points to the view of Vischer and others on the relationship of promise and fulfillment. The Christological content of the Old Testament consists in the fact that Christ was expected. But what is the content of the New Testament? Is it that the promise was fulfilled in a final way so that a "new time," a new *Aeon* dawned? No. The Christ event means that the promise was reinforced. Thielicke cites Vischer's approval of Barth's view:

Not that the kingdom of God has come, but that it has drawn near, is there *after as before* the appearance of Christ the meaning of the Word about the fulness of time . . . not the *presence* of a visible or invisible better world, but the *waiting* for a new heaven and a new earth, now first made necessary and powerful on the basis of the appearance of Christ. There is no other blessedness than just the blessedness in hope. . . . That the promise is fulfilled does not mean that the promise ends and that which is promised takes its place, but rather that the promise becomes completely, perfectly unambiguous and therewith powerful. If anywhere, so faith precisely in the light of the appearance of Christ becomes advent faith, a waiting for coming revelation.[7]

This means, says Thielicke, that both Testaments are subsumed under the same point of view—the expectation of Christ. The content of both is the same, and the New Testament simply reinforces what was less clear in the Old.

The result of all this is for Thielicke that the difference between the Testaments does not imply a radically new stage in the progress of the *Heilsgeschichte*. Thielicke saw this as an adaptation of the Calvinist view that the New Covenant does not differ from the Old in *substance* but only in the *mode* of its administration. One must ask, Thielicke says, in what sense this Barthian construction can speak of a freeing from the law at all.

The history of Christ is nothing other than a renewed, a particularly impressive, as it were, sealed, demonstration of the promise which already exists beforehand, which as such was from the beginning ordered before the law and therefore muted its judgment character. Therefore the gospel (in its nature as fulfillment) does not displace the law in that it frees from its character as curse, but rather the gospel reveals itself as the content of the law in that it establishes its character as promise. Therewith, however, practically and theoretically the temporal succession is dissolved. The once-for-all is eliminated for the sake of a docetic presence of Christ at all stages, a symbolism of the historical incarnation. Christmas becomes only an advent, perhaps a particularly illuminated advent with five can-

---

[7] Thielicke, *Zur Frage Gesetz und Evangelium*, p. 181.

dles, but not the festival of Christ with its turning point of the ages.[8]

The time line, says Thielicke, in which the year one takes a very special place, is "dissolved" *(aufgehoben);* he quotes Hellbardt's actual statement to this effect: "The fact that Jesus appears in the world temporarily after the Old Testament is theologically of secondary importance.[9] Thus, for Thielicke, in place of the word become flesh one finds a "historical docetism, a phantom-like incorporeality." [10]

In summary, the Barthian denial of the antithesis between law and gospel results, according to Thielicke, in a system which threatens the character of the gospel as the miracle of God's grace, threatens the historical nature of revelation, and turns the whole into a timeless idea, a monistic world-view.

It might be objected, Thielicke says further, that such a critique does not take adequate account of the development of Barth's theology, but he discounts this objection. In every phase of Barth's theology, he says, the monistic-timeless tendency remains the same; the emphasis merely comes to rest on different *loci* in different ways. Thielicke does not question the good intent of Barth's theology; but he believes that the conceptual form, which denies the sharp distinction between law and gospel, destroys the attempt to give a true picture of biblical revelation. Barth, he says, has imported a philosophical point of view which tries to understand the whole under one unifying principle. But for Thielicke it is just this possibility which is withdrawn in revelation and faith. The distinction between law and gospel provides a means of recognizing this fact. It is a distinction which remains removed from the realm of conceptual perfection—it is a tension which cannot be removed by any system.

> We are constrained to add: this in principle indisssolubility of the tension rests on the fact that the unity which stands behind it and "resolves" it is unknown. The bracket around the *deus*

---

[8] *Ibid.,* p. 182.

[9] *Ibid.,* p. 183.

[10] *Ibid.,* p. 183.

> *absconditus* and *revelatus*, the *auctor praedestinationis* and
> *evangelii* is invisible to us. Indeed it does not even have to enter
> into the horizon as a theme of our desire to perceive and of our
> speculation. The *verbum Dei quoad nos*—for only this is the
> concern of theological discussion—encounters us only in that
> "dualistic" unfolding. . . . The unity of law and gospel is al-
> ways simply the object of the movement of faith, in which
> the emphasis lies just as much on "movement" as on "faith."
> . . . But whoever makes that unity in a direct sense into a theo-
> logical theme seeks God beyond law and gospel, seeks God "in
> himself" and encounters thereby the illegal distinction between
> the *verbum Dei extrinsece* and *intrinsece*. [11]

The problem in Barth's theology is that he speaks of the Word
of God "in itself" whose essential content is always the same; which
can then be divided into law and gospel in its application to us.
This kind of construction, Thielicke says, is destructive of the true
nature of God's confrontation of man in the Word as law and gospel.
It seeks behind the Word as we know it a hidden unity which man
can "know" rather than believe.

Thus in Thielicke's work we find the same insistence upon the
dialectic of law and gospel we found in Elert, though Thielicke
attempts to draw out more fully the consequences of Barth's denial
of this dialectic. Once again he insists that the dialectic cannot be
resolved prematurely in thought or in conceptual construction.
Thielicke, like Elert, regards law and gospel as two opposite and
real possibilities which cannot be united under any common principle. They correspond also to the possibility of a twofold outcome
of the *Heilsgeschichte* for man—damnation or salvation. These two
possibilities cannot be reconciled speculatively by a theological
system; this would turn it into a timeless monism which would
lead necessarily to universalism. (Thielicke maintains that the
Barthian construction must logically lead to this if it is consistent
and that Barth has simply been ambiguous on this point.) The
only reconciliation possible is in the movement of faith. That there
is a higher unity can only be believed, not anticipated by the system. Simply put, this means that a theological system cannot deliver

---

[11] *Ibid.*, pp. 190-191.

one from the threat of the law and death by a favorable construction; only God can do this by creating faith.

Here again, it seems, the debate has suffered from considerable confusion. It is strange indeed that Barth, who has spoken so much about the miracle of God's grace, should be accused of a theological construction which obscures that miracle. One might well ask if Thielicke has really taken into account all that Barth has said about the nature of the Word of God as that over which God alone has sovereignty. Indeed, when the entire point of Barth's construction is to maintain God's freedom, the entire point of placing gospel before law is to insure that God not be bound by human constructions, it is strange that this should be the very charge made aganst him—a monism which limits God's freedom.

The crucial question which arises out of Thielicke's critique is the question of knowledge. Barth has said that it is only through faith that one can really know the law, because only then is its ultimate unity with God's purpose perceived. Thielicke, on the other hand, maintains that the ultimate unity of law and gospel, wrath and love, etc., can only be maintained by faith in the face of temptation *(Anfechtung);* it cannot be *known* or represented conceptually in the theological system. Barth wants to turn this around and say that only in the act of faith is true knowledge given, so that everything previous to this act is "misunderstanding." The debate at this point revolves around the question of the manner in which one is allowed to theologize. As we shall see, this problem was magnified by the subsequent debate.

Gustaf Wingren especially has pressed the question of knowledge in his critique of Barth's teaching on gospel and law.[12] Wingren believes that Barth, in reaction to the anthropologically centered theology of the nineteenth century, has simply taken over the same framework of this theology but attempted to turn it upside down.[13] This means that the main structural antithesis (God/man) remains the same, and that man's problem is that he lacks knowledge of

---

[12] Gustaf Wingren, *Theology in Conflict,* trans. E. Wahlstrom (Philadelphia: Muhlenberg Press, 1958) and "Evangelium und Gesetz" in *Antwort,* pp. 310-322.

[13] Wingren, *Theology in Conflict,* p. 27.

God. Revelation is then that which gives man the necessary knowledge. Since there can be no proper knowledge of God outside revelation, there can be no knowledge of the law. Law must then be forced into Barth's framework.

Wingren believes that Barth's position is a distortion of the biblical point of view. According to the Bible man's problem is not lack of knowledge but guilt. Man knows to a certain extent what is expected of him, and he realizes that he has failed to meet these expectations. What he needs is not knowledge, but justification. The biblical account does not center on the problem of the knowledge of God but on the *acts* of God in redemption, in rescuing man from the hostile forces which are arrayed against him. These hostile forces, Wingren says, are absent from Barth's theology, leaving the main problem merely that of knowledge. Wingren believes, therefore, in spite of all assertions to the contrary, that the center of Barth's theology is *man and his question* rather than God and his acts. This means that the Word of God is "imprisoned in an anthropology that is constructed independently of the Word of scripture," and that God loses his freedom.[14]

The fundamental mistake, Wingren seems to be saying, is to construe law as though it were supposed to be a source of knowledge about God rather than a government of this world which makes men aware of their guilt. This means that one becomes unduly preoccupied with the question of the clarity and correctness of this knowledge. Since knowledge is the way of salvation, law is an agency of salvation.[15] This results in the tendency to interpret gospel as law and law as gospel and to turn the whole into guidance for a certain political order or a social program. This is the manner in which the law takes its revenge when it is not properly placed in the theological structure. "When it is driven out from its proper and relatively modest place, where it is to be overcome by the gospel, it returns in another form. But now it aspires to enter the holy of holies, to overcome the gospel itself and to make the gospel its servant." [16] For Wingren this can be avoided only when

---

[14] *Ibid.*, p. 40.

[15] *Ibid.*, p. 43.

[16] *Ibid.*, p. 126.

the law and gospel are kept strictly separate and related dialectically, so that the gospel brings freedom from the law and not
merely knowledge about God.

Wingren insists that Barth's attempt to reverse the law-gospel
order and to make the law the form of the gospel runs the risk of
turning the gospel into mere information—knowledge about God—
which means that it is made into a new law. He accuses Barth of
committing those very errors which he is most concerned to avoid—
limiting the freedom of God and legalizing the gospel. Here again
we must ask whether there is not some basic confusion which makes
understanding difficult if not impossible.

A critique of a more profound nature can be found in Hans
Iwand's essay, "Jenseits von Gesetz und Evangelium?" [17] Written
in 1935 as a critical review of the first volume of the *Church Dogmatics,* it actually appeared before Barth's essay on gospel and
law. Nevertheless it anticipates that argument from a reading of
the *Church Dogmatics.* Iwand saw in the distinction which Barth
made between the Word of God and the word of man an attempt
to construct a doctrine of the Word of God which does more than
simply defend itself against nineteenth century immanentism. This
doctrine actually raises itself to the level of an "article of the stand-
ing or falling church" which threatens to displace the doctrine of
justification and the distinction between law and gospel which
accompanies it. Iwand saw this as an attempt to construct a doctrine of the Word of God which is "beyond law and gospel," one
which would undercut the certainty of faith.

The sharp distinction between the Word of God and the word
of man, Iwand maintained, reflected Barth's extreme reluctance
to allow a close union between the divine and the human word—
which leads to questioning the incarnation of the Word. To be sure,
Iwand said, the Word of God for Barth takes on a worldly form, it
becomes real for us in certain forms, it becomes earthly *(welthaft).*
But what is the relationship between the worldly form and the
Word of God? If this is not carefully defined, it would simply mean
that the Word of God becomes confused with the word of man.

---

[17] Hans Joachim Iwand, *Um den Rechten Glauben* (München: Chr. Kaiser
Verlag, 1959), pp. 97-109.

To avoid this, Barth was forced to make a distinction between the Word of God "in itself" (intrinsece), and the Word of God in earthly form (extrinsece). Behind the earthly forms of the Word of God (revelation, scripture, proclamation) is the Word of God in itself, the unapproachable divine "what" (Was). The earthly form of the Word of God is the human reflection (Spiegelbild) of the Word, which is in itself not available to us. Because of this, the revelation which is available to us is never completely transparent but always wreathed in a certain ambiguity.

Iwand attacked this formulation. He said that Barth's starting from the antithesis Word of God—word of man leads to a further distinction between the Word of God intrinsece and extrinsece which, Iwand believed, threatens the certainty of faith. It is not, Iwand said, entirely illegitimate to make this kind of distinction in theology, but when it is made, it must be subordinated to the distinction between law and gospel and to the doctrine of justification. It is not correct, first of all, to say that the Word of God merely assumes worldly form or becomes welthaft. Coupled with the distinction intrinsece and extrinsece this means that the Word of God intrinsece becomes the real object of our concern and our theologizing. But since this Word assumes earthly forms which are only human reflections and never completely transparent, one has introduced a distinction between a phenomenal and a noumenal mode of existence of the Word of God which makes the certainty of faith questionable.

Consequently these distinctions in the forms of the Word must be subordinated to the distinction between law and gospel and the doctrine of justification. Contrary to Barth's position, Iwand pointed out that it is precisely the humanity of the Word, the incarnation of the Word, which is the basis for certainty in salvation. God "in himself," as Luther put it, is the hidden God, the "devouring fire," about whom nothing certain can be known by sinful man. But God incarnate rescues men from this uncertainty and establishes faith on sure footing. Hence, said Iwand, it is the Word of God extrinsece which is the object of our concern, the source of assurance, and the basis for our theologizing. It is not correct to designate the Word of God intrinsece as a real Word and to say that the Word of God *extrinsece* is only a reflection of that inner Word. In so doing, one seeks a Word of God beyond law and gospel, the *logos* of the philosophers. The knowledge of the nature of the Word of God, Iwand said, can only come from the actual confrontation with Christ and not from a theological construction which seeks to penetrate behind that confrontation. One has life or death only as one hears the Word of Jesus Christ, not as one inquires about the essence of the Word of God in itself behind that hearing of the Word. In the encounter with Christ one hears either judgment or grace, and indeed, both at once:

> No one can hear God without hearing both. In this battle between faith and doubt, grace and sin, life and death, we are concerned in fact no longer with the distinction between man's word and God's Word, but with the impotence of the ordinary word of man, the human word that draws its understanding out of reason and the conscience, and with the authority of another Word which is also a human Word and yet dares to oppose that divine Word that condemns us. For when the condemnation of God meets us in his Word, we can do nothing other than acknowledge it.[18]

For Iwand, the distinction between Word of God and word of man cannot be made as Barth tries to make it. This is so because man never experiences the Word of God other than as a word of man; he knows it only as a seemingly nonsensical and irrelevant human speech about God. But that in itself is precisely man's judgment. If it occurs, then—as it did in the nineteenth century—that the Word of God becomes twisted and dimmed, this proclamation is not merely nothing, not merely a misunderstood word, "it is in fact the judgment, which this fallen church must carry out on itself and the world in its proclamation, it is the voice of God becoming audible in the speech of the church, on which this church itself must die." [19]

One cannot, Iwand said, reach the Word of God "in itself" merely by making dogmatic distinctions. Every word which reaches us is a "human word" and makes contact with us merely because we

---

[18] Iwand, *Um den Rechten Glauben,* p. 103.
[19] *Ibid.,* p. 104.

have ears to hear—it is speech from man to man. But it is only when I hear this word as a judgment which I accept that I can also hear it as grace. This is true because God emptied himself, the Word became flesh—really entered into human existence—not because behind the human word I can hear, however dimly, the Word of God "in itself." It is precisely because the Word really became flesh that in it the Word of God and the word of man became one in the event of revelation.

> The separation of the *verbum Dei intrinsece* and the *verbum Dei extrinsece* is not something that lies in the nature of the Word of God itself, but becomes an event at that point where God traps man in his own pride and foolishness. But where the Word of God becomes the judging Word and man comes under this judgment so that he understands himself in no other way than from this judgment which is pronounced on him, there the *verbum Dei extrinsece*—as the written and spoken human word—becomes the *verbum Dei intrinsece*. There God goes "out of himself" and man goes "into God" and this coincidence of the Word of God in its internality and externality is the certainty of faith. The distinction between human word and divine Word made by unfaith is then over, faith can no longer distinguish between them. To faith they have become one.[20]

Hence for Iwand the distinction between law and gospel is primary to all other distinctions—Word of God—word of man, *intrinsece* and *extrinsece*. This is so because God's Word does not encounter us in any other way than as a human word. This is the meaning of incarnation. But the very fact that it is a human word first is judgment. The Word encounters us first as law, as that which judges; only then, when this judgment is acknowledged, does this word of judgment become gospel.

The movement is incarnational. It is only in and through the human Word that one hears the Word of God. It is not that behind the human form one now perceives somehow the Word of God "in itself." The certainty of faith rests upon this incarnational movement. One must first experience the Word as law and as gospel. No

---

[20] *Ibid.*, p. 107.

dogmatic construction can anticipate or avoid this experience. The Word of God is not available to man "beyond law and gospel."

Iwand's critique touches one of the crucial questions of the debate—the question of theological method and the manner in which the distinction of Word of God—word of man affects the relationship of law and gospel. Iwand's charge is that Barth's method, his *fides quaerens intellectum,* has led him to attempt to reason from a word *extrinsece* to a word *intrinsece,* and that this attempt destroys the certainty of faith. Note again that Barth is accused of the very thing which he attempts to avoid. The purpose of his method and the consequent distinction between the word *intrinsece* and *extrinsece* is to assert that the inmost being of God is in fact grace, even though *extrinsece* his Word may (indeed must) take the form of judgment.

One of the reasons why Barth does this is to avoid the suspicion left in the thought of the reformers of a God who is "in himself" a devouring fire of wrath from which grace comes as a means of rescue—but only subsequently. The purpose of the construction in Barth is to make grace paramount and thus, supposedly, to strengthen the assurance of faith. Here again it would seem that there is some kind of basic misunderstanding which frustrates the real progress of the debate.

The reconstruction in social ethics which Barth has attempted on the basis of his reversal of the law-gospel order has likewise not escaped critical question. In his essay "The Christian Community and the Civil Community" [21] Barth describes how one is to derive concrete recommendations for the ordering of political and social life from revelation. The Christian community and the civil community are to be ordered as concentric spheres; one is to make recommendations for the political order (the outer sphere) by drawing analogies from the inner sphere, the Christian community. Through this method, Barth says, definite political tendencies take shape: because God becomes man and our neighbor, the state must be concerned about man and not abstractions like capital, state, national honor, etc. Because the Christian community witnesses to

---

[21] Barth, *Community, State and Church,* pp. 149-189.

divine justification, the state must be concerned about justice. Because the Son of Man seeks the lost, the state must be concerned about the weak and downtrodden. Because the Christian community sees all men as equal under one Lord, so there must be equality and freedom, and so on.

Several questions have been raised about this procedure of Barth's.[22] For our purposes, the most important objection is centered on the use Barth makes of analogy. Are the concrete prescriptions which Barth makes really analytical judgments? Do they really follow necessarily from revelation, or are they rather synthetic, that is, judgments of faith on an already given historical reality? As Heinz-Horst Schrey points out, political conclusions of widely differing sorts have been drawn through the use of analogy throughout history. Eusebuis, for instance, argued for the monarchy of Constantine because it was analogous to the monarchy of God. Both armed conflict and pacifism have likewise been justified by the same method. Examples can be multiplied in which the method has been used to justify diametrically opposing systems. It has been remarked that Barth did little more than to justify the present-day democracy of Switzerland by his use of analogy.

Barth has admitted that his results coincide with much natural law thought,[23] but he takes this merely as a sign that the *polis* is in the kingdom of Jesus Christ even when its office holders are not aware of it or refuse to admit it. In this case, Barth says, there is all the more reason why the church cannot and must not withhold its witness to a proper insight.[24]

But this clarification only makes the question more persistent. Is Barth's use of analogy really what he claims it to be, or is it not rather merely giving theological sanction to what has in fact developed in history? Is the revelation actually the source of the order thus established? As Schrey put it, does revelation ontically establish justice, or is it merely a noetic act in which the justice already present is known according to its essence, origin, and meaning? If

---

[22] See Heinz-Horst Schrey, "Die Wiedergeburt des Naturrechts," *Theologische Rundschau,* Vol. 19, No. 3, 1951, p. 199.

[23] Barth, *Community, State and Church,* p. 180.

[24] *Ibid.,* p. 181.

the latter is the case, wherein lies the critical function of revelation? It is extremely difficult, it would seem, to draw concrete prescriptions for the political order from Barth's view of revelation with any degree of assurance. For this reason, it is difficult to see how one can enter into a fruitful discussion with secular ethics; since the law is the "concrete form" of the gospel at a given moment, not a general command or principle available to all men, it is difficult to find a common basis for the discussion of ethical questions with the secular world.

Thus the debate over Barth's reformulation of the law-gospel problem has not been very satisfying. If anything, the confusion only seems to have increased and resulted in a stalemate. Nor is this one of those instances in which Barth has altered his position with time. In a later volume of the *Church Dogmatics* Barth reasserts his original position on gospel and law and insists that this belongs to the bedrock *(eisernen Bestand)* of his dogmatic.[25] He concedes that this does not necessarily mean that he is right, but it does mean that he is not convinced by his critics that he is wrong. "Too much," Barth says, "in the differing and opposed meaning and function of law and gospel in these authors is afterwards as before still completely unclear.[26]

Barth lists the points which he does not understand. First, he says, he cannot understand what biblical basis or which Christology could allow one to speak of two differing and opposed Words of God; second, he cannot grasp a concept of the gospel which could allow it to be exhausted in pure internal receptivity, or a concept of law as abstract demand which could on the one hand be mere external order and on the other be determinative in accusing man and preparing him for the gospel. Third, he does not see how one could ascribe to St. Paul a concept of divine law which runs contrary to the Old Testament view of the positive relation of law and covenant as evidenced by contemporary Old Testament scholarship (Noth, v. Rad, Kraus, etc.). Fourth, he says he cannot understand how one can arrive at such a concept of law without recourse to the idea of "natural law" and thus to a general revelation or a naive

[25] Barth, *Church Dogmatics,* IV, 3, pp. 427-428.
[26] *Ibid.,* p. 427.

Biblicism, with the fateful consequences which such things have for theology. Finally, he says, he does not understand how such an alleged "law" could result in a serious, precise, and inescapable knowledge of man's transgression, how it could be said to have God's authority and power to bring man into judgment, and thereby bring him to the knowledge of the gospel.[27]

There is no doubt justification for Barth's complaint. Barth's critics, at least in what we have seen so far, have not clarified some of the critical issues. It has not, for instance, been made clear how the concept of law espoused by a law-gospel rather than a gospel-law order differs from that of natural law idea of the sixteenth and seventeenth centuries. It has not been made clear how one is protected from the same difficulties the theologies of those centuries encountered (especially in relation to the root problems of history and atonement), as we saw in previous chapters. Barth is perfectly justified in asking for just such clarification. This bears out my contention that considerable confusion reigns and that the problem must be clarified against the background of its history before any real advance can be made. As we have shown, the law-gospel problem has undergone a kind of willy-nilly evolution in connection with the discussion of other problems; it has not received the kind of specific attention which could clarify its status. Barth, therefore, is justified to a certain extent in saying that he does not "understand" what his critics mean.

At the same time, however, it must be asked if Barth has really answered the questions of his critics. The basic question which they have asked has to do with the relationship of the law-gospel dialectic to the theological system which evolves from it. As Iwand put it, it appears that Barth seeks a Word of God "in itself" beyond law and gospel. Barth's critics are asking if such a Word is in fact available to man. In seeking such a Word Barth attempts to go beyond or behind the historical event with its double character as judgment and grace in order to reach the suprahistorical unity of God "in himself." In the process one discovers, according to Barth, that all the antinomies of existence have already been overcome in

---

[27] *Ibid.*, pp. 427-428.

the life of God and, indeed, that they have been posited in order to be overcome to the greater glory of God's grace. This means, Barth's opponents claim, that one is left with a system which is constantly in danger of being reduced to a timeless and universalistic world-view. This is the logical outcome of Barth's attempt to reverse the law-gospel order and to make the law the form of the gospel.

This is a serious charge, for it implies that Barth is guilty of a kind of thinking about law and gospel which runs counter to his own expressed intention. His obvious intention, we have seen, is to assure the eschatological act character of revelation by making the law the form of the gospel as it encounters man in the event of revelation. Indeed, for Barth revelation is so exclusively an "event" —so "new"—that it cannot be thought about in ordinary terms at all. The law which it brings must be distinguished absolutely from all other types of law, just as the gospel which it brings is entirely new.

This leads to the difficult question of how one is to think theologically about this new event—how one can say anything at all about this radically "other" Word of God. It cannot be spoken of, obviously, as the deliverance of certain infallible propositions as in orthodoxy. Nor can one speak of it in terms of practical and moral religion as Ritschl did. These were attempts to understand revelation in terms of man's systems of truth. Then, too, Barth eventually rejected the temptation coming from existentialism to speak of revelation only in terms of its "negative imprint" on man, for this also results only in "anthropology." Barth has chosen instead a *fides quaerens intellectum* after the manner of Anselm—a "thinking into" the event of revelation itself—as the only proper kind of thinking.

But this is where the difficulty arises in Barth's system. The act character of revelation depends upon the dialectical confrontation by the Word of God in its veiling and unveiling—law and gospel. Barth said earlier that this cannot be a matter of constructing a synthesis, nor even of a thinking of that synthesis as having taken place, but rather a "seeking and finding it in God." But if this "seeking and finding it in God" means that one discovers that all the antitheses were posed only to be overcome to the greater glory of God's grace, then the question is whether the original dialectic is not in fact seen through. "Thinking into" the event of revelation appears to lead Barth to a kind of undialectical theology of the "new age." There is no longer any way to speak theologically about the "old age" at all, for it has no real relevance. The "old age" simply falls away. When this happens, the dialectic is lost.

Perhaps this gives deeper insight into the complexity of the debate over law and gospel. It leads to basic questions about how one thinks theologically—questions to which I shall return in the two final chapters. For the moment the important thing is to note the Lutheran question to Barth: Does conceiving of law as the form of the gospel lead to a system which eventually loses the dialectic of judgment and grace? If this is so, Barth's opponents contend, theology will have to use a different approach.

Gerhard Ebeling perhaps more than anyone else has attempted to get at the real problem.[28] He has pointed out that it is quite evident in the contemporary debate that we have to do with differing uses of the concept of law.[29] This could mean, he says, one of two things. Either the difference is merely terminological, in which case one would merely have to take note of the differences and make the necessary adjustments, or it could mean that the differences are symptomatic of a much deeper difference in the entire method of theologizing. It is this latter which Ebeling thinks is the case, so that for him it is not enough merely to debate on the level of terminology.

This means, for instance, that the problem cannot be solved, as many biblical scholars assume, merely by exegetical analysis of the use of the word "law" in the Old and New Testaments. What is involved rather is the very difficult problem of the development of theological concepts in which one must consider both the history of conceptual usage and the thing itself which one wants to convey by means of the concepts.[30] It is therefore impossible for systematic theology simply to capitulate to biblical philology, especially in the

---

[28] Gerhard Ebeling, *Wort und Glaube* (Tübingen: J. C. B. Mohr (Paul Siebeck), 1960).

[29] Gerhard Ebeling, "Erwägung zur Lehre vom Gesetz," *Wort und Glaube* (Tübingen: J. C. B. Mohr (Paul Siebeck), 1960), pp. 255-261.

[30] Ebeling, *Wort und Glaube*, p. 256.

case of a concept like law, for two reasons. First, the biblical usage itself is not consistent; there is no such thing as *the* biblical concept of law. Second, the concept of law is bound to a history, which means it may have to be used differently today to convey what the text originally intended.[31] It is the task of systematic theology, Ebeling has said, to take account of the manifold character of the history of language and to work through this history to express clearly the reality inherent in the Christian proclamation.[32]

For Ebeling, it is not enough merely to point out that the Old Testament concept of Torah was much richer than its post-exilic corruptions, or that Paul must have misunderstood the Old Testament, or that Luther misunderstood Paul, etc. Interesting and valuable as such insights may be in themselves, they do not solve the systematic problem. It simply is not the case, as H. J. Kraus says, for instance, that the results of Old Testament exegesis must now be accepted by the systematicians to the advantage of the "gospel-law" order.[33] One cannot draw this kind of systematic conclusion from mere historical exegesis. One must go on to ask some systematic questions. One must ask whether the Old Testament exegete does not operate, as seems all too often to be the case, with a systematic conception of the *Heilsgeschichte* like Hofmann's which predetermines his answer. By the same token, one must ask if Barth, for instance, is justified in pointing to Old Testament exegesis to support his case when it becomes evident that he is using the term law in a very different sense. What is involved here is the systematic question, the question of how one can understand and use the concepts of law and gospel so as to convey adequately the eschatological proclamation of the Bible *today*. This systematic question cannot be settled simply by historical exegesis.

The real problem, therefore, is a systematic one which must be solved not by philology but only by taking careful note of the historical evolution of the concepts involved and then asking whether the concepts as they are used against this background actually serve the eschatological proclamation of the gospel.

---

[31] *Ibid.*, pp. 259-260.
[32] *Ibid.*, p. 261.
[33] *Ibid.*, p. 275.

It is this kind of historical evolution I have been attempting to trace in this study. Barth stands, I have asserted, at the end of a line of development in which law has been increasingly restricted until it becomes the form of the gospel in the event of revelation. The question which arises is whether this restriction of the concept of the law and the subsequent reversal of the law-gospel order really does service to the eschatological nature of the gospel. This is the question which Barth's critics have asked.

Is it proper to conceive of the law as the form of the gospel, and is it possible to reverse the law-gospel order? The critical point in Barth's construction here is his discussion of the "misunderstood" and the "properly understood" law. Barth argues that all law "prior" to the gospel is "misunderstood" law and that only in the light of its unity with gospel is it properly understood. But it must be asked if Barth is not hedging somewhat in his discussion. Barth admits that this "misunderstanding" is a result of the fact that God gives us his law "nevertheless," even though we are sinners. This "misunderstood" law "nevertheless" remains God's law; it becomes the instrument of his wrath which destroys the sinner. In his essay on "Gospel and Law" Barth says that when the "misunderstood" law has thus destroyed man as sinner, the gospel operates "fully for the first time" as "the really glad tidings for sinners." Here, Barth admits, is the sense in which the order law-gospel is legitimate; here it follows the order death-life.[34]

Thus there seems to be a sense in which one must speak of a law-gospel order. If it is true that only after the law has destroyed the sinner does the gospel operate "fully" as the "really glad tidings," then it would seem that this is much more important than Barth wants to admit in his system. Yet as far as I can see, Barth nowhere makes use of this fact in the *Church Dogmatics*. Barth simply goes on to say in his essay that this kind of law-gospel order is entirely unintelligible to us as an order. He says it can "only be *event* and *fact* and we of ourselves believe it only as the promise of what Jesus Christ does for us, and our belief will be a source of amazement to us.[35] With that, it seems, he dismisses it from

---

[34] Above, pp. 141f.
[35] Barth, *Gospel and Law*, p. 97.

further consideration. It is the "misunderstood" law, Barth says, which was rightly called the great antagonist of the gospel; this must be displaced entirely by the gospel. But this is not the true law, and it is a mark of our sin that we "do not hear the gospel in the law." [36]

This is the point at which the decisive question can be raised. Is it really correct to pose the question as one of misunderstanding versus understanding? How does man get beyond the situation of sin to see that law and gospel form a self-evident unity? Do we really understand the law differently after faith? Are we able to transcend that situation in which sin prevents us from hearing the gospel in the law merely by an act of understanding? Or is it rather the case that as sinners we do in fact *understand* the law, at least to some extent, but because of sin we overestimate our powers and *misuse* the law as a means of self-justification? Do we not by revelation become aware of the real depth of sin and through grace learn the proper *use* of the law? Do we not learn that law is not a way of salvation but rather that it has its function *prior* to the gospel and comes to its *end* in the gospel? If this is the case, then we must say that it is only in the act of faith that the law comes to its end, and therefore that faith puts the law in its proper place—that is, gives us insight into the proper *use* of the law.

This is a subtle but important distinction. For Barth the transition is from a misunderstood and misused law to an understood unity of gospel and law. The former law is rejected on the basis of a new understanding. In the latter view, in contrast, law is understood but misused. The transition is from law to gospel by faith, through which one learns the proper *use* of the law. The law, which man as sinner has in common with all mankind, is not rejected or dismissed but remains *in use*, as that which orders life and is a threat to man as sinner if he "loses faith." Man in this life can never transcend the situation of being a sinner; he can keep the law in proper perspective only through faith, and not by "sight." In this view law is excluded because it reaches its *telos* in faith. This faith, however, does not translate man to a realm where he has a new

---

[36] *Ibid.*, p. 95.

type of "understanding" beyond the dialectic of law and gospel; faith does not separate a man from the rest of mankind in this manner. Instead, faith affirms man's solidarity with mankind and assists him to put the law in proper perspective. In this view it is impossible to reverse the law-gospel order; such a possibility simply is not open to man as a sinner. And this disagreement is more than a strife about mere words; it reflects the basic manner in which one theologizes. As Ebeling has put it:

> It is a fundamentally different way of doing theology if one reasons from a standpoint where law and gospel form a self-evident unity rather than from a standpoint where this unity can be maintained only in the face of anxiety (Anfechtung). In these two instances, quite obviously, the concept of law will then be very differently defined.[37]

But what is this basically different way of theologizing, and how is it related to the concept of law? In order to answer this question we must look more closely at the kind of law-gospel dialectic which has resulted from the argument about Luther's theology. This is the concern of the next chapter.

---

[37] Ebeling, *Wort und Glaube*, p. 281. (Eng. Trans., *Word and Faith*, p. 270.)

CHAPTER XI

THE INTERPRETATION OF LAW BY LUTHERANS: GOSPEL AS THE END OF THE LAW

The current interpretation of law among Lutheran theologians is a result, mainly, of Luther research. Since the debate began with an argument about Luther's theology, this is a quite natural development. The argument, of course, is still continuing, since Luther interpreters do not all agree. It need not be our purpose here to discuss all the variant interpretations; many of them reflect positions we have already encountered in the course of the debate. Rather I shall select some representative interpreters who seem to me to set forth a definite advance in the debate about law. My main interest is in those men who claim to find in Luther an interpretation of law which runs counter to the interpretation we have found in the development from Hofmann through Ritschl to Barth. My concern here will be to point out a general development without dwelling on individual differences which may exist between these interpreters.

Perhaps the best place to begin is with the problem of Luther's relationship to orthodox Lutheranism, since this has been one of the major questions throughout the discussion. Clarification of this issue would also help to answer Barth's question of how the concept of law espoused by his Lutheran critics differs from the "natural law" he finds so destructive.

The Finnish Reformation scholar Lauri Haikola has devoted considerable attention to this question; his work represents the fruit of much contemporary Luther research, especially that done by Swedish scholars.[1] Haikola finds that the major difference between Luther and later orthodoxy lies precisely in the understanding of law.[2] In later Lutheran orthodoxy law was understood as an eternal, objective order, a *lex aeterna*, which described the ideal to which human life must aspire.[3] Law in this sense was defined as an objective scheme of demands and prohibitions which must be fulfilled. Since law was understood in this way, it was quite easy to conceive of the atonement as a substitutionary fulfillment, provided one did not press the logic too far.

Luther, on the other hand, says Haikola, understood law quite differently.[4] The proper relationship between man and God could not, in Luther's view, be understood in terms of an objective legal order. Luther's view, Haikola says, is quite different from the *lex aeterna* doctrine of later orthodoxy, even though Luther does on occasion use the term.[5] At no time, according to Luther, does man possess full knowledge of the divine will, but only a knowledge of the law appropriate to his actual historical situation. This is true both of man in his original state and in his fallen state. The prohibition of eating from the tree of knowledge, for instance, Luther takes as an indication that God has not revealed his absolute will to

---

[1] Laurel Haikola, *Gesetz und Evangelium bei M. Flacius* (Lund: C. W. K. Gleerup, 1952). *Studien zu Luther und zum Luthertum* ("Uppsala Universitets Aarsskrift," No. 2, 1958; Uppsala: A. B. Lundquistika Bokhandeln, 1958), cited hereafter as *Studien; Usus Legis* (Uppsala Universitets Aarsskrift, No. 3, 1958 Uppsala, A.-B. Lundquistika Bokhandeln, 1958).

[2] Haikola, *Studien*, pp. 9-12, 106-107.

[3] *Ibid.*, p. 9.

[4] *Ibid.*, p. 10 ff.

[5] Haikola points here to Heckel's study, *Lex Charitatis,* where it is maintained that the term *lex aeterna* means something quite different for Luther than it did for Aquinas. Haikola, *Studien*, p. 10, n. 8. Heckel says that for Luther divine law is in itself, to be sure, unchangeable and eternal, but in its working upon man it alters itself incessantly depending upon man's relationship to God at the moment and consequently appears as the most changeable thing conceivable. Johannes Heckel, *Lex Charitatis* ("Abhandlungen der Bayrischen Akademie der Wissenschaften." *Neue Folge,* Heft 36; München: Verlag der Bayrischen Akademie der Wissenschaften, 1953), p. 54.

man even in paradise. The will of God is not made known to man in once-for-all fashion, least of all can man capture this will in the form of eternal principles. Rather man must learn to know God's will anew in each new situation. God's command and God's continuing creation belong together. Law remains, in view of its potentially changing appearance, in a certain sense hidden. Its content will depend upon the concrete situation in creation at a given time; man cannot have it in the form of eternal principles in advance of any concrete situation.[6]

This means that for Luther law does not constitute, as it does for orthodoxy, a fixed scheme according to which God and his revelation can be "figured out." Rather law is a term for the manner in which the divine will confronts sinful man in his existence, in every concrete situation. Gerhard Ebeling concurs with Haikola:

> For Luther, law is not a revealed statutory norm to which man relates himself thus and so, but law is an existential category in which the entire theological interpretation of man's actual existence is comprehended. Law is not therefore an idea or a collection of propositions but the reality of fallen humanity.[7]

Law, according to this interpretation of Luther, is to be understood in terms of its immediate effect upon sinful man. Theologically, this means that it is understood as that which attacks and accuses man in his self-sufficiency. This means that law, for Luther, cannot be *identified* with any set of propositions or prescriptions, be it the decalogue or any other code. Law is *anything* which frightens and accuses "the conscience." The bolt of lightning, the rustling of a dry leaf on a dark night, the decalogue, the "natural law" of the philosopher, or even (or perhaps most particularly) the preaching of the cross itself—all or any of these can and do become the voice of the law.[8]

This means in relation to the discussion with Barth that it would be quite impossible to reverse the law-gospel order, or to penetrate

---

[6] Haikola, *Studien*, p. 12.

[7] Ebeling, *Wort und Glaube*, p. 65. (E.T. p. 75).

[8] See Ebeling, *Wort und Glaube*, pp. 288-291 (E.T. pp. 276-279). Cf. Rost, *Lutherischer Rundblick*, IX, No. 1, n. 29a, pp. 15-16.

beyond it to some kind of self-evident unity. Law cannot be dismissed simply as something "misunderstood" or erased, as one erases a code or group of propositions. Such attempts are purely theoretical exercises which may remove certain laws but which do not and cannot remove *the* law as Luther defined it. It is impossible to dispose of *the* law in that manner because the law is an existential category. It designates the manner in which God confronts sinful man in judgment. This confrontation in judgment must always and necessarily *precede* the gospel.

This argument can be illustrated by a significant passage from Luther's "*Wider die Antinomer.*" [9] The Antinomians of Luther's time, like Ritschl, insisted that repentance arises from the gospel; from this they drew the conclusion that the law should be removed from preaching. This affords an interesting parallel to the contemporary argument because here Luther is forced to define more carefully the place and function of the law. Whereas against the Roman Catholic position he argued against the law, here he had to argue for it. The manner in which he did this is very significant. To those who attempt to remove the law from preaching he replied:

> . . . Who would know what Christ is and why Christ suffered for us if no one knew what sin or law was? Therefore the law must be preached if one wants to preach Christ, even if one refuses to call the law by name. For the conscience will nevertheless be frightened by the law when the sermon declares that Christ had so dearly to fulfill the law for us. Why then should one want to remove it *when it cannot be removed, indeed, when it is even more deeply entrenched through the removal?* For the law terrifies even more frightfully when I hear that Christ, God's Son, had to bear it for me, than if it were preached to me outside of Christ merely as a threat without such great torture of the Son of God. [10]

---

[9] The writings of Luther against the Antinomians represent an important and relatively untapped source for Luther's view of the law. Ebeling has apparently recognized this and has promised a study of the disputes (*Wort und Glaube*, note 64, p. 65, also p. 68), but to my knowledge it has not yet appeared.

[10] H. H. Börcherdt and George Merz (eds.), *Martin Luther, Ausgewählte Werke* (München: Chr. Kaiser Verlag, 1957), IV, p. 196 (italics mine). Cited hereafter as *München Ausgabe*.

Here it is quite apparent that when Luther speaks of law, he does not mean merely a *code of laws,* but rather that which terrifies the conscience. The statement that Christ by his death fulfilled the law —a statement which ordinarily would be considered gospel—here is accorded the function of law because it threatens the sinner in his self-sufficiency. Law, in this sense, is not something which can be removed or placed after the gospel by some sort of theoretical rearrangement. Law will do its work first, prior to the gospel, regardless of what men may attempt to do with it in their theologies.

Those who attempt to get rid of the law by a theoretical construction, Luther says, ". . . do nothing more than throw out these poor letters, 'L-A-W,' but nevertheless establish the wrath of God which is indicated and understood through these letters . . ." [11] To speak about law means not merely to speak about it ". . . technically or materially . . . or grammatically . . . , but as it is and sounds in your heart, exhorting, piercing the heart and the conscience until you do not know where to turn." [12] Law is a power which threatens man because of sin, and remains a power until death. The following theses from Luther's disputes against the Antinomians point this out clearly:

1. The law has dominion over man as long as he lives.

2. But he is freed from the law when he dies.

3. Necessarily, therefore, man must die if he would be freed from the law.

. . . .

7. These three, law, sin and death, are inseparable.[13]

The "end" of the law, consequently, comes only in the death of the sinner in Christ and in participation in his resurrection:

10. Indeed, in Christ the law is fulfilled, sin abolished and death destroyed.

11. That is, when through faith we are crucified and have died

---

[11] Luther, *München Ausgabe,* IV, p. 198.

[12] *D. Martin Luthers Werke* (Weimar: Hermann Böhlaus Nachfolger, 1926), Vol. 39, 1:455. Cited hereafter as *WA.*

[13] *WA,* 39, 1:354.

in Christ, such things [law fulfilled, sin abolished, death destroyed] are also true in us.

. . . .

36. To one raised in Christ there is certainly no more sin, no death, no law—things to which he was subject while living.

. . . .

40. Now, in so far as Christ is raised in us, in so far are we without law, sin and death.[14]

It is therefore impossible to remove the law by some sort of "theological erasure":

14. Necessarily, therefore, in as far as they are under death, they are still also under the law and sin.

15. They are altogether ignorant and deceivers of souls who endeavor to abolish the law from the Church.

16. For that is not only stupid and impious, but *absolutely impossible*.

17. For if you want to remove the law, it is necessary at the same time to remove sin and death.[15]

The question which arises at this point is one which we have already encountered in Theodosius Harnack's interpretation of Luther. What Haikola, Ebeling, and others point to as the existential character of the law Harnack would have referred to as the "office" of the law in relation to sinful man. But is there not also a sense in which Luther speaks of the eternal "essence" of the law, the unchanging content of the divine will, as Harnack maintained? This question, to my knowledge, has not really been answered satisfactorily.

Closely related is the problem of the "third use" of the law. The idea of law as an eternal ideal and the "third use" of the law go hand in hand. For if the law is the eternal ideal, it stands to reason that this must be man's guide even after justification. If the foregoing analysis is correct, however, it would seem that law can

---

[14] WA, 39, 1:355-56.

[15] WA, 39, 1:354.

never be taken merely as an abstract ideal which man can isolate and fix in his "system." Taken in its absolute seriousness, law is always an accuser from which man cannot escape on his own. It is always law in this existential sense which concerns Luther. What he seeks is *actual* deliverance from the threat of the law.

In the face of the concrete existential situation, the question about a distinction between essence and office is beside the point. The point is that "under the law" man cannot escape the accusation; the "essence of the law" for the sinner is that it always accuses. The sinner cannot dispose of the law by making theoretical distinctions. He cannot "break through" by means of some theoretical tour de force to a position where he can recognize an abstract will of God which does not threaten him. The problem is not that of a distinction between essence and office, but whether a man hears the will of God as law or as gospel. The will of God is indeed eternal, but the question is how man as sinner hears the will of God as it confronts him in the Word. For man "under the law" a distinction between essence and office is impossible, and for man "under the gospel" it is unnecessary.

This conclusion can be documented by some further passages from the disputations against the Antinomians. In the second set of theses for disputation, the question was whether law, like circumcision, was only temporal and thus came to an end after Christ: that is, whether one can dispose of law by means of a *heilsgeschichtliche* scheme. Luther states in his theses that this is not so, that the law remains to all eternity because it discloses sin and must be fulfilled:

45. For the law as it was before Christ did indeed accuse us; but under Christ it is placated through the forgiveness of sins, and thereafter it is to be fulfilled in the Spirit.

46. Accordingly after Christ, in the future life, [law] will remain, having been fulfilled, and then the new creature himself will be what [law] in the meantime demanded.

47. Therefore the law will never in all eternity be abolished but will remain either to be fulfilled by the damned, or already fulfilled in the blessed.

48. These pupils of the devil, however, seem to think that the
     law is temporal only, ceasing under Christ just as did
     circumcision.[16]

Here it would seem that Luther is arguing for law as an eternal
ideal, but it is important to see the sense in which this is meant.
The Antinomians had argued that if the effect of a thing ceased,
then the cause of that effect ceases. Since the effect of the law
ceases in Christ, as Luther seems to have said previously, then the
law itself ceases and must consequently be abolished.[17]

It would appear, then, that the Antinomians argued just as Luther
did. If the law is defined in terms of its effect, then law would
surely cease when the effect ceases. Indeed, Luther begins by con-
ceding the point,[18] but he goes on to make some important quali-
fications:

> Where sin ceases, there law ceases, and to that degree that sin
> ceases, to that degree law ceases, so that in the future life the
> law ought completely to cease, because then it will be ful-
> filled.[19]

Where sin ceases, there law indeed ceases. But this is an eschatological possibility and can be realized fully only *in the future life.*
The end of the law cannot therefore be fixed according to some
historical scheme. To do this is not a possibility for man; as long as
sin is present, the law will continue to accuse.

But what then does Luther mean when he says that the law is
eternal? What does he mean when he says on the one hand that
the law will never in all eternity be abolished and on the other
that where sin ceases, there law ceases? The reason is the close
connection between law, sin, and death. It is not enough to say,
as the Antinomians did, that the appearance of Christ at a point
in time does away with the law, for the law is a power which

---

[16] WA, 39, 1:349-350.

[17] "When the effect ceases then the cause in actuality ceases. The effect of the
law ceases. Therefore the law itself ceases and is consequently abolished and
removed." WA, 39, 1:430.

[18] WA, 39, 1:43, 4-5.

[19] WA, 39, 1:431, 6-7.

can never be erased by an objective theoretical arrangement. This is true to all eternity. The law has its end only where it is fulfilled *in actuality*, and where it is fulfilled, there sin ceases. And where sin ceases, the law also ceases because it ceases to accuse. It is very significant that Luther, whenever he insisted upon the impossibility of removing the law, always based this on the fact that the law is "written on our hearts" and not on a theory about the eternal will of God. The persistence of the law is due to the fact that it is utterly impossible for man to escape it in this life.

Luther's defense of the eternality of the law is thus quite different from Harnack's "essence-office" distinction. The law is eternal because man as sinner cannot escape it. One might say indeed that for man as sinner, the "essence" of the law *is* the "office" precisely because, as sinner, man cannot distinguish between them. As long as sin remains, the law will *always* accuse; it will never be a neutral "essence." Only when it is fulfilled does it cease.

But does not the fact that law must be fulfilled before it ceases mean that it is "in essence" still in effect and therefore remains in effect throughout eternity? Must not Luther finally make the same distinction that Harnack makes? Luther is finally driven to make a distinction of sorts, but it is important to note the manner in which he conceives of this distinction.[20] One must distinguish, Luther says, between an "empty or quiescent . . . law and a law which accuses us or a decree inscribed in our minds." [21] The distinction Luther makes here is not between the essence and the office of the law, but between an empty or quiescent law and an accusing law written in man's heart or mind. Only the angels and saints in heaven, he says, know the law as empty *(vacua)*, because in them it is fulfilled.[22] Eschatologically, therefore, the law ceases because it is empty *(vacua)*—no longer active.

In another instance Luther argued that the law in the sense of the decalogue can be said to be eternal, but only because the reality, the *res*, which is its fulfillment, is eternal. In this case the An-

---

[20] Cf. Ebeling, *Wort und Glaube*, p. 65.
[21] *WA*, 39, 1:433, 1 ff.
[22] *WA*, 39, 1:433.

tinomians had held that the law, like circumcision, is abolished at a point in time. Luther replied that circumcision, like baptism, is temporal, "but only the decalog is eternal, *in its reality*, however, *not as law*, because in the future life those things which the law demands will be realized." [23] The decalogue remains eternally in the sense that the reality demanded remains, but *not as law*. Here the distinction is between reality *(res)* and law, but not between the essence of law and the office of law. The term "law" applies only to the "office," and not to the *res*.

The point seems to be that Luther did not want to grant eternal status to the law as law. Instead, he defined law in its existential sense as that which accuses. Quite naturally he did not allow that such a situation (that of being under accusation) should last eternally. But then how does it end? Certainly not by an abrogation of the divine will, and not by some theoretical cancellation of the law. The law "ends" only when it is fulfilled—when the state which the law demands is realized in actuality. The law ends (the accusation becomes powerless) when the new situation, the *res* to which the law points eschatologically, breaks in. When law no longer accuses, it is emptied of its power and becomes what Luther called a *lex vacua*. The fulfillment of the law is the end of the law, [24] and an entirely new situation obtains: man lives under the gospel. By faith man participates in the new situation under the gospel even though as a sinner he still lives in this age and still hears the voice of the law. Only the angels know the law completely as a *lex vacua*.

But is not this really the same as the distinction between essence and office or, at the most, only a quibbling about words? The difference, no doubt, is a subtle one, but still it is exceedingly important, for it reflects one's whole theological approach and thus affects one's entire system. The essence-office distinction can ostensibly provide man with a theoretical scheme according to which

---

[23] *WA*, 39, 1:413, 16 ff. Cf. Ebeling, *Wort und Glaube*, p. 65.

[24] Qui enim implent Euangelium, non sunt sub lege. Quia iam nulla est super eos, cum eam impleverint et iam ei adequati sunt. Lex enim non dominatur nec est supra eos, qui eam implent. Sed potius ad eam ascendunt et pertingunt ad eam. ("Impletio legis est mors legis." Rom. 7 Quamdiu vir vivit.) *WA*, 3, 463:33-37.

he can place himself apart from the law, view it in the abstract, and construct theories about how God's eternal will is satisfied. This allows man to place himself *above* the law and to look at it from God's point of view. The law is therefore disposed of theoretically, and faith consists of man's "understanding" how this has taken place. An eternal static order is posited which is objectively fulfilled; the paradigm for faith is the act of cognition.

To distinguish between a powerless law *(lex vacua)* and an accusing law *(lex accusans)* or between the dialogue as *lex* and as *res*, however, is quite different. To know the *lex* as *vacua* or to participate in the *res* of the decalogue is strictly an eschatological possibility. Man as sinner can never escape the *lex accusans*. He can never place himself above the law. Insofar as he is sinner, he is always under the law. Only actual death and resurrection can deliver him from this predicament. Only, therefore, as he participates in the death and resurrection of Christ in faith and hope is deliverance possible. The paradigm for faith is death and resurrection. In faith and in hope man is free from law. The eschatological possibility is made a present possibility only through faith in Christ.

The theological systems which result from these two ways of defining law are also quite different. In the first instance, law "in its essence" remains the basic structure of the system. It provides an eternal structure for the speculative doctrine of the atonement which we have described in earlier chapters. In the second instance there is a decisive break. The law comes to its *end* in the eschatological event, the *res* which the law demands breaks in and brings the law to an end. This means that in place of a one-membered eternal scheme, a two-membered dialectical scheme governs the system. Only by participation in the eschatological event does the law come to its end for the believer. This gives the terminology of the system a basically different thrust, even though that terminology may in many instances be the same.

The basic test for this distinction is the doctrine of the atonement. If what modern Luther interpreters have been saying is accurate, then it should be reflected especially in Luther's doctrine of the atonement. There has been some debate over Luther's doctrine of the atonement in recent years especially among Swedish Lutheran interpreters.[25] The question at issue has been whether Luther's manifold statements on atonement can be entirely comprehended under what Aulén has called the "classic" view of the atonement.

This modern debate is in many ways a repetition of the debate precipitated by Hofmann. Several interpreters argue that essential aspects of Luther's view can be understood only from the Anselmic or "Latin" point of view.[26] To support this contention these interpreters point to Luther's repeated assertion that Christ bore the punishment of the law which man deserved, that the wrath of God was appeased through Christ's satisfaction, etc.[27] Once again the decisive question is that of the place of law in the system.[28] Aulén, opposing the Latin theory, insists that however one looks at the matter, one thing is certain: for Luther atonement means the abolition of the judicial order (Rechtsordnung), the removal of all legalism from one's relationship to God. Atonement through Christ means the casting off of the religiosity of the judicial order, the setting aside of the power and tyranny of the law. In Luther's view, Aulén admits, the law indeed must be fulfilled, but it is fulfilled in order to be *removed* and *cancelled*, not because it is the eternal standard of justice according to which God *himself* must be satisfied.[29]

It is beyond the scope of this study to attempt a solution to this argument among Luther interpreters. It is important to point out, however, that the decisive issue in the debate is the question of *how* the terminology is used. It is not enough merely to point out that Luther did in fact use much of the terminology of the Anselmic theory. If what the several Luther interpreters we have cited have said about Luther's understanding of the law is correct (and the

---

[25] Edgar Carlson, *The Reinterpretation of Luther* (Philadelphia: Westminster Press, 1948), pp. 58-77. This is the only instance as far as I can see, where debate about atonement again becomes a substantial part of the discussion. It is important to note that the whole debate now hinges on the interpretation of the nature of the law.

[26] *Ibid.*, p. 66.

[27] *Ibid.*, p. 66.

[28] *Ibid.*, pp. 68-70.

[29] G. Aulén, *Das Christliche Gottesbild* (Gütersloh: C. Bertelsmann Verlag, 1930), p. 205.

illustrations cited would seem to bear them out), then it is quite possible, indeed probable, that all of the "Anselmic" terminology could be used within a different systematic framework and given quite a different thrust. For if the law is understood in a different way, then it follows that such terms as satisfaction and fulfillment will have to be understood quite differently. This is no doubt what Aulén is attempting to say.

This is also the position taken by Haikola in his comparison of Luther and Lutheran Orthodoxy. In his chapter on "Christ's Fulfilling of the Law," Haikola tries to spell this out more completely. He says that the fact that Luther did not understand the law merely as an objecive scheme of commands and prohibitions means that fulfillment must be understood differently. It cannot be understood as though the law could be *quantitatively* fulfilled by a "substitute." [30] Rather the entire law is summed up in the First Commandment, which demands a *qualitative* subjection of man to God in faith and love. No quantitatively measurable limits can be set for the fulfillment of such a law. The demand of the law is so understood that every thought of quantitative equivalence or supererogatory merit is excluded. The Anselmic alternative satisfaction or punishment *(satisfactio aut poena)* cannot arise; God is not one who allows himself to be "bought off" by a quantitative fulfillment.[31] The atonement occurs indeed through "fulfillment" and "satisfaction" of the law, indeed even by "placating the wrath of God," but everything depends upon how this is understood. If it is understood in the sense that Christ suffered and died under the absolute qualitative demand and thus bore the "punishment," therein coming to his *absolute end,* then it becomes quite a different matter. Then

---

[30] Haikola, *Studien,* pp. 106-110.

[31] Haikola cites Holl, *Gesammelte Aufsätze I,* pp. 69-70: "One ought not allow himself to be deceived by the fact that Luther for his part also uses the Catholic expressions 'satisfaction' and 'merit' because he assigns to them a different meaning from the Catholic Church. There *satisfactio* means a substitutionary accomplishment, a substitute payment to God. I recall here the Anselmian either/or: either satisfaction or punishment. Anselm rejects the second as impossible. Luther on the other hand finds precisely in it the true meaning of the death of Christ in explicit connection with his stricter conception of God and of sin. Sin is something that can never be made amends for and God is not one who allows himself to be bought off."

Christ's "satisfaction" is not the quantitative satisfaction of a "substitute" but the qualitative satisfaction of one who totally identified himself with man and died, as Hofmann said, "in our place." Then it is the resurrection which "brings the victory," and at the same time brings law to an "end." This is quite different from the vicarious satisfaction or the fulfillment which leaves law intact as an eternal juridical order. The same terms are used, but they mean something quite different. The terminology taken from the Latin view of the atonement is given basically a different thrust.

This difference in focus comes from a basic difference in the manner in which one approaches theology. The orthodox view, leaning heavily on the Latin theory, is based on a theology which attempts to reconcile divine attributes on God's level.[32] Atonement is an "example of rational justice" which expresses God's "calculation" rather than the mystery of his immeasurable love. As Haikola says:

> The love which comes to expression in Christ's cross is not an expression of God's own sacrifice but of God's calculation. Since the agreement between righteousness and mercy is thought of as having happened already in eternity, so also that which happens in history becomes merely a demonstration of the eternal atonement. Atonement retains a docetic character in spite of the realistic description of the suffering.[33]

In Haikola's view, such thinking is excluded by Luther's conception of the atonement. Such thinking would mean speculation about God's majesty—a vain enterprise.

> In Luther's theology, all thought, including that which is valid of the atonement, must proceed from the historically given and not from God's eternal attributes. . . . Theology should speak only of the revealed God (deus revelatus), of God "in relatione." In the historical revelation through his acts and words, God appears as wrath and love. On the plane of history he reveals himself as the one who in his love "conquers" wrath. This historical fact, that God in the cross of Christ actually submits to the might of the powers, of sin, death, the devil, the law,

---

[32] Haikola, Studien, p. 112.

[33] Ibid., pp. 111-112.

and wrath . . . that is the only starting point for thinking about the atonement.[34]

Thus Haikola maintains that the entire outlook on atonement took a different shape for Luther. This can be seen at several crucial points. First, God's wrath against sin retains its character as real wrath. It is not, as in the orthodox scheme, that man knows in an objective factual sense that God's righteousness has already received its "due" by a legal satisfaction. God's wrath is no mere demonstration which can be stilled by "objective" knowledge of a transaction; it is real, and it destroys utterly. Man's only hope is participation in the mystery of Christ's triumph over this wrath through faith.

Second, God's love retains for Luther its character as pure, unfathomable mercy. It is the *power* which in resurrection wins the victory in the actual historical battle on the cross.[35]

Third, in this view atonement retains its perpetually actual character. When wrath, law, death, etc., are understood as actual historical forces, atonement can never be understood merely as an objective transaction completed in the past. For it is not merely some objective, abstract and suprahistorical wrath which is atoned and conquered, but precisely that power which attacks man in his own life situation.[36] Atonement is release for man in his actual historical need. The "subject-object" impasse is avoided. Atonement is a unified action in which the real reunion of the opposed parties occurs. "The 'subjective' reception of redemption (faith) is contained in the objective act of redemption." [37] The "subjective" never occurs without the "objective," and vice versa. There is no "objective" atonement apart from faith, apart from actual participation in the action.[38]

Finally, Luther's insistence upon thinking strictly in terms of the actual historical forces means that the problem of history is more easily handled. Since Christ enters into this world, dies under and

---

[34] *Ibid.*, p. 112.
[35] *Ibid.*, pp. 113-114.
[36] *Ibid.*, p. 114.
[37] *Ibid.*, p. 108.
[38] *Ibid.*, p. 108.

wins the victory over the actual historical forces which continue to enslave man as long as he remains in sin, atonement is an on-going work in history. The Word, the proclamation of Christ's victory, is not merely intellectual information about an objective transaction but is itself the bearer of ongoing atonement. The proclaimed Word is, so to speak, the end and the new beginning wherever and whenever it is heard. It announces *and realizes* the end of the old and the beginning of the new when it is heard in faith.[39] The history of the old has its end when Christ is received in faith. The fulfillment of the law and the stilling of the divine wrath are thought of in terms of end and new beginning, not in terms of a timeless legal structure.

The conclusion of these interpreters, therefore, is that Luther's use of Latin or legal terminology by no means proves that Luther can or even should be understood in terms of the Latin or Anselmic view of the atonement. Rather, they say, the entire nature of Luther's thought excludes this view. The decisive point, especially for Haikola, is the understanding of law in Luther's theology. Law in Luther's thinking, Haikola says, simply does not provide the kind of structure necessary to support a Latin theory of the atonement.

The interpretation of the atonement by these men may be taken as indicative of the present status of the argument about Luther's doctrine that began with Hofmann. Perhaps that argument is not yet over, but it is extremely significant that these men find a view of the atonement which is neither that of the orthodox (vicarious satisfaction), nor, strictly speaking, that of a *Heilsgeschichte* like Hofmann's. That which makes it differ from both of these is the understanding of law. Law is neither an eternal framework for a transaction nor is it merely part of a historical dispensation. Law is an existential power from which man cannot escape without a real deliverance in the present. Atonement is the actual end of the law through faith. The atonement has, as Haikola points out, a more actual character. It is a view which, though critical of previous views, nevertheless attempts to do justice to the legitimate concerns in those views. As Otto Wolff remarks of Aulén's interpretation:

---

[39] *Ibid.*, p. 115.

Here Hofmann's energetic insistence upon understanding God's action exclusively as a line running from above to below comes to its historical fulfillment. The battle cry first taken up by him, in which this insistence found its most manifest expression, becomes here the center of the entire composition. But neither is Harnack's counter-complaint forgotten. God is not pictured in colorless one-sidedness, but the tension of the great polarities of wrath and love, etc., permeate throughout. Also Ritschl's basic concern for an independent thinking about faith which grows from its own roots comes in a happy manner to fruition.[40]

Let me sum up our findings on the understanding of law in Luther's thought among these interpreters: These interpreters point to the fact that law and gospel for Luther must be related eschatologically rather than in terms of a continuous or timeless scheme. We are led to the idea here that the relationship and tension between law and gospel should be understood in terms of the relationship and tension between the old and the new age. Haikola, for instance, says:

> When Luther places these antithetical total judgments on man (judgment and grace), he means at bottom the fact that man belongs to two opposing kingdoms, to two ages, between which there is at present perpetual struggle, but which will finally end with the victory of the one kingdom. The totality of the judgment stems therefore from the fact that the two eschatological entities are so utterly opposed and yet both really penetrate into the life of man and determine it.[41]

Likewise Ebeling maintains that the actuality of faith in the present can be maintained only through an eschatological scheme, to the exclusion of both the static-ontological scheme and the *heilsgeschichtliche* scheme. To support this contention he points to Luther and quotes Luther's own words about the distinction between the ages:

> "Christianity is divided into two times: in so far as it is flesh, it is under law; insofar as it is spirit, it is under the gospel."

---

[40] Wolff, *Die Haupttypen*, p. 394.
[41] Haikola, *Usus Legis*, p. 125.

But mark well, with this distinction: "The time of law is not
forever . . . the time of grace is to be eternal." "They are utterly distinct times, and nevertheless it is fitting that sin and
grace, law and gospel be most closely conjoined.[42]

Others as well, among them Wilfred Jöst and Helmut Thielicke,
claim this eschatologically oriented understanding to be the key
to Luther's view of the law.[43]

For these interpreters, therefore, law is understood as an "existential category" which describes man's actual situation in "this
age." It cannot be removed by theological erasure or by theological manipulation, but only by the actual breaking in of the "new
age" in Christ through faith. Insofar as man, even in faith, remains
a citizen of "this age" the law continues in its "office" as that which
constantly drives him to Christ. Existence under the gospel is the
new possibility which breaks in in Christ. Faith makes one a participant in the new age. The implication is that all the paired terms
in Luther's theology—law-gospel, wrath-love, flesh-spirit, hidden-
revealed, etc.—are to be understood in terms of this eschatological
dialectic.

This eschatological orientation helps to clarify the position of
these men in their argument with Barth as well as to shed light
on the Lutheran position in general. The question of the order of
law and gospel, as well as the problem of the nature and function of law, will be fixed by the eschatological scheme. Just as the
old age precedes the new, so also law will precede gospel. Just as
the old age comes to its end and *telos* in the new age, so also law
has its end in the gospel.

The nature and function of law, consequently, must be defined
in terms of an eschatological dialectic. Law is a general term for
the manner in which the will of God impinges upon man in the
old age, both in nature and in the words of Scripture. It is the
demand and the judgment which confront him as a sinner. Even
the words about the cross will initially be heard as demand, as a

---

[42] Ebeling, *Wort und Glaube*, p. 292.

[43] Cf. Wolfgang Berge, *Gesetz und Evangelium in der Neueren Theologie*
("Aufsätze und Vorträge zur Theologie und Religionswissenschaft") (Berlin:
Evangelische Verlagsanstalt, n. d.), pp. 38-42.

threat to his being. It is important to note here that law is defined almost exclusively in terms of its function. Nature and function are taken together. The nature of law is that it terrifies.

The corollary to this definition of law is that in the "old age" there is no really decisive break between "natural" and "revealed" law. Both are *law*, both impinge upon man in the same way. This, no doubt, can be seen as the reason for Luther's apparent haziness on the question of natural law and the fact that he can at times make a rather easy identification between the laws of nature and the decalogue.[44] For Luther, law is "natural" to man in the sense that it represents the way he naturally thinks and reacts; this cannot be escaped apart from faith. The law is "written in the heart." But this does not mean that everyone (or anyone, for that matter) has an innate and accurate knowledge of the divine in the form of a timeless moral code; this is ruled out.[45] Law is, on the one hand, "in its expressly rational character the form of being of the reality of man as a reasonable creature in this world"; it is also the "mask" through which God works.[46] One may have only a dim knowledge of law, or he may have a highly refined ethical system derived from the philosopher. He may even derive his ethical code from the Bible which is *quantitatively* more correct. But whatever it is, his code is still law, and on this level there can only be a question of degrees of correctness at a given time. Hence the decalogue is the best statement of the natural law. If man does not know the law, he must be taught. But on this level, within the old age, it remains, it would seem, only a question of the relative appropriateness of a course of action in a given situation. On this level there is no decisive break between what is natural and what is revealed.

The only really decisive break comes in the transition through faith from law to gospel, from the old age to the new age. The true function of law is seen in the light of this break. Law is limited to the old age. The new age is the age of the gospel. It is not strange, therefore, that our interpreters hold that Luther spoke almost exclusively in terms of the first two uses of the law to the exclusion of

---

[44] Cf. Ernst Wolf, *Peregrinatio* (München: Chr. Kaiser Verlag, 1954), p. 195.
[45] Above, p. 176.
[46] Wolf, *Peregrinatio*, pp. 196-197.

the third. In the new age, the reality to which law points is given and law reaches its end. Law is therefore accorded the political use in ordering the life of the old age and the theological use of driving the sinner to Christ. To be sure, the law remains in effect even for the believer, but only because he is still also a sinner; that is, he still lives out his life in the old age. But when law is understood in terms of the dialectic between the old and the new age, it makes little sense to attempt to reintroduce it again *after* the gospel. To do so would be to fail to recognize the radical nature of the break between the two ages.

Thus modern Luther interpretation has led to a view of law which differs somewhat from that of Barth. Instead of an increasing particularization of the law, as in the line which began with Hofmann and goes through Ritschl to Barth, here there is an increasing *generalization*. Law is a *general* term for describing the nature of man's existence in this age. It is the command which man meets in society, demanding order, and it is also the judgment of his way of life which drives him to the cross. It is defined in a general sense, as that which afflicts the conscience. Nothing *material* is said about the *content* of law as such; that, apparently, may depend upon concrete circumstances. Since law is defined in this general way, no great point is made about a distinction between a natural or a revealed law. It is simply taken for granted that law is natural for man.

This difference between a particularized and a generalized law is one source of the difficulty in the contemporary debate. It means, for one thing, that when the participants in the debate speak of law, they may be speaking of quite different things. It is not strange that a good deal of confusion has resulted.

This generalized concept of law is the outcome of the second line of development which began in Hofmann's interpretation of Luther's theology. The reinterpretation of Luther's concepts of wrath and hiddenness (which we have traced from Harnack through Kattenbusch and Holl) has reached its completion in a reinterpretation of Luther's understanding of law. Harnack, as we saw, opposed Hofmann and Ritschl with his interpretation of Luther's understanding of wrath. But Harnack based his concept of divine wrath on the idea that God "outside of Christ" was a hidden God—that is, a God of law—and used the distinction between essence and office to reinstate the orthodox concept of natural law. Kattenbusch showed that God's hiddenness did not apply only to the natural revelation outside of Christ but also more precisely to God's revelation *in* Christ. Karl Holl rediscovered the dialectic of God's alien and proper work in Luther's view of the relationship between wrath and love.

As I have pointed out, though, these advances did not come to grips with the real problem of law.[47] The work of the contemporary interpreters has more successfully dealt with the problem of law in Luther, and hence has completed this line of development. For when law is understood as an existential category, many of the difficulties in understanding Luther can be dealt with more fruitfully.

This eschatological understanding of law necessitates a fundamental reorientation at a number of crucial points. First, of course, it means that the orthodox concept of law is displaced. Law cannot be understood as a *lex aeterna* in the sense that the orthodox held—an eternal standard which governs the system. Insofar as this is true, there is agreement with the original contention of Hofmann.

Second, however, law is not displaced merely by an objective historical dispensation. For law remains always as that which afflicts the conscience of sinful man in the old age. Here there is a fundamental criticism of Hofmann's scheme of *Heilsgeschichte.* Law is neither an eternally fixed standard nor merely a part of a limited historical dispensation.

Thirdly, some adjustments must be made in Harnack's interpretation. It is misleading to identify law, as Harnack did, with God's revelation of wrath "outside of Christ." For if law is defined as that which afflicts the conscience, then God's action in Christ (as Luther saw) will become the most powerful manifestation of law to the sinner in the old age. Here there is some justification for the Ritschlian position—that true repentance does, indeed, arise from God's action (not, however, from God's action as *gospel,* but God's

---

[47] Above, p. 131.

action as *law*), and that "the same fact that increased our grief . . . will nevertheless be perceptible to us as a word of God convincing us that he has reached down to us."[48]

Here Harnack's view must be found wanting, for law must be extended to include also God's action in Christ. Law as that which judges and terrifies is not and cannot be limited to a "natural revelation" outside of Christ. When law is defined existentially, it certainly includes the natural, but at the same time it includes more—God's judging action in Christ. In the terms of the eschatological dialectic, what is natural is included in the old age, but it is also in this old age that Christ appears and brings the work of the law to its climax. It belongs to man's naturalness in the old age that he apprehends the divine will in all its manifestations as law.

This means also that Harnack's use of the distinction between the essence and the office of law must be rejected. Man cannot get behind the office of the law to find a neutral essence which could be used as a means for reinstating the orthodox view of the atonement. To do so would mean a return to an abstract objectivity which destroys the reality of the atonement. Saying this, however, does not mean that Harnack's insistence upon the dialectic of wrath and love is denied; instead it is reinforced and given a more actual character than his own understanding would allow.

Fourthly, the Ritschlian approach must be revised. The eschatological understanding of the relationship between law and gospel can more fully realize the essential concerns of Ritschlianism; at the same time it can more adequately deal with the criticism of that position. For the eschatological interpretation of law and gospel stresses actuality, actual atonement, actual renewal in the present through participation in Christ's death and resurrection. The framework is eschatological; so that the Ritschlian attempt to affirm the distinction between theoretical and practical reason, beween "nature" and "spirit" is discarded. After all, the actuality of the gospel is assured not by these distinctions but only when it is seen as the power which breaks in and defeats the powers which enslave man in the old age. One cannot rid oneself of the "natural" or the

---

[48] Above, p. 124.

"theoretical" by making a further *theoretical* distinction. The "natural" is accepted as a part of man's existence "under the law." "Under the gospel" man learns to see nature in its proper perspective and to realize that it is both impossible and unnecessary to attempt to exclude nature in the Ritschlian manner. From this point of view the Ritschlian polemic against nature and natural law must be judged as mistaken; one does not serve the gospel by that kind of polemic.

So also with the concept of wrath. Love is not served by attempting to erase wrath from the system. The reality and actuality of the divine love is rather asserted most strongly when it is seen as the power which breaks in and overcomes wrath. When law and gospel are related eschatologically the abstract and theoretical nature of theology (which Ritschl abhorred) is overcome, but the problems with which he was concerned are more adequately solved.

Finally, the work of Kattenbusch and Holl must be appended and modified. The eschatological dialectic of law and gospel provides a more viable systematic structure for Kattenbusch's interpretation of the hidden-revealed dialectic in Luther and also for Holl's interpretation of the alien and proper work of God. The contemporary interpretation has simply completed the work they began and has freed it from Ritschlian presuppositions. Kattenbusch's interpretation of the hidden-revealed dialectic receives a more fixed systematic structure: God is indeed hidden—both in nature and in Christ—because man in the old age experiences him as a God of law and wrath. God is *revealed* in Christ because in faith he is received as the God whose power has overcome and brought about the decisive inbreaking of the new age. The hidden-revealed dialectic, therefore, does not refer merely (as Kattenbusch said) to the mystery of God as "the incomprehensible." [49] It relates more precisely to the eschatological nature of God's action.

Likewise Karl Holl's Ritschlian moralism in his interpretation of Luther [50] is overcome. "Consciousness of the imperative" may indeed play an important part in Luther's thought, but it is not the basis of his religion. The eschatological dialectic of law and gospel

---

[49] Above, p. 127.
[50] Above, pp. 129ff.

shows that the imperative is overcome by the radical nature of the gospel. It is misleading, therefore, to say that the imperative is the basis for Luther's religion; this only creates the impression that the law is the foundation of the system and that the gospel is merely that which makes the law work. The eschatological dialectic gives the law an entirely different function from the gospel, a function as different from it as death is from life, old age from new age. Likewise it is misleading to say that the command which confronts man is in its basic content nothing other than the gospel.[51] To be sure, if the *res* to which the law points is realized in the gospel, then there is a sense in which this is true. But when the eschatological framework is missing the statement is misleading. The eschatological dialectic cuts through the underlying Ritschlian moralism.

The eschatological dialectic is also able to handle Holl's difficulty with the wrath-love problem more effectively. While it is true, as Holl said,[52] that wrath serves love in the sense that its purpose is to drive the sinner to Christ, it is impossible to seek a unity behind the paradox by neglecting or ignoring the fact that wrath can also lead to eternal death. Man simply cannot remove this possibility by his system, for if wrath does not lead to real death, one returns to the docetic tendencies of Hofmann's interpretation of the atonement; love becomes a foregone conclusion and the eschatological nature of the gospel is lost. Leaving open the possibility of a "stringent wrath"[53] better protects Holl's own assertion that the unity of wrath and love can be held only in *faith*.

To sum up, the concept of law and gospel which emerges from the argument over the interpretation of Luther makes possible a systematic reorientation which can absorb the legitimate concerns of the various participants in the debate from Hofmann down to the present. It is of great significance to note that the debate over Luther's theology has been carried out in living dialogue with the developing demands of systematic theology. This is no doubt the reason why in many Lutheran circles Luther research has been

---

[51] Above, p. 130.

[52] Above, p. 128.

[53] Above, p. 129.

almost a substitute for systematic theology, or at least a determinative factor in it.

One might well ask, I suppose, whether the theologians we have investigated have not read into Luther a theology consonant with their own systematic prejudices. This question can also be asked, no doubt, of the emerging eschatological interpretation in present-day interpreters. Have they not, perhaps, read into Luther a theology which meets the demands of the current emphasis on eschatology? Interesting and important as this question may be, it is beyond the scope of this study to attempt an answer. The point which I seek to make is that Luther *has* been interpreted this way and that this interpretation exerts its pressure on present-day systematic conclusions.

The relation of Luther research to the systematic debate, however, means that this research can best be understood in terms of its contribution to the solution of the problem of law and the act character of revelation. Quite clearly, affirming the eschatological character of the relationship between law and gospel is an attempt to deal with this problem. This is especially evident in the work of a man like Gerhard Ebeling. The act character of revelation is maintained through the idea that the gospel is the eschatological *event* which brings men freedom from the law in the present. Law is a general term which describes man's bondage in the old age and which leads to "death." Gospel is the eschatological advent of freedom and life.[54]

---

[54] Ebeling, *Wort und Glaube,* pp. 290-293.

CHAPTER XII

ESCHATOLOGY AND LAW

We have reached the point now where we must attempt to assess more precisely the nature of the Lutheran argument with Barth. Just where and how does the difficulty arise? First of all, the problem has been the attempt to give proper expression to the eschatological act character of revelation. *Both* the Lutheran and the Barthian reformulations of the doctrine of law and gospel are the result of this attempt. Both recognize that the eschatological nature of the gospel posits a break so radical that it cannot be interpreted as simply the realization of potentialities inherent within the "old age." What this means systematically is that the law cannot be understood as a scheme whose fulfillment provides for a continuous transition from the new to the old age. This means that for the sake of a proper understanding of the gospel, *the continuity in the system of law must be broken.*

The sign of this agreement is that both sides in the debate interpret faith in terms of the death of the "old man" and the resurrection of the "new man." As Barth put it, the subject "Adam" dies and the subject "Jesus Christ" takes his place.[1] Both sides recognize that the gospel demands the eschatological dialectic between the two ages. This means that there is unity in theological intent whatever differences arise in subsequent formulations. Failure to recognize this only renders the debate fruitless and sterile.

---

[1] Above, p. 147.

But because the continuity of law must be broken for the sake of the gospel, one question immediately arises: To which side in the dialectic is law to be assigned? Does law really belong exclusively to the side of the old age, or does it belong essentially to the side of the new age? Here the protagonists in the debate have taken different roads. Most Lutheran theologians have limited law strictly to the old age; they stand, as I have contended, at the end of a line of development in which law has been increasingly generalized as that which characterizes man's existential predicament in the old age. They define law as "that which accuses the sinner." Since the gospel means the eschatological advent to faith of the new age, such accusation must "end" when Christ is received in faith. Law must therefore emphatically and radically be excluded from the new age. The gospel is the end and *telos* of the law.

Barth, on the other hand, has taken the road of limiting law in its *true* sense to the new age. He has defined law as the command of *freedom*, the law *in* the gospel; this law, of course, cannot in any way be mixed or combined with law in the old age. It is the command which can be apprehended only in faith, only by the new man. Barth realizes, of course, that there is a "law" in the old age, a law which accuses and tyrannizes man, but since this is a law which accuses and does not set free, it must be excluded from the law of the new age. The law which accuses (which man always takes to be a law by which he can justify himself) is the misunderstood and misused law which must be displaced entirely by the law which is the form of the gospel, "the law of the spirit of life." The *true* law—law properly understood and properly used—belongs only to the new age and is known only to faith. Barth, then, stands at the end of a line of development which has led to increasing particularization of the law. For him law in its "true" sense must be limited entirely to the new age.

It is obvious at this point that some of the difficulty in the debate is simply the result of a difference in definition. The Lutherans define law as "that which accuses"; quite naturally, they limit it to the old age. The Barthians seek to define law in its true sense as "the law of liberty" and hence must limit it to the new age. This terminological confusion must be noted carefully for proper prose-

cution of the debate; some of the confusion arises simply because
the opponents are operating with different definitions of the term
"law."

The natural question which arises is whether the differences are
only terminological. If that were so, all that would be necessary
would be to take note of the differing definitions and make the
proper systematic adjustments. One might well say, for instance,
that both systems seek through the gospel to exclude the law
which accuses, and that this is the essential point. For the Lutheran
it is the law as such, whereas for the Barthian it is the "misused"
law. And the difference between the law as such and the "misused"
law is virtually removed when it is seen that for Barth even this
"misused" law derives its power and authority from the fact that
it is God's law nevertheless. Furthermore, one might well say that
Luther's idea of the *res* of the law, to which the law points and
which displaces law, is simply the counterpart of Barth's idea of the
"law of liberty" given to man in Jesus Christ. Indeed, once it is
realized that both systems have a common theological intent one
could go a long way towards ameliorating the differences by such
systematic comparisons.

Despite this superficial agreement, though, the entire tenor of
the debate insists that the problem is not merely one of definition.
Barth cannot rid himself of the suspicion that the Lutheran concept of a law, distinguished as it is from the gospel, not only sanc-
tions the fateful idea of a *Volksnomos* as a revelation of "God's
will" apart from the gospel but also leads to a perversion of the
gospel itself. For a law understood apart from the gospel leads inevitably, for Barth, to a gospel which merely becomes a crutch for
man's attempts at self-justification. On the other hand, the Lutherans see in Barth's idea of the law as the form of the gospel a fatal
tendency to unify law and gospel which threatens to destroy the
dialectic and to lead to an optimistic, monistic world-view. As
Ebeling has put it, it represents a "fundamentally different way of
doing theology." [2] We must look into this problem more carefully.

Quite obviously, the main point of contention is Barth's insis-

---

[2] Above, p. 174.

tence that the law apart from the gospel and faith is necessarily "misunderstood" and "misused" by man, so that only the use of the law in faith can be considered its proper use. Against this the Lutherans maintain that since the gospel is the advent of eschatological freedom, law can find its proper function only *prior* to the gospel. Thus the debate centers around the problem of the knowledge and use of the law. Again the trouble arises because of a common theological concern—the necessity of a break in the continuity of the law. Theologically, the Lutheran rejection of the "third use" of the law serves the same purpose as the Barthian rejection of the first two uses of the law.

Again it must be asked whether the differences are as absolute as the disputants have made them appear. After all, Barth holds that even in the "misuse" of the law man has to do with God— the God who is not mocked and who sees to it that man inevitably reaps what he sows. Thus even the "misuse" of the law apparently "destroys." It is for Barth "the law of sin and death" which must be displaced by the life-giving law in the gospel; this is very close to the Lutheran idea of the first two uses of the law.

From the Lutheran side there are also approaches to Barth's position. It has been pointed out, especially by Ebeling and Ernst Wolf, that the Lutheran view of the uses of the law can be held *only* from the point of view of faith,[3] for the doctrine of the two uses of the law implies that the law must be limited strictly to this age. The proper use of law, then, can be grasped only in the light of its eschatological limitation. This means that only from the point of view of faith can one come to speak of a civil or theological use of the law. It is only from the viewpoint of faith—that is, only in the light of the gospel—that one can recognize the eschatological limit and hold law "in its place" in this age. Apart from faith and the gospel, man will inevitably attempt to extend the use of the law beyond this age as an instrument for either utopian aspirations or self-justification; only from the viewpoint of the gospel and faith can a distinction be made between law and gospel at all. This distinction cannot mean a *separation* between law and gospel because

---

[3] Ebeling, *Wort und Glaube*, p. 66; Wolf, *Peregrinatio*, pp. 201-208.

it is faith in the gospel which *alone* holds the law in its place and insures its proper use. Apart from the gospel, man uses the law to serve his own ends; it becomes for him a vehicle for either presumption or despair.

This Lutheran interpretation of the use of the law undoubtedly takes a long step toward approximating Barth's position. It admits (as Barth has insisted all along) that apart from the gospel and faith, law will inevitably be misused by man, and it agrees that only the gospel insures proper use of the law. It is significant that the Barthian Hermann Diem concedes that this kind of interpretation virtually removes the objections Barth would have to the Lutheran position.[4]

But does this mean that the differences between the two views have been resolved? No doubt at this point it becomes increasingly difficult to locate the exact sources of the disagreement, but perhaps all we have done so far is to clear the ground of *apparent* obstacles in order to get closer to the *real* issues. From what we have discovered it can be seen that many of the arguments are indeed the result simply of terminological confusion, misunderstanding, or insufficient clarification, but there are still some points of disagreement. Focusing on these points should enable us to get closer to the real issue.

Perhaps the best place to begin is with Barth's somewhat complex and confusing stand on the idea of the "misused" law. For Barth, the law is misused when man uses it as an instrument of self-justification. This misused law is therefore to be distinguished not just relatively but *absolutely* from the true law, the command of God. Yet at the same time Barth insists that in the misused law man still has to do with God. The misused law still accuses; it derives its authority and power from the fact that it remains God's law even in its misuse. It seems that God somehow acts upon man even through the misused law as the God of wrath, the God who

---

[4] Hermann Diem, *Karl Barths Kritik am deutschen Luthertum* (Zollikon-Zürich, Evangelischer Verlag AG., 1947), pp. 15-27. Diem goes on, however, to express preference for Barth's formulation because he feels that the socio-political presuppositions for Luther's law-gospel view are no longer present and that as a consequence Luther can no longer be used to reconstruct a viable political ethic.

is not mocked. Even the misused law, therefore, does assault and accuse man.

The command of God also assaults and seizes man,[5] indeed, the command of God kills.[6] Yet Barth says that the command of God is to be distinguished absolutely from the misused law. It is not even to be considered the infinitely multiplied intensity of the "infernal assault" of other commands. That is so because the command of God kills *only* to make alive. It differs from other commands in that it is the command of a "friend" and not, apparently, an enemy. What Barth means, no doubt, is that only the law in the gospel, only the law as it assaults and seizes man in the event of Jesus Christ, can be the occasion of a final and serious conviction for man. Hence *this* law must be distinguished absolutely from other law.

Here too there are parallels with the Lutheran view. Barth's assertion parallels the Lutheran view that the hiddenness of God —that is, God as wrath and law—comes to its final and decisive climax *only* in the cross. For the Lutheran, too, the ultimate and final proclamation of law comes only in the cross; man can accept this final judgment only when he knows that it is the judgment of love.

Still, there is one essential difference. For the Lutheran there is no *absolute* distinction on the *level of law* between the law as it meets man "outside of Christ" and the law in the Christ event. There can be no absolute break between some "other" law and God's law, for the essence of both is that they accuse. Since law is a term which denotes man's existence in this age, there can be no such break. Furthermore, since the incarnation means that Christ is born "under the law," the Christ event is for men of the old age the ultimate and final statement of that law—the point of view which Barth rejects. Incarnation means that Christ is born into *this* world, under "the law of sin and death" to which man in this world is subject. The death which Christ dies is *man's* death under that law. Only the resurrection—the gospel—brings that law to its "end." The decisive and absolute break comes between law and

---

[5] Barth, *Church Dogmatics*, II, 2, p. 594.
[6] *Ibid.*, II, 2, p. 623.

gospel, not between law and law. Only the gospel is the end of the law.

The crucial problem is the question of the misunderstanding and misuse of the law. Barth, in his concern to exclude the misunderstood and misused law, must introduce *another* law which is the *true* law. Barth, of course, is entirely correct in maintaining that man's misuse of the law is the basic mark of his sin, and that it is precisely from this misuse that he must be rescued; as we have seen, there should be no quarrel on this point. A Lutheran, if he is to be true to his principles, would certainly agree that man apart from faith misuses the law.

Nevertheless, there is a crucial question which has been overlooked in the discussion. That is the question of who really is the one who *uses* the law.[7] Is it God as the author of the law or is it man upon whom the law impinges? Ebeling, in an essay on the three uses of the law is surprised that this question has never been discussed in Protestant theology.[8] This point is crucial to the debate about the misuse of the law, for Barth builds his whole case for the difference between the kinds of law on the fact that *man* misuses the law. His presupposition seems to be that *man* is the one who is supposed to use the law, and that since in sin law is misused, what man really needs is a new kind of law—a law *in* the gospel where the proper use will be restored. But if—and this Ebeling finds in Luther's theology[9]—God through Christ is really the one who uses the law, then the situation is considerably altered. Then it can be readily admitted that man in sin misuses the law. Indeed, it is the very mark of his sin that he arrogates to himself the position of being the one who uses the law. The point is that even though *man* misuses the law, *God* does not. God is, after all, the sovereign of the law; what man needs, then, is not another totally different law, but rather the faith to submit to God's use of the law

---

[7] The idea of the use of the law, or *usus legis*, refers to the traditional Protestant teaching that the law has two (or three) functions. It is "used" (1) politically to establish civil justice and order, (2) theologically, to convict of sin, [and (3) as a guide to the life of the Christian]).

[8] Ebeling, *Wort und Glaube*, p. 64.

[9] *Ibid.*, p. 65.

and in the light of the gospel to become a proper steward of his sovereign.

To be sure, the Lutheran would agree with Barth that only in faith can one gain insight into the proper use—God's use—of the law. The only problem is the attitude which man *in faith* is to have toward the law. The Lutheran argument is—or should be—that in faith man realizes that God remains sovereign over the law in *this* world, and that the man of faith must deport himself properly in accordance with that fact. Barth, on the other hand, argues that faith means the radical exclusion of law outside of the gospel. It is because Barth has not clarified the question of who uses the law that his statements about law are so confusing.

On the one hand the law "misused" by man still is in some sense "God's law." On the other hand this misused law is excluded by God's *true* law. Further, God's "true law" comes to man only in the "garment" of some seemingly "human" command, but is to be recognized as "Gods law" because it manifests the proper conjunction of permission and obligation. This confusion is the result of Barth's attempt to posit another law in addition to the law that man misuses. Once it is realized that God, after all, is sovereign over the use of the *law,* the necessity for speaking of another law is removed. The law which confronts man in the event of Jesus Christ is not *another* law; it is simply the final crescendo of God's use of the law which judges and accuses. It is God's final judgment of the sinner, the judgment that the way to life leads through the death and resurrection of Jesus Christ. For the law is not the form of the Gospel; it is rather, the form of *this age.* The gospel is its end and *telos.*

Perhaps now we are in a better position to evaluate the real issue in the debate—why the concept of law will be different according to whether one thinks from a point of view in which law and gospel form a self-evident unity or from a point of view in which this unity can be maintained only by faith in the face of *"Anfechtung,"* and why this difference leads to a fundamentally different way of doing theology.

When Barth insists that the "true" law—the command of God—must be distinguished absolutely from all other law, a number of theological consequences follow. First of all, law and gospel form a unity and constitute a "real world" over against which "this world" under the "other law" appears to be the result of a misunderstanding. This means in turn that a very specific type of theologizing is demanded, for the gospel with its own special "form" can have no point of contact with "this world." One can only "think into" the event of revelation. But the Word of God which comes to man in law and gospel can have only one content—grace. This means that there is a unity of law and gospel beyond the dialectic to which faith, supposedly, can penetrate. The law of God, in distinction from other law, "kills" *only* to make alive. Upon "thinking into" the event of revelation faith discovers that all the antinomies of existence have already been overcome in the life of God himself; indeed, that they have been posited in order to be overcome to the greater glory of God's grace. This means, Barth's critics say, that Barth's system is in constant danger of being reduced to an undialectical, timeless, universalistic world-view. To be sure, Barth can insist that it will not do this as long as the act character of revelation is maintained and as long as it is clear that such a view is possible *only to faith*. But the difficulty is that this conception of law and gospel leads to a point of view which threatens the act character it is supposed to protect.

Thus from his starting point, Barth has been led to seek, as Iwand put it, a Word of God "in itself" "beyond law and gospel." [10] This has led him to assert that there are "two worlds"—this world and God's "real" world. From the point of view of grace, the fallen world in which the law is misunderstood and misused can only appear as an "unreal" world, a world of non-existence, a "shadow-world" which God rejects. The real world is the world which from all eternity is posited by God's free grace, a world which cannot be lost. It is somewhat difficult to see just how these worlds are related. If the world of sin is the world of the misused law and the world of grace is the world of the true law, in which world and under what law did Christ suffer? Where did the event of the cross take place? It would have to take place either in the "unreal world,"

---

[10] Above, p. 161.

where it could have no reality, or in the "real world," where it could not be an event. As Regin Prenter asks:

> One asks himself here in which world we lead our real life. One asks himself here further which world God has loved so that he sent his Son into that world. Is it so that we all live somehow in a world which God rejected . . . , that God on the other hand created only that other world . . . , that God took on a human nature which belongs only to that other world? In which world does Golgotha's cross stand? [11]

Barth can, of course, say that there are not two worlds but only one world which cannot be lost, and that the "other world" exists only insofar as men have fallen and do not know God's "real world." But that does not really help matters, for then the impression is given that man's problem is simply lack of knowledge—sinful ignorance that this world really *is* the world of grace which cannot be lost. If this is the case, one is driven to a universalism in which it is difficult to explain how sin is serious at all or how man could be lost. And if man cannot really be lost, then nothing *happened* in the "event" of Jesus Christ other than that man received the knowledge that God has from all eternity posited and overcome sin in himself.

We are confronted here with a rather impossible either/or in the problem of the relationship of the "two worlds." Either revelation is an *event* which entirely negates this world and which can have no positive relationship to it at all; or else this world is the world embraced by grace all along, so that revelation is not really an event but only a demonstration of an eternal truth of which man was ignorant. Since law and gospel are a unity there is no way to speak theologically of God's relationship to "the world" apart from grace. Thus the theology of grace must either reject the world completely or embrace it completely.

To be sure, one can sympathize with Barth's intent in all this. He has tried to establish the theology of grace on firm ground by making it "the real" over against which life apart from grace can only

---

[11] Regin Prenter, "Die Einheit von Schöpfung und Erlösung." *Theologische Zeitschrift*, Vol. II (May/June, 1946), No. 3, p. 175.

appear as "unreal" or "ontically impossible." But does one really serve a theology of grace by obscuring its act character in *this* world, the only world which man knows? One is accustomed to hearing of the "triumph of grace" in *Barth's theology*, but the triumph of grace *in the actual life of this world* is quite another matter. It is not difficult to construct a *theology* in which grace triumphs. It is more difficult, however, to have a theology which fosters the triumph of grace *in actual life*.

This is the burden of the Lutheran complaint against Barth. It is not that the Lutherans do not share a common theological concern with Barth; certainly they do. Nor is it merely that they have chosen apparently different formulations to express their common concern. Often these formulations obscure rather than reveal their basic agreements, so that with sufficient analysis one can discover these agreements. It is rather that Barth in his haste to exclude the "misused" law has been forced to posit another law which forms a unity with the gospel. He has been driven to seek this higher unity "beyond law and gospel," which threatens the act character of revelation in *this* world.

The Lutheran position on law results in a quite different point of view. Even though it recognizes, with Barth, that law inevitably is misused by man in sin, the Lutheran view holds that nothing is gained theologically by attempting to speak of some "new law." Indeed, a good deal may be lost, for the real problem is that man arrogates to himself the position of the *user* of the law and thereby tries to extend law beyond its proper use. Man uses law as an instrument for self-justification and for his utopian designs; law becomes an instrument for presumption or despair or both. The problem is that man as sinner must learn the proper use of law, and that means learning to accept both the limits of law and his own limits as a creature in this world. What man needs is to be saved for existence in *this* world.

What is needed in the Lutheran view, therefore, is not a new law but rather a faith which heals from presumption and despair and which insures the proper use of the law. This, of course, can be no merely "theoretical" matter. Proper use of the law can come only through a faith which accepts Christ as the real and personal eschatological limit to one's existence. In other words, no theology as such, no set of assertions—however cleverly constructed—can "save" man. Only Christ can do that. Only when the gospel is heard as God's *final* word in Christ in a concrete existential sense can this come about. Only when faith accepts the fact that Christ is the end of the law is law put in its proper perspective, for only then will man realize what it means to live in *this* world under the sign of the eschatological limit and promise. The gospel means that man's entire hope is given in Jesus Christ; because of this, man can live in faith in this world and apply himself to being a proper steward of God's law.

This means that in the Lutheran view law is, in the good sense of the word, "natural." That is to say, for faith law is divested of its *super*natural pretensions and limited to this age. Law is the theological term denoting the manner in which God relates himself to this age. Law is the "form" of *this* age. This explains the Lutheran tendency to limit law to the first two uses—civil and theological. The law gives form to this age and it accuses the sinner. As such it is an existential power which will continue to accuse as long as man remains in his sin. Only a living faith in Christ as the end of the law can hold the law in its proper perspective. Faith alone makes and keeps the law "natural."

This means that for the Lutheran it is misleading to speak about the sinner's relationship to the law under the category of "misunderstanding." This gives the impression that the Christian has some special epistemological advantages over the non-Christian when it comes to "knowledge" of the law. It is precisely faith, however, which tells the believer that this is not so. Faith tells him that law is something he has in common with the rest of mankind. To be sure, the Christian also has the laws of the Bible, but even these *as laws* are available to the non-Christian, to say nothing of non-Christian parallels of biblical law.

What the Christian *is* given is a faith that clarifies for him the nature of his existence under the law in this age. Faith tells him that the "naturalness" of the law means that he does not have access to the will of God in the form of some eternal *law of being*, but rather that in common with the rest of mankind he must use his reason in the context of his situation to work out the best practical solutions possible to his problems.

But does this not mean that Lutheranism falls into the danger which Barth was seeking to avoid, namely the fatal error of sanctioning a "natural law" apart from the revealed will of God, the mistake of separating out a part of existence not subject to the lordship of Christ? The history of Lutheranism demonstrates that this is an ever-present danger which must not be overlooked, but on the basis of Lutheranism's own principles it is a gross mistake for Lutherans to look upon the distinction between law and gospel as though it could mean a *separation*.

It is only from the point of view of faith that the distinction between law and gospel can be made at all. And faith then should see that the gospel, for the time being, does not separate out another realm into which man is prematurely translated; instead the gospel places the believer in this world as the steward of God's use of the law.

This means that the Christian's task is to bear witness to the proper use of the law. To do this is no insignificant accomplishment, for it means that all misuse of the law must be resisted. All false idealism, whether personal, social, or political, must be excluded. Whenever law is used to tyrannize man for false ends it is misused; the Christian is called upon to expose such misuse. Perhaps if this had been realized in the days of the *Kirchenkampf*, some of the disastrous errors could have been avoided. For the Christian knows that Christ is the end of the law and that a use directed to any other end is a misuse. Thus quite clearly there can be no question of separation, of setting up a realm over which Christ's lordship does not extend. But at the same time faith cannot construe Christ's lordship according to some theocratic ideal, some "new law," for that too is excluded. Christ rules as no other Lord rules—through a gospel which fixes the end of the law. The problem is not *whether* Christ is Lord over all, but *how* Christ exercises his lordship.

From this it should be apparent why the Lutheran position leads to a way of doing theology different from Barth's. The task of theology is not to "think into" the event of revelation in order to discover the inner unity of law and gospel. The task of theology is both more modest and more difficult. Its task is to serve a proclamation of the law and the gospel in such a way that the proclamation is the bearer of the same event that Jesus Christ is. It is a more modest task because it realizes that theology too remains under the eschatological limit, that it is a thinking in this age which remains subject to the laws and limitations of this age. As man remains "under the law" in this age, so does theology. It is simply human reflection on the event of Jesus Christ; it does not differ in principle from profane thinking, and it must attempt to be as systematic as possible according to the laws of thought in this age. But theology is also more difficult than Barth would have it, for it realizes that like all man's thinking its temptation will be to transcend its limits, to be "misused." It is difficult because of the nature of its object—the event of Jesus Christ—and because it realizes that the greatest temptation is for theology itself to take the place of that event.

Thus theology in the Lutheran view must realize that it too operates in this age under the strictures of the uses of the law. It cannot present itself as a new and perhaps higher kind of law which supposedly "saves" man. It must foster a proclamation which points to Christ. It must therefore apply the distinction between law and gospel *to itself*. It must strive to be, as Luther insisted, a theology *of* the cross, not merely a theology *about* the cross which subtly takes the place of the cross. It must realize that it can never get rid of the law by any kind of theological device, however clever; only Christ can do that. Theology must therefore seek to insure that the law and the gospel are properly distinguished and proclaimed in their ultimate and final sense. It must realize that the unity of law and gospel—that is, that the God of the law and the God of the gospel are one and the same—is something which can be grasped in the final sense only by faith or, as Ebeling put it, only in the face of *Anfechtung*. Theology, of course, asserts this unity, but faith does not consist ultimately in believing the assertions of theology, but rather in trusting in the Christ who alone makes it possible to *believe* the unity.

Thus Lutheranism has attempted to foster a theology which preserves the eschatological dialectic of the two ages. This, in sum, is what the distinction between law and gospel is really about. It means that for the Lutheran one cannot theologize in terms of a one-membered, eternal, ontological scheme, one must instead learn to think in terms of two ages and the fact that the Christ event itself can be the only point of transition between these two ages. All attempts to think in terms of the *lex aeterna* of orthodoxy, the historical process of Hofmann, the practical religion of Ritschl, or an undialectical theology of the new age must be rejected. And they will be rejected precisely because these theologies do not think stringently enough in terms of the dialectic. In the Lutheran judgment, all of these attempts invariably tend to enclose the gospel in the systems of this age and thus to present it as a "new law." None of these theologies *intend* this, of course, but it is the inevitable result of their failure to apply the distinction between law and gospel to theology *itself*.

The Lutheran also realizes that theology can only work with the "systems" or the thought forms of this world. He insists, though, that "working with the thought forms of this world" be *strictly* adhered to—that is, that these be recognized as the thought forms of *this* world and not of some other world. For the promise of the new age is given in Christ only to faith, not to "sight"; this is so because the Christ event itself makes it so. The Christ event is the bearer of absolute judgment and absolute grace; indeed, it is one only because it is also the other. The fact that it is absolute judgment means that man cannot attempt to anticipate the eschatological vision or to translate himself prematurely into the new age. But the fact that it is also absolute grace given here and now means that there is no need for such an attempt. Under the sign of this absolute judgment and grace the believer can be content to remain in this age until God sees fit to change things. Thus Lutheran theology by its very this-worldliness reflects its belief in the other world, the new age.

This is Lutheranism's charter for a "different" kind of theology. Perhaps this difference can be seen most clearly in the problem of form and content introduced by Barth. Whereas for Barth the "true" law is the form of the gospel and thus the form of the "new age," for Lutheranism the law is, strictly speaking, the form of this age. But there is also a sense in which Lutherans could speak of the law as the form of the gospel, for the gospel involves the fact of incarnation. Christ enters into the form of *this* age, "under the law." He takes the "form of a servant." For the time being man has access to the gospel only under this form. But the gospel also involves the fact that Christ could enter the form of this world only to die and to break the bonds of this form by the resurrection. Christ became the *end* of the old form, and he now offers to faith the promise of a new "content." But because of the nature of Christ's appearance in this world, faith enjoins man to live for the time being where he is and to become a proper steward of the form of this age.

Undoubtedly there are perils in this type of theology too. There is always the danger that attempting to speak in terms of the two ages will lead, as Barth fears, to an illegitimate separation, to speaking in terms of "two realms" in which the relationship is not clear and the critical function of the gospel is not brought to bear in this age. There is also the danger that speaking of Christ as the "end" of the law (and thus of this age) will become almost exclusively a kind of *negative* theology, a kind of "negative theology of glory" in which it is difficult to give positive content to the new life in this age. These are, of course, difficulties that arise from the same source as the difficulties in Barth's theology: the fact that in order to preserve the act character of revelation it has been necessary to break the continuity in the doctrine of law. We shall attempt to deal with them more fully in the final chapter.

CHAPTER XIII

CONCLUSION AND PROSPECT: THE CHURCH AS THE LOCUS OF CONCERN FOR LAW AND GOSPEL

It has been my concern to investigate some aspects of the historical background of the contemporary discussion of law and gospel. We have found that the difficulty began with the transition from the older orthodoxy to the *Heilsgeschichte* of the 19th century. This transition made necessary a fundamental systematic reorientation which is most evident when one considers the doctrine of law. In *Heilsgeschichte* theology law was no longer understood as the static-ontological structural component of the system but became instead a part of a historical dispensation. The place of law was preempted by a philosophy—or, if one prefers, a theology—of history. This precipitated a crisis which has been most evident in the debate over the doctrine of the atonement.

When the orthodox view of law and atonement was rejected, two alternatives emerged. One could, perhaps, seek to understand God's action in terms of a view of history. This presupposed the ability to arrive at a view of God's action in history as a continuous stepwise process in which law is peculiar only to a specific historical dispensation superseded by the next stage of development. This means, though, that the eschatological nature of God's action is obscured by the idea of history as a continuous process. One could, in contrast, try to understand God's act in Christ in terms of an interpretation of religion. This meant to Ritschl that Christianity was "the perfect moral and spiritual religion." Here law is understood as the imperative of the practical "kingdom of God." It is to be understood only within the community established by Christ as the command of love. Here again the eschatological nature of God's action is obscured; it is difficult to see how the "kingdom of God" is anything more than a purely historical community realizing man's inherent capacities for "practical religion." In both alternatives, therefore, the eschatological nature of the divine action is obscured.

Contemporary theology has attempted to overcome the difficulties of these systems by asserting the eschatological act character of revelation. In doing so it has challenged both the idea of a *Heilsgeschichte* as Hofmann conceived it and the idea of the kingdom of God as a purely historical community set forth by Ritschl. It has introduced instead the idea of God's action as an eschatological in-breaking to faith in the living present. It has not been sufficiently realized, however, that criticism of the kind of theology suggested by Ritschl and Hofmann also involves one in a criticism of the corresponding concepts of law. A vital factor in the theologies of both Hofmann and Ritschl was a reinterpretation of the orthodox concept of law. Criticism of these theologies must therefore concern itself with the concept of law. Thus it is not strange that the debate over law and gospel has once again come to the surface in contemporary theology and that because of the obscurity of the historical background considerable confusion has resulted. It has been my contention, therefore, that if the debate about law and gospel is to be understood and to progress, it must be seen against its historical background.

Studying this background leads us to several conclusions. The first is that the recovery of the eschatological act character of revelation is quite necessary for the proper understanding of the gospel. For if my analysis has been correct, the demand to understand revelation in this way is not due merely to pressures which are external or accidental to theology. That is to say, it is not due merely to such historical "accidents" as the advent of historical criticism and the failure of the "search for the historical Jesus," nor to such external pressures as the influence of existentialism and the drive to be "relevant." Such factors have no doubt been influential, but it is an oversimplification to see the development of the eschatological act character of revelation only in that light. For my investigation has shown that there has been a constant pressure exerted from *within* theology itself which has called for a more viable formulation of the nature of revelation. This pressure began in the days of the atonement controversy and has continued until the present.

The assertion of the eschatological act character of revelation is the result of a long development. Both Hofmann's demand for a revelation which is self-authenticating in the present and Ritschl's demand for actuality were only steps along the way. The assertion of the eschatological act character of revelation comes as the solution to a systematic problem internal to the tradition itself, not merely as a concession to external pressures. It has been the attempt to clarify problems centering around the doctrines of law and atonement which have plagued Protestant theology from the very beginning.[1]

But even though contemporary theology has asserted this eschatological act character in no uncertain terms, it has not given enough careful attention to what this involves for the doctrine of the law. From the theologies we have investigated we have seen that in order to assert the eschatological act character of revelation it has been necessary to break the continuity in the law. A proper understanding of eschatology has involved, for these theologies, the idea that the *eschaton* posits a break so absolute that law as it was formerly understood (i.e., in orthodoxy, Hofmann, or Ritschl) cannot survive the break. The *eschaton* brings a qualitatively new kind of existence to the man of faith. This, of course, radically questions the place of

---

[1] In this connection it is interesting and extremely significant to note that Martin Werner has suggested that one of the most difficult problems even for the early church in the shift from eschatology to ontology due to the non-occurrence of the *parousia* was precisely the problem of law. The fact that the church never really settled this problem, Werner says, meant that it was bound to flare up again. Martin Werner, *The Formation of Christian Dogma*, tr. S. G. F. Brandon (rev., New York: Harper and Bros., 1957), p. 76, cf. pp. 77-94.

law and calls for a careful reevaluation of the relationship of the Christian to the law. The debate over law and gospel is a recognition of this need for reevaluation, but the unsatisfactory result of the debate indicates need for further work.

The conclusion to which we are led, therefore, is that the relationship of law and gospel must be carefully defined in accordance with the eschatological act character of revelation. Failure to do this would leave theology in one of the previous historical positions we have investigated with its attendant difficulties. But how is such careful definition to be made? In our study we have dealt with two divergent attempts to deal with the problem. Both attempts, we have seen, have found it necessary to break the continuity in the doctrine of law in order to protect the act character of revelation. But the manner of doing so is quite different in each case. One, the Barthian, seeks to assure the act character by placing law in its true sense entirely on the side of revelation. Law is the "form" of the gospel event in the particular moment of its occurrence. All understanding of law prior to or outside of the event is "misunderstanding" and "misuse," and it must be strenuously excluded. The other attempt, under the influence of Luther research, interprets law as the existential power under which man lives "in this age" which is broken and comes to its "end" in the gospel event. The difference can be summed up by saying that, for the Barthian, law in its true sense belongs solely to the "new age," whereas, for the Lutheran, law belongs properly only to the "old age."

This difference characterizes quite well the current status of the debate. It is reflected in the fact that the debate has crystallized around opposing formulas: "gospel and law" versus "law and gospel." The opposition represented by these formulas indicates that there are a number of problems remaining, and it accentuates the need for further thinking. In the remainder of the chapter I shall attempt to point up these problems and to suggest lines along which such thinking might proceed.

There is, first of all, the persistent problem of the knowledge of the law. Barth has asserted that true knowledge of the law is given only in the event of revelation. All knowledge of law prior to or outside of the event of revelation must then be rejected as "misunderstanding" and "misuse." Barth's Lutheran opponents, however, argue that knowledge of the law is "natural" to man even in his unregenerate state, and that it is precisely this knowledge of law which drives man as a sinner to the gospel. But there is some lack of clarity on both sides. This is evident in Barth's view when he says that God "nevertheless" gives his law to sinful men and that consequently this "misused" law remains the instrument of God's wrath; as a result, the gospel is understood "really for the first time" as gospel when this misused law is excluded. This seems to indicate that there must be some theological necessity for speaking of a knowledge of law prior to the event of faith, even if that knowledge is somehow a "misunderstanding."

The lack of clarity in the Lutheran view is evident when they hold that the finally decisive proclamation of the law comes only in the death of Christ. Even if it is true that apart from faith man will experience law as an existential threat to a greater or lesser degree, is it really possible to maintain that *apart from faith* Christ's death can become the finally decisive proclamation of the law? Does not the ability to experience and interpret the death of Christ in this manner *presuppose* faith? And if this is so, must not one admit with Barth that apart from faith it is impossible really to know the law? There are points here where the opposing views converge, but there is still a lack of clarity.

The problem of knowledge relates directly, of course, to the second problem, the problem of order. Should law precede or follow gospel? Barth argues that law must follow gospel, since true knowledge of the law is possible only after the gospel event. His opponents argue that the law must precede the gospel just as in the saving event death precedes life and the old age precedes the new. This problem needs more precise definition.

Our study has pointed out, in the first place, that the antagonists in the debate are really operating with quite different concepts of law. But we have also found that the difference is not merely due to terminology. It has its roots in different ways of thinking about the law-gospel problem. Barth refuses the traditional order because of his stand on the problem of the knowledge of the law—that proper knowledge is not possible prior to faith. But this seems to presuppose that faith as such brings a knowledge of law which was not previously available. Is this really the case? As we have seen, especially in the area of political and social ethics, Barth is hard pressed to demonstrate that faith has a new or distinctive knowledge of law. On the other hand, it would seem equally perilous to insist on placing law before gospel on the grounds that man can and does know the law prior to faith, as some Lutherans argue. There is certainly no guarantee that this *must* be the case in every instance.

This raises the question of the real basis for the order of law and gospel. Is it perhaps not a mistake altogether to ask the question in this manner? Is it not a mistake to attempt to answer the question in terms of the knowledge available to man "before" or "after" faith? To do so, it would seem, is to involve oneself in some rather fruitless and inconclusive arguments—either attempting to demonstrate that one does automatically gain new knowledge after faith, or that one can—perhaps even must—have proper knowledge of the law prior to faith.

This points to the need for further clarification. What is the relationship of faith to the law? What alteration does faith bring to man's relationship to the law? What, precisely, does "before" and "after" faith mean in this connection? Perhaps the answers to these questions would help to determine more carefully the solution to the problem of the order of law and gospel.

There is also the problem for ethics, the problem of separation. The breaking of the continuity in the law means that the message and influence of the gospel threaten to become radically separated from the "everyday" world. The "new age" is in no way to be understood as the realization of the potentialities inherent in the "old age." Unless it is carefully handled, this leads to an unfortunate cleavage between Christian ethics and secular ethics. This can happen in Barth's theology when it is held that the knowledge of the law is possible only to faith. This can result in a tendency for theology to withdraw until there is no common ground with the secular world for dealing with ethical problems. The tendency is apparent in Lutheran thought, of course, in the distinction between the "two kingdoms." Here too there must be more careful thought.

Can these problems be resolved? It is not my purpose here to attempt exhaustive solutions. What I shall attempt in the light of our study, is to offer some suggestions for further thinking. These suggestions will be based, quite naturally, on the conclusion I have drawn: that thinking about law and gospel since the time of Hofmann has led inexorably to the assertion of the eschatological act character of revelation and that as a consequence this thinking must consciously and explicitly be brought into line with the eschatological two-age dialectic.

The problems which remain are the result of a failure to think rigorously enough in terms of this eschatological dialectic. As we have seen, this has been the constant source of difficulty throughout the debate, and our study indicates that this is still the point where the difficulties arise. For on the one hand the objection to Barth is that he tends in his thinking about law and gospel to lose sight of the dialectic and to lapse into a monistic theology of "the new age." And on the other hand the criticism of the Lutheran view is that by placing law before gospel it tends to accept uncritically the "law" of the "old age" and to separate the gospel from it so radically that the positive impact of the gospel on the life of this age is lost. In both instances the difficulty arises at the point of defining the nature of the dialectic of the two ages. It is indicated therefore that this is the point at which further thinking is called for.

What should such thinking involve? Several points must be emphasized. First of all, if justice is to be done to the gospel one cannot think in terms of a "de-eschatologized" monistic system of whatever sort, whether that be a system based on the thinking of the "old age" or a supposed attempt to think exclusively in terms of the "new age." One must learn to think in terms of two ages, in terms of a two-membered ontological framework rather than a one-membered scheme.

Secondly, it must equally be emphasized that the nature of this two-membered scheme must be *exclusively* determined by the nature of the eschatological revelation itself. When the term "dialectic" is used here it must be understood that this is a dialectic determined entirely by eschatology, and not by other concerns. Problems arise here primarily because "this age" already has its own types of duality, its own contrasts between "this world" and the "ideal world"; thinking in terms of two ages often tends to become confused with these dualisms. Indeed, this is no doubt the greatest source of difficulty in attempting to think in terms of two ages. One thinks immediately here of Bonhoeffer's criticism of Barth to the effect that Barth's concept of the dialectic, at least in its early stages, is influenced too much by Kantian transcendentalism and by a purely formal definition of God's freedom.[2] It must also be recognized that the Lutheran dialectic of wrath and love can lapse into a dualism of the Marcionite type.

Everything depends, therefore, upon thinking *theologically* about the dialectic. This implies that thinking in terms of two ages must be carried out only in the light of God's eschatological act of judgment and grace in Jesus Christ. It is this act alone which defines the limits and the relationship of the two ages. It is only in the light of faith that the dialectic between the two ages becomes apparent. That is to say that the dialectic is not based on any merely formal ideas of God's transcendence, non-objectivity, "wholly otherness," or whatever, but on the kind of distinction which God himself has made materially in the act of revelation itself. God himself sets and defines the limits of this age, and he gives the gift of the new age to faith in the death and resurrection of Jesus Christ. There is no "system" as such which can distinguish between the ages or can provide a continuous transition from this age to the next. Only the death and resurrection of Christ, the act of judgment and grace, is "the way."

Thinking *theologically* about the dialectic involves the fact that this act is at once *total* judgment and *total* grace. The fact that it is total judgment means that there can be no attempts on man's part to translate himself prematurely into the new age either by his action or by his thinking. Man's acting and thinking in this life remain an acting and a thinking in this age, under the eschatological limit. The fact that it is also total grace means that man can be content to allow his acting and thinking to remain as it is, totally in this age; he can trust in Christ entirely for the gift of the new

---

[2] Dietrich Bonhoeffer, *Act and Being*, trans. Bernard Noble (New York: Harper and Bros., 1961), pp. 79-107.

age. The importance of this will become apparent later when I spell out its significance for the problem of law and gospel.

But if man's acting and thinking remain an acting and thinking in this age, then the problem arises of how the new age takes on any kind of positive reality in this age. This brings us to the third point that must be emphasized in thinking in terms of two ages: the doctrine of the church as the eschatological community existing in this age. Everything we have said about the dialectic of the ages is possible only if one includes also the reality of the church, for the church is the point, the place, where the new age "breaks in" in the old age. It exists in the old age, but at the same time in faith it participates in the new age. The church is therefore the locus of concern for the two ages and also therefore the locus of concern for the proper distinction between law and gospel. As Bonhoeffer put it, it is in and through the church that revelation, even though it can be conceived of only as "act," takes on the form of "being" appropriate to it in this age, "Christ existing as community."[3]

Theological thinking in terms of the two ages must therefore concern itself with the reality of the church. We can see from our study that there is good precedent for this.

A major facet of the thinking of both Hofmann and Ritschl was the concern of each for the church as the community within which proper theologizing could be carried out. It has been my judgment, however, that they failed to understand the eschatological act character of revelation and consequently the eschatological nature of the church. The line of thinking started by Hofmann and Ritschl must therefore be taken up and completed with the eschatological corrective.[4]

In the light of the eschatological act of judgment and grace it becomes apparent that one must define the nature of the church somewhat differently. It is not, as Hofmann supposed, that one is

---

[3] *Ibid.*, pp. 117-151.

[4] An admirable example of the type of thinking demanded here is afforded by Dietrich Bonhoeffer's *Act and Being*. More than any other thinker, Bonhoeffer has completed the line of thinking about the church begun in Hofmann and Ritschl.

prematurely translated into a new historical dispensation, nor, as Ritschl held, that one realizes the possibilities of practical religion inherent in the old age as such. Rather in faith one finds himself a participant in the new age at the same time as he continues to live in this age. One finds oneself, in the church, under the totality of judgment and grace. In the church the believer comes to understand his existence in terms of *two* ontological determinations of his being, being "in Adam" and being "in Christ." This corresponds exactly, of course, to the dialectic of the two ages. From the point of view of faith, man confesses that his everyday existence is an existence in Adam, in sin and guilt. But he can make this confession as a *total* confession only insofar as he is also totally in Christ. And this confession of the double ontological determination of his being characterizes the nature of the church, the eschatological community in this age.[5]

Theological thinking about the two ages must be, therefore, a thinking in the light of faith, and that means a thinking in the church, the community which cleaves to the eschatological Word and which understands man's existence in terms of the dual ontology of sin and grace, Adam and Christ. Nevertheless, it is not a "new" kind of thinking in the sense that it has some special method or epistemological advantages over other kinds of human thinking. It differs only in that it attempts to be obedient to the eschatological word of judgment and grace and to serve the proclamation of that Word.

Having made these suggestions for further thinking, I can return to the problems pointed out at the beginning of this chapter. I can now indicate how these suggestions might lead in more fruitful directions. First let us look at the closely related problems of the order of law and gospel and the knowledge of the law. It is evident from what I have said that it is *only to faith* that the distinction between law and gospel is apparent. This much, at the outset, must certainly be conceded to Barth. There is no possibility of speaking about law *and* gospel prior to faith. At the same time, however, it is apparent that it is precisely faith which grasps the gospel as God's

---

[5] For a fuller discussion of what is involved here we must again point to Bonhoeffer, *Act and Being*, pp. 117-184.

final Word and that from this standpoint law must be ordered *before* gospel. It must be emphasized, however, that the order of law and gospel is established *theologically*, not by arguments about the possibility or impossibility of man's "natural knowledge" of the law "prior to" faith. That is quite another matter. In the ordering of law and gospel we have to do with the *theological* problem of the dialectic of the two ages in which both components must be considered. Quite obviously it is only by faith in God's eschatological act that the believer sees that his existence must be understood in terms of the two ages, where being in Adam under the law is always before being in Christ under the gospel. Faith grasps the gospel as God's "last Word"; thus it places law before gospel.

It might be objected, however, that if one does grasp the eschatological dialectic of the ages and all that that means, then it is a relatively harmless thing to speak of another use of law *after* the gospel, perhaps a "third use" of the law. Here there are several things which must be said. First, such a use of the term law cannot be made without drastic modification and rather tortuous redefinition. This is quite evident from the lengths to which Barth must go in order to define what such a "law" could mean. It is modified to the extent that it has little or no relationship to what is ordinarily meant by the term. Perhaps it is possible to speak of the admonitions *of the gospel*, but little is gained by using the term law in that connection. Second—and this is a more serious objection—when such a use of the term law is made so as to *discredit* or *rule out* other uses as a "misunderstanding," then, as we have pointed out, one is threatened with a loss of the dialectic altogether and the old age simply drops out of the picture. It is far from harmless to use "law" in this way. Theologically, therefore, it seems much more advisable to order law before gospel.

The history of the idea of the "third use of the law" offers little encouragement for its use in a truly evangelical ethic. It has its roots ultimately in the orthodox concept of the *lex aeterna* [6] and has hardly served any other purpose than to impose a new kind of

---

[6] It was initiated, apparently, by Melanchthon. See Ebeling, *Wort und Glaube,* p. 50.

legalism. Ragnar Bring has pointed out that the idea of a "third use of the law" presupposes a pietistic concept of conversion in which the believer supposedly is already translated into a new and different kind of existence, where *he* now uses the law in a "third way" in distinction from the rest of mankind.[7] Not only does this foster an illegitimate kind of separatism, but it also confuses the nature of the dialectic between the two ages and encourages the Christian to think in terms of a premature translation into the "new age." Furthermore, it does not consider the question of the real subject of the use of the law.

Paul Althaus has made an attempt to rescue the idea by making a distinction between "command" and "law" *(Gebot* and *Gesetz).*[8] God's gracious "command" belongs, for Althaus, to the situation of man before the fall. After the fall, the command becomes the "law" which accuses man. With the advent of faith, the law once again becomes the gracious command. It is difficult to see, however, how such a scheme really offers much more than the distinction between the essence and office of the law made—with rather unfortunate consequences—by Theodosius Harnack. Furthermore, Althaus' scheme presupposes the believer's ability to place himself beyond the real threat of the law simply by disposing of it in a neat *Urstand,* fall, and *Endzeit* scheme. Intending, no doubt, to establish the command of God, it simply makes it harmless.

It cannot be our purpose here to investigate the various attempts to rescue a "third use of the law"; that would involve us in quite extensive additional study. It seems quite evident, however, that once the eschatological act character of revelation has been asserted, the law which is now to be used in a "third way" must be redefined so radically that it bears little or no relationship to the former uses whatsoever. Such redefinition can only have unfortunate results. Either the "new use" is so "other" that it discredits the old uses altogether—to the extent that "this age" ceases to have any theological viability whatsoever—or there is, simply by virtue of the

---

[7] Heinz-Horst Schrey (ed.) and Helmut Thielicke, *Glaube und Handeln* (Bremen: Carl Schünemann Verlag, n.d.), pp. 157-166.

[8] Paul Althaus, *The Divine Command,* trans. F. Sherman ("Facet Books: Social Ethics Series," N. 9; Philadelphia: Fortress Press, 1966).

fact that the term "law" is used, a hidden continuity between the other uses and the "third use" which serves only to foster an illegitimate legalistic separatism—a special group using the law in a "third way" which is after all only the old way in disguise. It is difficult to see that any theological purpose is served by these attempts.

The *problem*, of course, is evident. The assertion of the eschatological act character of revelation has created a crisis for the doctrine of law, a crisis so severe that one can perhaps speak even of a bankruptcy in the attitude of Protestantism towards the law. The purpose of all these attempts, no doubt, has been somehow to rescue the concept of law in a theologically viable way. The success of these attempts, however, is dubious. Not only do they obscure the nature of the eschatological dialectic of the two ages, but they also produce what can be called a disguised antinomianism—an antinomianism carried out under the disguise of redefining the law so as to make it virtually synonymous with gospel. If Protestantism wants to rescue the idea of law it must find better ways of doing it than that.

If the law is to mean anything at all, therefore, it must be placed before and distinguished from the gospel. But does this mean that it is possible *prior to faith* to know the law really as law? Not necessarily. It is only *in* faith that one becomes aware of the *real* distinction between law and gospel and therefore hears the law for what it really is. It is also precisely in faith that one sees that law must be ordered before gospel. It is only in faith that one becomes aware of the ontological order where being "in Adam" is always "the old," "the past," while being "in Christ" is the new, "the future." The ordering of law and gospel is therefore the result of reflection in the light of faith. It is not based on fruitless arguments about what man can or cannot know prior to faith.

But what does this mean for the problem of the "natural knowledge" of the law? Here we must press the question of what man comes to know in faith so as to establish more precisely the relationship of faith to the knowledge of the law. Does faith involve some sort of translation into a new state in which the believer enjoys epistemological advantages over the unbeliever? Does faith bring some new or special knowledge of the law? It is always tempting, apparently, for theology to assert this, but it is difficult to see how this can be anything more than a kind of theological *hybris*. For faith means precisely *faith* and not some sort of supernatural *sight*.

Here we must refer back to what was said previously about the totality of judgment.[9] Faith means acknowledging this totality of judgment. Since faith accepts the being of man in Adam, it knows that its formal possibilities of knowing are not altered. Faith does not separate the believer from his fellow man in such matters; instead it drives home to him his solidarity with all mankind. In the problem of the knowledge of the law, the man of faith must join with the rest of mankind in searching for knowledge in given situations as best he can. Nor should the Christian refuse to recognize the possibility that certain of his "unbelieving" brothers could be blessed with better insight than he is. Even the laws of the Bible give the Christian no warrant for superiority, for as laws they are fully as available to man apart from faith as they are to man in faith. These laws too must be interpreted in their context and applied with the best skill and knowledge at man's disposal.

What faith should do, however, is to enable man to make the *distinction* between law and gospel. Apart from faith man is bound to look for his own "gospel" in the law and thus to refuse to accept law for what it is. In faith man learns to distinguish law from gospel and thus to allow law to be used in its proper manner. Faith sees that man apart from faith *misuses* the law, which then becomes for him the source of either despair or presumption. Faith sees that man's real problem with the law is that in unfaith he attempts to use what knowledge he has to gain heaven for himself, or to tyrannize his fellow men, or perhaps even to attempt to bring in a "heaven" on earth in the form of some sort of utopia. Faith, because it trusts totally in God's grace, sees that all these uses are in fact misuses of the law because they are presumptuous. They attempt to use the law for "supernatural" rather than "natural" ends. They extend law beyond its intent. What faith brings to man's knowledge of the law is the same thing it always brings: healing. Faith

---

[9] Above, pp. 223ff.

heals because it sets the proper limits to law. It prohibits supernatural pretension and consequently guards against despair.

But what does all this have to say about the problem of man's
knowledge of the law "before" faith? Does the reception of the
gospel presuppose and therefore *depend* upon a knowledge of the
law and hence of sin before faith? First of all, it should be clear
that it is only in faith that Christ is accepted as both absolute judgment and grace. It is only to faith therefore that the absolute totality
of the qualitative judgment is apparent. That is simply to repeat
what we have already said: that it is only to faith that God's use of
the law is clear. But the acceptance of judgment and the reception
of grace is, we can only say, simultaneous. One can accept the judgment of the law as total and qualitative only when in faith one sees
simultaneously the totality of redemption. But this "dialectical"
simultaneity is the situation in which man always remains in this
life. He never gets "beyond it" to a situation where he can speak
of a difference of "before" and "after" with regard to his knowledge
of the law. The transition (if one can use that term) which faith
brings is not such that his capacity for knowing the law is altered.

From this point of view, there is no theological reason for denying to man "prior" to faith the possibility of knowing the law as
such. Some men may, and no doubt do, have more knowledge and
others less. The proclamation of Christ does not, strictly speaking,
depend upon such knowledge because this proclamation is by its
very nature a proclamation of *both* law and gospel. What the proclamation does presuppose, at the very least, however, is the capacity
to *hear* the law. The idea of a "point of contact" is a *theological*
necessity, for the gospel must make contact with man *in this age.*
If it does not, the dialectic of the two ages is lost altogether.

Along with the capacity to hear the law there seems to be no
theological need to deny man the ability to know the law in varying
degrees. Indeed, this is all that man has in "this age." Likewise, it
does not seem necessary to deny to man "prior" to faith some knowledge of his sins. This will, of course, always be a knowledge of sin
as "act" and not as "being"; thus it will always foster the presumption that by avoiding the "act" man can avoid sin. But man's confession of sin as "being" is never engendered by a quantitatively

better knowledge of law as such. Rather this is born only by the proclamation and acceptance of Christ's qualitatively total judgment and redemption. It is still true that it is only by faith that we know ourselves to *be* sinners even though it is not necessary to deny some quantitative acknowledgment of sins prior to faith. As long as it is clear that the gospel is the "end" of the law, and that the only really decisive and qualitative break comes *between* law and gospel, there is no danger in allowing both the capacity to hear the law and varying degrees of the knowledge of law. Indeed, it is a theological *necessity* if the dialectic of the two ages is to be preserved.

The final problem to discuss is the ethical problem. The difficulty is that the distinction between law and gospel has usually led to various types of fateful separation or divorce between the "realms" or "kingdoms" of law and gospel. But if our analysis is correct, the source of this error should be apparent. A divorce between the "realms" becomes possible only when it is believed that faith somehow means a translation *in re* from one realm to another. Then faith becomes an event which separates the believer from the rest of mankind rather than bringing home to him his solidarity with all mankind. But such a view of faith is the result of a failure to comprehend the eschatological character of the relationship between law and gospel and consequently between the two realms. When it is seen that law and gospel must be understood in terms of the *totality* of judgment and grace, then it is apparent that faith does not mean a premature translation into a realm which separates the believer from the rest of mankind and its concerns. For to acknowledge the totality of judgment means to acknowledge the solidarity of all mankind "in Adam" at the same time as one believes in the universal application of God's grace. It is precisely because the believer is "in Christ" that he can at the same time see the solidarity of all mankind "in Adam."

This qualitative totality of judgment guarantees for faith that there can be no premature divorce or separation between the two realms. A *distinction*, indeed, must be made, but it is a distinction which is meant to "heal" and "save," not to divorce or separate. The realms must be held together, therefore, in what Bonhoeffer has termed "a polemical unity." [10] The relationship between them can never be one of static independence. The man of faith must be the one who sees this. The new age can be the redemption of the old precisely because the distinction between them is made. The new age fixes the eschatological limit to the old so that the old age can be cured of its supernatural pretensions and be "saved" by being more "natural." The proper distinction between the realms assures both a better Christianity and a better secularity.

On this basis it should be possible not only to rescue the concept of law from its bankruptcy but also to arrive at a better understanding of the responsibility of the church in the world. For the church is the locus of the concern for law *and* gospel. The church is the community created by God's eschatological act which understands the duality of existence, the dialectic of judgment and grace. Because it accepts the totality of judgment in the light of the totality of grace, the church knows that there can be no premature separation from the world, either in its thinking or its acting. Because the church is aware of the eschatological limit, it knows that it has the responsibility of bearing witness to the proper use of the law.

This is an area of the church's witness which has been almost totally neglected, one which deserves much more attention than it has received. The church is not a legislative body for the world, but it is a body which must be concerned for the *proper use* of the law. And this should be its concern as a *church,* not just as isolated individuals. Wherever law is used to tyrannize men for the sake of the state or for personal aggrandizement, wherever men are sacrificed for the sake of an ideology, wherever earthly power of any sort becomes an end in itself, there law is being misused, and there the church has both warrant and responsibility to bear its witness. The church must bear witness to the fact that the law ultimately is God's, that *he* is the one who "uses" it, and that his use of the law has its *end* in the gospel. In the light of the gospel, the church is called to eternal vigilance over the use of the law. It is not my

---

[10] Dietrich Bonhoeffer, *Ethics,* ed. Eberhard Bethge, trans. Neville H. Smith (New York: The Macmillan Co., 1962), p. 65.

task here to attempt to outline fully what this would mean, but I do want to suggest that in the much neglected concept of the use of the law there are great possibilities for understanding the *positive* relationship of the church to the problems of social justice.

This concludes our investigation. No doubt many problems remain. Not the least of these is the problem of communication. Speaking in terms of law and gospel always seems to invoke all or at least part of the unfortunate legacy of the problem. I have tried to locate some of these difficulties in the tradition and to indicate how they could be corrected. No doubt other ways of communicating what is intended must be sought and found. It is my hope that an eschatological understanding of the dialectic of law and gospel will provide a starting point for thinking about such communication. That, however, could be the subject of another book.

Bibliography

Althaus, Paul. *The Divine Command*. Translated by F. Sherman. "Facet Books: Social Ethics Series," No. 9. Philadelphia: Fortress Press, 1966.

Aulén, Gustaf. *Das Christliche Gottesbild*. Gütersloh: C. Bertelsmann Verlag, 1930.

———— *Christus Victor*. Translated by A. G. Hebert. New York: Macmillan Company, 1951.

Bachmann, Paul. *J. Chr. K. v. Hofmanns Versöhnungslehre*. Gütersloh: C. Bertelsmann Verlag, 1910.

Barth, Karl. *Church Dogmatics*. Edited by G. W. Bromiley and T. F. Torrance. Translated by G. T. Thompson, *et al.* 4 vols. New York: Scribner, 1956-1961.

———— *Community, State and Church* ("Anchor Books"). Garden City: Doubleday and Company, 1960.

———— *The Humanity of God*. Translated by Thomas Weiser and John Newton Thomas. Richmond: John Knox Press, 1960.

———— *Die Protestantische Theologie im 19. Jahrhundert*. 2d ed. revised. Zollikon/Zürich: Evangelischer Verlag A.G., 1952.

———— *Eine Schweizer Stimme*. Zollikon/Zürich: Evangelischer Verlag A.G., 1945.

———— *Theology and Church*. Translated by L. P. Smith. London: SCM Press, 1962.

Berge, Wolfgang, *"Gesetz und Evangelium in der Neueren Theologie" (Aufsätze und Vorträge zur Theologie und Religionswissenschaft)*. Berlin: Evangelische Verlagsanstalt, n.d.

Bonhoeffer, Dietrich. *Act and Being*. Translated by Bernard Noble. New York: Harper, 1961.

———— *Ethics*. Edited by Eberhard Bethge. Translated by N. H. Smith. New York: The Macmillan Company, 1962.

Carlson, Edgar. *The Reinterpretation of Luther*. Philadelphia: The Westminster Press. 1948.

235

Diem, Hermann. *Karl Barths Kritik am Deutschen Luthertum.* Zollikon/Zürich: Evangelischer Verlag A.G., 1947.

Delitzsch, Franz. *Commentary on the Epistle to the Hebrews.* Translated by T. L. Kingsbury, Vol. II. Edinburgh: T. & T. Clark, 1876.

Delitzsch, F. und Hofmann, J. v. *Theologische Briefe. Herausgegeben von W. Volck.* Leipzig: J. C. Hinrichs, 1891.

Dillenberger, John. *God Hidden and Revealed.* Philadelphia: Muhlenberg Press [Fortress], 1953.

Ebeling, Gerhard. *Wort und Glaube.* Tübingen: J. C. B. Mohr (Paul Siebeck), 1960.

Ebrard, Johannes. *Die Lehre von der Stellvertretende Genugthuung in der heiligen Schrift begründet.* Koenigsberg: A. W. Unzer, 1857.

Elert, Werner. *Der Kampf um das Christentum.* München: C. H. Beck'sche Verlagsbuchhandlung Oskar Beck, 1921.

———— *The Structure of Lutheranism.* Translated by W. A. Hansen. St. Louis: Concordia Publishing House, 1962.

———— *Zwischen Gnade und Ungnade.* München: Evangelischer Pressverband für Bayern, 1948.

Flechsenhaar, G. *Das Geschichtsproblem in der Theologie von Hofmanns.* Giessen: O. Kindt, G.m.b.h., 1935.

Gollwitzer, Helmut. "Zur Einheit von Gesetz und Evangelium," *Antwort.* Zollikon/Zürich: Evangelischer Verlag, A.G., 1956, pp. 287-309.

Grützmacher, R. "Der ethische Typus der Erlanger Theologie," *Neue Kirchliche Zeitschrift,* 28, No. 6 (June, 1917), pp. 441-453.

Haikola, Lauri. *Gesetz und Evangelium bei M. Flacius.* Lund: C. W. K. Gleerup, 1952.

———— "Studien zu Luther und zum Luthertum" (*Uppsala Universitets Aarsskrift,* No. 2, 1958). Uppsala: A.-B. Lundquistika Bokhandeln, 1958.

———— "Usus Legis" (*Uppsala Universitets Aarsskrift,* No. 3, 1958). Uppsala: A.-B. Lundquistika Bokhandeln, 1958.

Harnack, Theodosius. *Luthers Theologie.* 2 vols. *Neue Ausgabe.* München: Chr. Kaiser Verlag, 1927.

Haussleiter, Johannes. *Grundlinien der Theologie Joh. Christ. K. v. Hofmanns in seiner eigenen Darstellung.* Leipzig: A. Deichert'sche Verlagsbuchh. Nachf., 1910.

Heckel, Johannes. "Lex charitatis." (*Abhandlungen der Bayrischen Akademie der Wissenschaften, Neue Folge,* Vol. 36). München; Verlag der Bayrischen Akademie der Wissenschaften, 1953.

Heintze, Gerhard. *Luthers Predigt von Gesetz und Evangelium.* München: Chr. Kaiser Verlag, 1958.

Herrmann, Wilhelm, "Christlich-Protestantische Dogmatik," *Kultur der Gegenwart.* Edited by P. Hinneberg. 2d ed. Part I, Sec. IV, 2. Berlin: B. G. Tübner, 1909.

―――― *The Communion of the Christian with God.* Translated by J. S. Stanton. New York: G. P. Putnam's Sons, 1906.

―――― *Ethik.* 2d ed. Tübingen: J. C. B. Mohr (Paul Siebeck), 1923.

Hirsch, Emmanuel. *Geschichte der neueren Evangelischen Theologie*, Vol. V. Gütersloh: C. Bertelsmann Verlag, 1954.

von Hofmann, J. C. K. "Begründete Abweisung eines nicht begründeten Vorwurfs," *Zeitschrift für Protestantismus und Kirche.* Neue Folge. 15 (1848), 89-97.

―――― *Biblische Hermeneutic. Nach Manuscripten und Vorlesungen herausgegeben von W. Volck.* Nördlingen: C. H. Beck, 1880.

―――― *Der Schriftbeweis.* 2 vols. Nördlingen: C. H. Beck, 1852-1855.

―――― *Der Schriftbeweis.* 2 vols. 2d ed. rev. Nördlingen: C. H. Beck, 1857-1860.

―――― *Die Heilige Schrift Neuen Testaments zusammenhängend untersucht.* 11 vols. Vols. 9-11 edited by W. Volck. Nördlingen: C. H. Beck, 1862-1886.

―――― *Encyclopädie der Theologie. Nach Vorlesungen und Manuscripten herausgegeben von H. J. Bestmann.* Nördlingen: C. H. Beck, 1879.

[von Hofmann, J. C. K.] "Lutherische Ethnik," *Zeitschrift für Protestantismus und Kirche. Neue Folge.* 45 (1863), 251-256.

―――― "Pfarrer Franz von Ingenheim, der ehrliche Schriftausleger," *Zeitschrift für Protestantismus und Kirche. Neue Folge.* 31 (1856). 175-192.

―――― *Schutzschriften für eine neue Weise, alte Wahrheit zu Lehren.* 4 parts. Nördlingen: C. H. Beck, 1856-1859.

―――― *Theologische Ethik.* Nördlingen: C. H. Beck, 1878.

―――― *Weissagung und Erfüllung.* Nördlingen: C. H. Beck, 1841.

Holl, Karl. *Gesammelte Aufsätze.* 3 vols. Tübingen: J. C. B. Mohr (Paul Siebeck), 1928.

Hübner, Eberhard. *Schrift und Theologie.* München: Chr. Kaiser Verlag, 1956.

Iwand, Hans Joachim. "Um den Rechten Glauben," *Theologische Bücherei*, No. 9. Edited by K. G. Steck. München: Chr. Kaiser Verlag, 1959.

Jöst, Wilfred. *Gesetz und Freiheit.* Göttingen: Vandenhöck & Ruprecht, 1956.

Kähler, Martin. "Geschichte der Protestantischen Dogmatik im 19. Jahrhundert." Edited by E. Kähler. *Theologische Bücherei*, Bd. 16. München: Chr. Kaiser Verlag, 1962.

Kant. Immanuel. *Kant Selections.* Edited by T. M. Greene. New York: Charles Scribner's Sons, 1929.

―――― *Religion Within the Limits of Reason Alone.* Translated by T. M. Greene and H. H. Hudson ("Harper Torchbooks"). New York: Harper, 1960.

Kantzenbach, F. W., *Die Erlanger Theologie.* München: Evang. Pressverband für Bayern, 1960.

Kattenbusch, Ferdinand. *Deus Absconditus bei Luther, Festgabe für Julius Kaftan.* Tübingen: J. C. B. Mohr (Paul Siebeck), 1920, pp. 170-214.

Keller-Hueschemenger, Max. *Das Problem der Gewissheit bei J. Chr. K. von Hofmann im Rahmen der Erlanger Schule. Gedenkschrift für D. Werner Elert.* Edited by F. Huebner, et al. Berlin: Lutherisches Verlagshaus, 1955, 288-295.

———— "Das Problem der Heilsgewissheit in der Erlanger Theologie im 19 und 20 Jahrhundert," *Arbeiten zur Geschichte und Theologie des Luthertums,* Vol. X. Berlin: Lutherisches Verlagshaus, 1963.

Lipsius, R. A. "Luthers Lehre von der Busse," *Jahrbücher für Protestantische Theologie,* XVIII, No. 2 (April, 1892), pp. 168-177.

Loewenich, Walter v. *Luther und der Neuprotestantismus.* Witten: Luther-Verlag, 1963.

Luther, Martin. *Ausgewählte Werke.* Edited by H. H. Borcherdt and Georg Merz. Vol. 4. München: Chr. Kaiser Verlag. 1957.

———— *D. Martin Luthers Werke.* Vol. 39. 1. Weimar: Hermann Böhlaus Nachfolger, 1926.

Marty, Martin E. (ed.). *The Place of Bonhoeffer.* New York: Association Press, 1962.

Paton, H. J. *The Categorical Imperative.* London: Hutchinson Publishing Group Ltd., 1948.

Philippi, F. A. *Commentar über der Brief Pauli an die Römer.* 2d ed. Frankfurt: Heyder u. Zimmer, 1856.

———— *Herr D. von Hofmann gegenüber der lutherischen Versöhnungs- und Rechtfertigungslehre.* Frankfurt: Heyder u. Zimmer, 1856.

Prenter, Regin. "Die Einheit von Schöpfung und Erlösung," *Theologische Zeitschrift,* II, No. 3 (May/June, 1946), pp. 161-182.

Ritschl, Albrecht. *A Critical History of the Christian Doctrine of Justification and Reconciliation.* Translated by John S. Black. Edinburgh: Edmonston and Douglas, 1872.

———— *Rechtfertigung und Versöhnung.* 3 vols. Bonn: Adolph Marcus, 1889.

———— *Rechtfertigung und Versöhnung.* 3 vols. 3rd ed. Bonn: Adolph Marcus, 1889.

———— "Die Rechtfertigungslehre des Andrias Osiander," *Jahrbücher für deutsche Theologie,* II, No. 4. (1857), pp. 785-829.

———— "Review of Theologische Ethik by J. C. K. v. Hofmann," *Theologische Literaturzeitung,* III, No. 21 (October 12, 1878), pp. 514-516.

———— "Über die methodischen Prinzipien der Theologie des Herrn Dr. v. Hofmann," *Allgemeinen Kirchenzeitung,* Vol. I, No. 12, 1858, pp. 353-364.

———— *Unterricht in der Christlichen Religion.* 2d ed. Bonn: Adolph Marcus, 1881.

Ritschl, Otto. *Albrecht Ritschls Leben.* 2 vols. Frieburg: J. C. B. Mohr, 1892.

Rost, Gerhard. "Der Zorn Gottes in Luthers Theologie," *Lutherischer Rundblick,* Vol. IX, No. 1 (February, 1961), pp. 2-32.

Schellbach, Martin. *Theologie und Philosophie bei v. Hofmann.* Gütersloh: C. Bertelsmann, 1935.

Schlink, Edmund. "Gesetz und Paraklese," *Antwort.* Zollikon/Zürich: Evangelischer Verlag A.G., 1956, pp. 323-335.

Schmid, Heinrich. *Dr. v. Hofmanns Lehre von der Versöhnung in ihrem Verhältnis zum Kirchlichen Bekenntnis und zur Kirchlichen Dogmatik geprüft.* Nördlingen: C. H. Beck, 1856.

Schrey, Heinz-Horst. "Die Wiedergeburt des Naturrechts," *Theologische Rundschau,* XIX, No. 3 (1951), pp. 192-221.

Schultz, Robert. "Gesetz und Evangelium in der Lutherischen Theologie des 19. Jahrhunderts." *Arbeiten zur Geschichte und Theologie des Luthertums,* Vol. IV. Berlin: Lutherisches Verlaghaus, 1958.

Seeberg, Reinhold. *Die Kirche Deutschlands im 19. Jahrhundert.* 2d ed. Leipzig: A Deichert, 1904.

Senft, Christoph. *Wahrhaftigkeit und Wahrheit. Beiträge zur historischen Theologie,* No. 22. Tübingen: J. C. B. Mohr (Paul Siebeck), 1956.

Thielicke, Helmut. "Zur Frange Gesetz und Evangelium, eine Auseinandersetzung mit Karl Barth," *Auf dem Grunde der Apostel und Propheten.* Stuttgart: Quell-Verlag der Evangelischen Gesellschaft, 1948. pp. 173-197.

Thomasius, Gottfried. *"Das Bekenntnis der lutherischen Kirche von der Versöhnung und die Versöhnungslehre D. Chr. K. v. Hofmanns. Mit einem Nachwort von Theodosius Harnack.* Erlangen: Theodor Bläsing, 1857.

Troeltsch, Ernst. *Vernunft und Offenbarung bei Johann Gerhard und Melanchthon.* Göttingen: Vandenhöck und Ruprecht, 1891.

Wach, Joachim. "Die theologische Hermeneutik von Schleiermacher bis heute," *Das Verstehen.* Vol. II. Tübingen: J. C. B. Mohr, 1926.

Wapler, Paul. "Die Genesis der Versöhnungslehre J. von Hofmanns," *Neue Kirchliche Zeitschrift,* 25. No. 3 (March, 1914), pp. 167-205.

———— *Johannes von Hofmann.* Leipzig: A. Deichertsche Verlagsbuchhandlung Werner Scholl, 1914.

———— "Die Theologie Hofmanns in ihrem Verhältnis zu Schellings positiver Philosophie," *Neue Kirchliche Zeitschrift,* 16 (September, 1905), pp. 699-718.

Weber, F. *Vom Zorne Gottes.* Introduction by F. Delitzsch. Erlangen: Andreas Deichert, 1962.

Weber, Hans Emil. *Reformation, Orthodoxie und Rationalismus.* Part II. Gütersloh: C. Bertelsmann Verlag, 1951.

Weizsaecker, C. "Um was handelt es sich in dem Streit über die Versöhungslehre?" *Jahrbücher für deutsche Theologie.* Vol. III 1858.

Wendebourg, E. W. *Die Heilsgeschichtliche Theologie J. C. K. v. Hofmanns,* Dissertation. Göttingen: 1953.

Wendebourg, E. W. "Die Heilsgeschichtliche Theologie J. C. K. v. Hofmanns in ihrem Verhältnis zur romantischen Weltanschauung," *Zeitschrift für Theologie und Kirche,* Vol. 52. No. 1. (1955), pp. 64-104.

Werner, Martin. *The Formation of Christian Dogma.* Translated by S. G. F. Brandon. rev. New York: Harper, 1957.

Weth, Gustav. *Die Heilsgeschichte*. München: Chr. Kaiser Verlag, 1931.

Wingren, Gustaf. "Evangelium und Gesetz," *Antwort*. Zollikon/Zürich: Evangelischer Verlag A.G., 1956), pp. 110-322.

———— *Theology in Conflict*. Translated by E. Wahlstrom. Philadelphia: Muhlenberg Press [Fortress] 1958.

Wolf, Ernst. *Peregrinatio*. München: Chr. Kaiser Verlag, 1954.

Wolff, Otto. *Die Haupttypen der neuen Lutherdeutung*. Stuttgart: W. Kohlhammer, 1938.

Index